# CONTEMPORARY FARCE ON THE GLOBAL STAGE

*Contemporary Farce on the Global Stage* provides audiences and practitioners a detailed survey of how the genre of farce has evolved in the 21st century. Often dismissed as frivolous, farce speaks a universal language, with the power to incisively interrogate our world through laughter.

Unlike farces of the past, where a successful resolution was a given and we could laugh uproariously at adulterous behaviour, farce no longer guarantees an audience a happy ending where everything works out. Contemporary farce is no longer 'diverting us' with laughter. It is reflecting the fractured world around us. With a foreword by award-winning playwright Ken Ludwig, the book introduces readers to the Mechanics of Farce, and the 'Four Ps,' which are key elements for understanding, appreciating, and exploring the form. The Five Doors to Contemporary Farce identify five major categories into which farces fall. Behind each door are a wide selection of plays, modern and contemporary examples from all over the world, written by a diverse group of playwrights who traverse gender, race, ethnicity, and sexual orientation. Supplementing each section are comments, observations, and reflections from award-winning playwrights, directors, actors, designers, dramaturgs, and scholars.

Designed specifically to give theatre-makers a rounded understanding that will underpin their own productions, this book will also be of use to theatre and performance studies students.

**David Gram** is an Assistant Professor of Theatre at Oakland University in Rochester Hills, Michigan, USA. He has been a theatre and opera director, actor, dramaturg, and playwright for over 25 years. Other research interests include contemporary musical theatre, Elizabethan and Jacobean drama, and new play development.

# CONTEMPORARY FARCE ON THE GLOBAL STAGE

or, Serious Laughter

*David Gram*

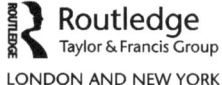
LONDON AND NEW YORK

Designed cover image: © Jeremy Barnett

First published 2024
by Routledge
4 Park Square, Milton Park, Abingdon, Oxon OX14 4RN

and by Routledge
605 Third Avenue, New York, NY 10158

*Routledge is an imprint of the Taylor & Francis Group, an informa business*

© 2024 David Gram

The right of David Gram to be identified as author of this work has been asserted in accordance with sections 77 and 78 of the Copyright, Designs and Patents Act 1988.

All rights reserved. No part of this book may be reprinted or reproduced or utilised in any form or by any electronic, mechanical, or other means, now known or hereafter invented, including photocopying and recording, or in any information storage or retrieval system, without permission in writing from the publishers.

*Trademark notice*: Product or corporate names may be trademarks or registered trademarks, and are used only for identification and explanation without intent to infringe.

*British Library Cataloguing-in-Publication Data*
A catalogue record for this book is available from the British Library

ISBN: 978-0-367-21927-7 (hbk)
ISBN: 978-0-367-21928-4 (pbk)
ISBN: 978-0-429-26880-9 (ebk)

DOI: 10.4324/9780429268809

Typeset in Times New Roman
by SPi Technologies India Pvt Ltd (Straive)

*Dedicated with love…*
*to my parents, Bruce and Seena*
*and*
*to my wife Kristina, whose laugh I treasure most*

# CONTENTS

*Acknowledgements*   *xi*
*Foreword*   *xiii*
by *Ken Ludwig*

Introduction   1

*Why Write about Farce? 2*
*The Book... 6*
*Works Cited 7*

Entrances: The Foundations of Contemporary Farce   8

*What is Farce? 8*
  *Defining Contemporary Farce 10*
*The 'Four Ps' of Farce 13*
  Passion *13*
  Persistence *14*
  Panic *15*
  Preservation *16*
*The 'Mechanics' of Farce 16*
*Structure and Farce 17*
*Character and Farce 19*
*Physical Comedy & Comedic Violence in Farce 20*
*Language and Farce 21*
*Themes and Farce 22*
*The Five Doors to Contemporary Farce 23*
*Works Cited 24*

1 Domestic Farce 25

   *Domestic Farce in the 21st Century 27*
     Rire Domestique: French Domestic Farce *28*
     Marc Camoletti: *Boeing-Boeing* (1960) *30*
     Yasmina Reza: *God of Carnage* (2008) *33*
   *Farce and Chips: British Domestic Farce 37*
     British Domestic Farce in the 21st Century *41*
     Moira Buffini: *Dinner* (2002) *41*
     Joe Penhall: *Birthday* (2012) *42*
   *Farce Americana: Contemporary Domestic Farce in the United States 44*
   Ken Ludwig's *'Two Tenors' 44*
     Deborah Salem Smith: *Faithful Cheaters* (2017) *48*
   *Feckin' Farce: Irish Domestic Farce 50*
     Enda Walsh: *The Walworth Farce* (2006) *51*
   *A Few More Contemporary Domestic Farces 54*
   *Works Cited 57*

2 Social Farce 61

   Joe Orton: *Farceur of Misrule 62*
     *Loot* (1966) *64*
     *What the Butler Saw* (1969) *65*
   *Farce and Identity 68*
     Jean Poiret: *La Cage aux Folles* (1973) *68*
     Sabina Berman: *The Agony of Ecstasy* (1985) *69*
     Terrence McNally: *The Ritz* (1975) *70*
     Marius Von Mayenburg: *The Ugly One* (2007) *71*
     Nell Benjamin: *The Explorer's Club* (2013) *73*
   *Farce and Class 75*
     *Bourgeois Farce 75*
     *Working-Class Farce 81*
   *Farce and Race 85*
     David Henry Hwang: *Yellow Face* (2007) *85*
     Thomas Bradshaw: *Intimacy* (2014) *89*
     Nakkiah Lui: *Black is the New White* (2017) *92*
     Larissa FastHorse: *The Thanksgiving Play* (2018) *94*
   *A Few More Contemporary Social Farces 95*
   *Works Cited 97*

3   Political Farce                                                                101

   Dario Fo: Farsa Politica  *102*
      *Morte accidentale di un anarchico* (Accidental Death
         of an Anarchist, *1970*) *103*
   *Farce and the Government  110*
   *Farce and the British Government  111*
      Tom Stoppard: *Dirty Linen* (1976) *112*
         Alistair Beaton: *Feelgood* (2001) *114*
         James Graham: *The Culture* (2017) *115*
         Lucy Kirkwood: *Tinderbox* (2008) *117*
      *Farce and the American Government  120*
         Tracy Letts: *The Minutes* (2017) *120*
         Selina Fillinger: *POTUS* (2022) *123*
      *Farce and the Radical  125*
         George Tabori: *Mein Kampf: Farce* (1987) *126*
         Mustapha Matura: *The Coup – A Play of Revolutionary
            Dreams* (1991) *128*
         Martin McDonagh: *The Lieutenant of Inishmore* (2001) *130*
      *Two Modern and a Few More Contemporary Political Farces  135*
   Works Cited *141*

4   Cultural Farce (or 'Farce Remixed')                                            144

   *Farce and the Novel  146*
      Peepolykus & Le Navet Bete *147*
      The Goodale Brothers: *Jeeves and Wooster in Perfect Nonsense*
         (2013) *149*
      Tom Basden: *The Crocodile* (2015) *149*
      Ken Ludwig's *The Game's Afoot* (2011) and *Baskerville*
         (2015) *150*
      Patrick Barlow: *The 39 Steps* (2006) *152*
   *Farce and the Silver Screen  155*
      Graham Linehan: *The Ladykillers* (2011) *155*
      Sandy Rustin: *Clue* (2020) *157*
      Mel Brooks & Thomas Meehan: *The Producers* (2001) *159*
   *Farce and the Theatrical Adaptation  161*
      Phil Porter: *Vice Versa* (2017) *162*
      Taylor Mac: *Gary – A Sequel to Titus Andronicus* (2019) *164*
      Richard Bean: *One Man, Two Guvnors* (2011) *169*

*Farce and the Cultural Icon 173*
    Terry Johnson: *Hysteria* (1993) *173*
    Itamar Moses: *Bach at Leipzig* (2005) *174*
    Liz Duffy Adams: *Or* (2009) *175*
    Steve Thompson: *No Naughty Bits* (2011) *176*
*A Few More Contemporary Cultural Farces 176*
*Works Cited 179*

5   Backstage Farce     182

    Michael Frayn: *Noises Off* (1982) *183*
*Farce in Rehearsal 188*
    Sarah Ruhl: *Stage Kiss* (2011) *189*
    Peter Houghton: *A Commercial Farce* (2009) *190*
    Anne Washburn: *10 out of 12* (2015) *192*
*Farce in Performance 194*
    Farce Goes Wrong: *'Mischief Theatre' 195*
    Ben Ashenden and Alex Owen: *The Comeback* (2020) *200*
*Farce and the Understudy 202*
*Farce and the Critics 205*
*One Modern and a Few More Contemporary*
   *Backstage Farces 209*
*Works Cited 212*

Exits: Farce and the Future     214
*Works Cited 221*

*Appendix: List of Modern and Contemporary*
   *Farces from Around the World*     *222*
*Index*     *229*

# ACKNOWLEDGEMENTS

Over the course of writing this book, I have mentioned to numerous people that this has been one of the most challenging endeavours in my career. It has also been one of the most rewarding.

One of the great pleasures this book has afforded me is the opportunity to speak with playwrights, directors, actors, designers, stage managers, agents, and scholars from all over the world. Some provided me with instrumental connections and resources, while others generously took time out of their schedules to answer questions about their work and farce.

Although I was unable to quote everyone I spoke with, I would be remiss not to thank all of my interviewees who generously shared their time and insights about farce and comedy. Your stories, wit, observations, and passion not only for farce, but for the role of laughter in the theatre, are part of this book's DNA.

Thank you to:

Jeremy Barnett, Richard Bean, Jenna Berk, Judy Blazer, Lisa Codrington, Bryony Corrigan, Sinead Crowe, Jessica Milner Davis, Matt DiCarlo, Jytte Drue, John Treacy Egan, Matthew-Lee Erlbach, Selina Fillinger, Sean Foley, Amanda Giguere, Sarah Giles, Michael Grandage, Dave Hearn, Jeremy Herrin, Ravi Jain, Eamonn Jordan, David Josefsberg, Julie Kelleher, Michael Kostroff, Leslie Littell, Whitney Locher, Ken Ludwig, Danielle Maas, Alex Mandell, Rob McClure, Meredith McDonough, Priscilla Melendez, Gary Mickelson, Simon Nye, Jill Paice, Emma Parker, Michael Perlman, Lorenzo Pisoni, Phil Porter, Mark Price, Jemima Rooper, Sandy Rustin, Kat Sandler, Karen Sheridan, Deborah Salem Smith, Don Stephenson, Moritz von Stülpnagel, Greg Vinkler, Tommy Wedge, Eric Weitz, Nick Whitby, Paula Wing, and Brandon A. Wright.

Thank you to my grad school colleagues and faculty in the School of Theatre at Boston University; specifically Jim Petosa and Judy Braha for their guidance and mentorship, and for encouraging me to pursue my love of farce as a director.

Thank you to my colleagues in the School of Music, Theatre, and Dance at Oakland University, with an extra special thanks to my faculty in the Department of Theatre for their support and encouragement.

Thank you to my students, past and present, who have helped me wrestle with the ideas in this book. You are all excellent teachers.

Thank you to my research assistants, who provided immeasurable help in various areas of this book: Annika Andersson, Sophia Cannella, Krissy Castellese, Kori Fay, Gabrielle Keen, Olivia Kiefer, and Emily Nichter.

Thank you to Ben Piggott, Zoe Forbes, and Steph Hines at Routledge for this opportunity, and for their ongoing encouragement, guidance, and patience, as I navigated unfamiliar and scary territory as a writer. Thank you to Nick Brock for his keen editing eye.

A big thank you to Ken Ludwig for graciously agreeing to write the Foreword.

I want to thank my family for all their love and cheerleading: my sisters, Robyn and Michelle; and my parents, Bruce and Seena. A special shout-out to my Dad for his expert advice and help, especially throughout the revision process.

My 'kids', Oslo, Lulu, and Gatsby, for keeping me company during early morning and late night writing sessions.

And finally, thank you to my wife Kristina, for being my rock, for the tough love when I needed it, and for believing in me every step of the way.

# FOREWORD

By Ken Ludwig

The subtitle of this book, *Serious Laughter*, gets it just right. As a playwright who has devoted his life to both the creation and the study of stage comedy, I can attest that farce is serious business. The plays that David Gram explores in this monograph are often maligned by critics and ignored by scholars, tagged with that insidious little word: *just*. They are *just comedy*. But as Gram ably demonstrates, these plays aren't *just* anything. They are intricate works of art. They are meticulous in their architecture and invaluable in their consistent ability to reflect our anxieties back at us in a way that relieves despair rather than compounding it. And they are long overdue for a serious treatment like this one.

Art is discipline. For me, that means spending solitary hours each day putting pen to paper to craft each of my plays by developing what Gram so aptly calls a "blueprint" for the productions that will be built from my scripts. My writing process begins by reading and seeking to understand the great comedies of the past: how are they structured? What's at stake for the characters? What do they teach us about our own humanity?

I couldn't hope to write a romantic comedy like *Dear Jack, Dear Louise* without studying *Much Ado About Nothing*, a boulevard comedy like *Leading Ladies* without reading *Blithe Spirit*, a comedy of chaos like *Lend Me A Tenor* without understanding *A Flea In Her Ear*, or an Aldwych-style farce like *A Fox on the Fairway* without first knowing Goldsmith's *She Stoops to Conquer*. Perhaps because Shakespeare, Coward, Feydeau, and Goldsmith have stood the test of time, we recognize the value of studying their work, even if others might label that work *just comedy*.

This book extends our understanding of the long tradition of farce to include plays of the 21st century. It therefore demonstrates that the art of farce is not valuable simply because it persists, but because the form itself continues to evolve. Farce continues to be an essential dramatic structure, one to which both playwrights and audiences repeatedly return. As a playwright who has sought to tell some of his stories in this form, I'm indebted to Gram for his scholarship.

Stage comedy is both my profession and my passion. Its artistic impetus is vital to our collective emotional health: farce invites us to wrestle with our own fear of failure within a context that allows us to still hope for a happy ending. It allows us to remain optimistic in the face of a chaotic world. And it is a special pleasure to see it get the book-length analysis it deserves.

Ken Ludwig<br>
Washington, D.C.<br>
August 2023

**Ken Ludwig** has had six productions on Broadway and eight in London's West End. His plays are produced in 20 languages in more than 30 countries. His first play, *Lend Me a Tenor*, won two Tony Awards. His first musical, *Crazy For You*, won the Tony and Olivier Awards for Best Musical. Ludwig has also won the Edwin Forrest Award for Contributions to the American Theatre, two Laurence Olivier Awards, two Helen Hayes Awards, the Charles MacArthur Award, and the Edgar Award for Best Mystery of the Year. His 34 plays and musicals are staged around the world and throughout the United States every night of the year.

# INTRODUCTION

I love to laugh.

I mean, really laugh.

The kind of unbridled, uninhibited laugh that feels like an otherworldly experience. Your body shakes. Your chest contracts and tightens. Tears stream down your face. Catching your breath seems impossible. To put it bluntly, you feel as if you're never again going to regain control over your senses or bodily functions.

That's the kind of laugh I'm talking about.

Farce, when done well, elicits that kind of response. There is nothing quite like sitting in a darkened theatre with an audience of strangers, sharing a communal laugh at the expense of a group of people onstage fighting so hard for something, their rational selves all but disappear into the ether. We delight in those who are forced, through circumstance, to make ridiculous decision after ridiculous decision, which inevitably gets them and the people around them into more and more trouble.

As outside observers we are given permission to laugh at the absurdity of these characters, the choices they're making and the escalating situation before us. What is the cumulative effect of all of these elements? A wall of laughter is generated that is so visceral, so infectious, so thunderous, you'd think the proscenium arch would crack open, and ceiling plaster would rain down on everyone in the building.

And as long as that plaster doesn't fall on *you*…it's even funnier!

Mel Brooks, the award-winning director, actor and writer of some of the funniest films ever put on screen, including *Blazing Saddles*, *The Producers* and *Young Frankenstein*, once said: "Tragedy is when I cut my finger. Comedy is

DOI: 10.4324/9780429268809-1

when you fall into an open sewer and die." This quote typifies the very nature of farce and the relationship that is established between what's happening onstage and what we're witnessing in the audience. When something awful happens to us that causes unspeakable pain, it's not funny. However, there is a unique and unquestionably guilty enjoyment in seeing someone endure harm, especially when it is completely unexpected, or when it happens in a high-stakes situation. I recognise that sounds callous, but as someone who readily trips on sidewalks, bangs his head, and has been defecated on by geese – I know exactly what Brooks means. When these things happen, and no one is around to witness them, I feel like an idiot – and yes, it is tragic – with me cursing the day that sidewalk had the audacity to trip me up, that cupboard decided to remain open as I lifted my head, or that goose chose to offer its 'gift.' On the other hand, when these perfectly-timed pieces of pain and slapstick offer a friend or relative a front row seat and subsequently a hearty laugh at my expense, it's easy to see from their perspective where the mirth lies.

**Why Write about Farce?**

Putting aside my role as an 'enthusiastic audience member', my interest in farce is a direct result of my work as a stage director, actor, writer, dramaturg and voracious reader of the genre. As a professor, I have discovered that the study of comedy – let alone farce – is rarely given its due in course curricula. This means that actors, directors, and designers are left to their own devices when approaching this kind of work. They must find their way through comedy via practical experience. They are forced to discover the 'style' demanded of comedic scripts through trial and error or via the guidance of a director – hopefully one who has the requisite knowledge, background and sense of play. It is perfectly legitimate, given the physical nature of farce, that practical exploration be one of the best ways to learn how to approach the form.

My own introduction to the study of farce has, for the most part, not been via textbooks. In fact, much of what I have learned about farce is the direct result of watching farces (stage and screen), reading scripts and novels, directing and acting in productions, and listening to other professionals discuss their craft. Unlike many other theatrical genres that are consistently studied in school or have provided leading authors a wide scope of written discourse, farce does not lend itself to 'serious' academic study. Perhaps it's because one of its sole aims is to make people laugh. And that's not always a priority for 'serious' study. Perhaps it's because the plays do not carry literary weight. The scripts themselves are often seen as blueprints, maps for a total theatrical experience that needs to manifest itself in a highly physicalized form onstage. Perhaps it's because farce is hard.

In her seminal book *Farce*, Australian author and scholar Jessica Milner Davis not only examines the genre's history and evolution, but also defends its status as "an essential component in both the comedic and tragic traditions" (Davis 2003). Yet the question remains: why does farce intimidate or dissuade companies from producing it, playwrights from writing it, or scholars from writing about it? In conversation, Davis offers two potential answers:

> The first one is the inherited tradition of [farce as] mean, lowly, degrading …'it isn't civilised to laugh', you know – so uproariously that you fall out of your chair…'gentle' people, well-bred people don't really 'show their teeth' – -just a smile. There is something felt to be atavistic or bestial about gales of laughter….And farce is a machine for making you laugh. So that has two denigratory elements to it…For the general public, one is the broad laughter and it's uncivilised, while wit is a higher form of humour. And for the second one, [there is] something mechanical about it. And, well, that means it's got to be despised [as being less than human].
> But the truth is, if you ask any experienced actor or director – and this is another reason why it's not done so much – it is the utmost test of skill. So, it's not like any other drama form where you can sort of half succeed and you can get a review that says, 'Oh, well,' you know, '"there were good bits and there were bad bits but I enjoyed this.' [Or] …'You will enjoy it, but it's not brilliant.'" A farce either works, or it falls flat on its face, and there's nothing in between.
>
> *(Davis 2020)*

Farce can produce a euphoric response in an audience bordering on the sublime. When a farce hums on all cylinders, it can literally leave people rolling in the aisles. In a 1954 article entitled "Farce is Far More Serious", Danish philosopher Soren Kierkegaard writes "anyone who wants to do a pathological study of laughter at various social and temperamental levels should not miss the opportunity offered by the performance of a farce" (Kierkegaard 3).

Speaking about why he is continually drawn to farce, award-winning British director Sean Foley believes:

> …when you get it right, it's the effect on an audience. It's what is so magical about farce…over and above any other form of theatre. I love all sorts of comedy. But with farce, when you get it right, there comes a point of utter delirium and then ultimately…you get this catharsis because the entire audience collectively goes through this convulsion of hilarity. And that is a wonderful, wonderful thing to have provoked in a group of people. It's very, very satisfying.
>
> *(Foley 2020)*

What is it that draws us to this centuries-old theatrical form? In essence, it's watching characters in a constant state of 'acting'. Not necessarily 'pretending to be someone else' (though many farces include characters putting on a disguise or taking on an alternate persona), but in a state of responding without thinking about what lies ahead. Farce is predominantly 'of the body' and the body's relationship to space and its circumstances. Generally, farce does not allow for deep, considered thinking.

Farce and its elements tap into our base nature. Citing the work and writings of Russian theatre-maker Vsevolod Meyerhold, Davis says:

> I'm absolutely convinced that [Meyerhold] is right when he says that farce – meaning mime, improvisation, stereotyping, demanding physical acting, making people laugh, make them weep as well but make them laugh, mostly – that is the lifeblood of the theatre. And whenever the theatre is running out of steam, it needs to return to its roots. It might not return for a glorious period of yet more pure farce. But it will return to those techniques and will use them in order to reinvigorate a kind of exhausted tradition.
>
> *(Davis 2020)*

There is also something satisfying about producing a difficult farce. A good farce should feel like a death-defying circus act in which the audience finds themselves constantly asking "How will they pull this off?" or "Will they pull this off?" This question should not only apply to the characters but to the production. Foley thinks

> …that real sense of danger is part of what the audience enjoys…in a way, farce is the most purely theatrical form. There's a visceral, palpable sense that this thing is happening live in front of you…it's exciting for an audience. That's why it feels so alive and dangerous.
>
> *(Lawson 2012)*

The genre requires a level of exacting and precision. It's not tied up in psychologically complex characters. Farce doesn't have the luxury to live in an emotionally fluid or liminal world. For the play to succeed, it's crucial that the elements of production go right, for everything else to successfully 'go wrong.' British director Josie Rourke surmises that,

> …farce is a reassuring form for both audiences and directors. You're dealing with absolutes: either that door will open on cue or it won't. It's actually a relief not to be standing around in rehearsal for 30 minutes, discussing why something happens. I think it's also a satisfying form for audiences, in that you are rewarded for listening and understanding. There's a particular laugh of satisfaction when something set-up early on, pays off later.
>
> *(Lawson 2012)*

Yet, farce is not a genre that easily satisfies. It's a type of theatre that elicits divided responses. Whenever I mention my affection for farce, the reaction is rarely centrist. People love it or loathe it. This includes theatre people. For many it conjures up poorly realised or groan-worthy productions: contrived or misogynistic writing, over-the-top or 'hammy' performance work, and unevenly paced direction. For some, watching half-naked people running in and out of rooms, adopting ridiculous disguises and falling over furniture is simply not their idea of an enjoyable night at the theatre. True, these clichéd images still populate contemporary farce plots, but, as we will see, these elements are no longer the driving force behind what defines farce today. Instead, playwrights are drawing on the conventions of the form (even subverting them) in order to address contemporary issues in humorous ways. And yes, the barometer for a successful farce must include how funny it is or isn't. However, contemporary farces are reinvigorating the form by harnessing the power of laughter to examine social and political agendas through a serious and virtuosic lens. We may marvel (and laugh) at the craftsmanship required to execute a piece, but deeper issues lie beneath the laughter.

Even for the seasoned artist, working on a farce can be daunting. As playmakers we are constantly being asked to 'expose' ourselves for an audience. Comedies, and especially farces, ask the artist to risk 'looking the fool' in order to get a laugh. There is something vulnerable about doing that and receiving nothing in return from an audience. Silence in a drama is one thing. Silence in a comedy, where laughter is expected, makes you want to slink away to a very dark place. Ask any actor working on a comedy – the sound of laughter is a reward and, yes, addictive! We hear laughter, we want more. Not hearing it can be dispiriting and may generate dangerous self-doubt. That's the risk we take as artists signing up for a comedy. The risk that we will not be funny. For this reason, farce scares away many artists. It's a challenging form requiring hard work – to create a product that appears seamless. Farce begins with the text but requires the actor, director, and designer to engage, innovate, and fill critical gaps – including the play's structural rhythm, characterisation, stage business, design elements and the audience's role in the event. As Davis says, farce has a machine-like quality, where the machine has to be firing on all cylinders to produce its intended effect of uncontrollable laughter or unbelievable shock. There is nothing like feeling impending dread while working on a comedy – that moment where everyone in the rehearsal room stops and looks at one another, thinking the same thing: 'Is this thing actually funny??'

It is a form that only reveals itself when skilled artists collaborate as an ensemble to tell a comedically complex story and make it look effortless. And then we share it with a paying audience that lets us know how well we did, based on their vocal hilarity. Easy, right?

---

## The Book…

Over the years, there have been a few publications written about farce, or specific farceurs. My desire in writing this particular book stems from a paucity of studies on how farce has evolved into the 21st century.

In the last twenty years, we have seen playwrights worldwide embrace, and even explode, the form. As I surveyed these contemporary plays and playwrights, I began to see patterns emerge from an anthropological perspective. The types of stories and thematic ideas being treated within the farce construct were edgier, challenging, and unafraid to upend or play with farcical conventions. Contemporary farce was no longer offering just an entertaining night at the theatre or means of escape. It was drawing on the world around it, steeping itself in social and political commentary like Larissa FastHorse's *The Thanksgiving Play*, Marius von Mayenberg's *The Ugly One* and Kat Sandler's *The Party/The Candidate*. Historically-set farces like Richard Bean's *The Hypocrite* or John Guare's *A Free Man of Color* help draw parallels between the past and the present. Most notably, more farces are finding inspiration in cultural touchstones as seen in plays like Patrick Barlow's *The 39 Steps*, or Taylor Mac's *Gary: A Sequel to Titus Andronicus*.

At the heart of all of this work remains laughter. Like tears, a good farce offers us the opportunity to purge through laughter; to experience a cathartic release over which we have no control. Sometimes it's uproarious, sometimes it's sweet, and sometimes the comedy is uncomfortably dark.

My observations have led me to identify what I call **The Five Doors to Contemporary Farce**: Domestic Farce, Social Farce, Political Farce, Cultural Farce, and Backstage Farce. These Five Doors are designed to offer alternate entrances into the genre. They invite audiences and practitioners to see the form with fresh eyes. These Five Doors will expand the parameters of how farce can encompass a wide range of thematic ideas.

Farce has the power to incisively, and sometimes sneakily, interrogate our world. My goal is to reframe any biases toward the genre and affirm that there is both theatrical and humanistic weight embedded within these plays.

For our purposes, I am employing the phrase 'contemporary farce' to reference pieces written since 2000. The plays I discuss and/or mention throughout the book may have prior reference for context, but we shall focus predominantly on farces written since the start of the millennium. The book seeks not only to honour those exemplary plays and playwrights who have left their mark on the genre, but also to highlight lesser-known works and writers whose plays should be seen as similarly excellent.

One important observation I wish to address upfront, that the keen reader and socially aware citizen is bound to notice: among playwrights globally, the ratio of female playwrights and playwrights of the global majority, to their white male counterparts, is quite lopsided. This has not gone unnoticed.

The farce form has been a white male-dominated genre. In each chapter, you will see farces penned by underrepresented playwrights whenever possible. In the future, my hope is that we will see even more women and playwrights of the global majority taking up the farce gauntlet and bringing their unique perspectives to the form.

Finally, it was important to hear from those closest to the genre. Through interviews conducted over the last three years, international playwrights, directors, actors, designers, stage managers, dramaturgs, and scholars shared unique perspectives on the rewards and challenges of farce, and offered constructive, personal, and pointed words of wisdom to anyone considering engaging with contemporary farce.

My sincere wish is that within the contours of this book, I may ameliorate some of the more extreme responses to the idea of farce, and reduce the anxiety level for those artists taking the plunge into farce.

The opportunity to write about an aspect of theatre I enjoy and believe in has been a privilege. By sharing this enthusiasm and love of farce with *you*, the reader and potential farceur, I hope to shine a new light on an often-neglected genre of theatre, showcasing work that hasn't been given its full due. In addition, I want to invite prospective artists, imaginative scholars, and future audience members to seek out and embrace this challenging, yet enormously rewarding theatrical form.

With apologies to Edmund Gwenn, if dying is easy, and comedy is hard, farce is making the hard look easy.

## Works Cited

Davis, Jessica Milner. *Farce* (Second Edition). Transaction Publishers, 2003.
Davis, Jessica Milner. Personal Interview. 15 Jul. 2020.
Foley, Sean. Personal Interview. 18 Aug. 2020.
Kierkegaard, Sören, and Mackey, Louis. "Farce Is Far More Serious." *Yale French Studies*, no. 14, 1954, pp. 3–9. JSTOR, https://doi.org/10.2307/2928955
Lawson, Mark. "Farce Is Everywhere on Stage – But Why?" *The Guardian*, 10 Jun. 2012.

# ENTRANCES

## The Foundations of Contemporary Farce

**What is Farce?**

Think about a strange, awkward or uncomfortable situation you found yourself in, and reflect upon how you survived or at least extracted yourself from it. The date from hell. That text message you accidentally sent to the wrong person. Or that time nature called during a presentation. We all find ourselves in potentially farcical situations every day. Certainly you've done things you're not proud of to protect your dignity and retain some sense of self-respect. Perhaps you succeeded. Perhaps you failed. But in the moment, you did the only thing you could do, given the 'truth' and 'reality' of your situation. That's what characters in a farce do as well. Now, for dramatic effect, a good farce will distort the situation a little, squeeze more complications into the plot, cast an 'eclectic' ensemble of characters, add time pressure, raise the stakes and ramp up the passion. When all is said and done, though, farce is a mere laugh or two removed from our own lives. If comedy offers us ridiculous characters in real circumstances, farces feature real characters in ridiculous situations.

Consider the following scenario: You have an important job interview tomorrow morning at 9 a.m. in another city. The first leg of your flight is delayed, resulting in a late landing. Your original two-hour layover has now vanished and your connecting flight is set to leave in 20 minutes. You deplane from a gate on the other side of the airport and need to traverse the entire terminal to make your connecting flight. What do you do? Do you wait for the tram? You look up at the clock. Time is ticking away. The tram is nowhere in sight. You decide to run. But you're wearing heels and trying to manoeuvre a rolling suitcase. You hear your passenger name called over the loudspeaker. The doors are closing in ten minutes. The heels are slowing you down. You decide to take them off and begin to run in your stockings! The wheels of your carry-on bag are flip-flopping on the ground. You're trying to hold onto your shoes, your hair is falling into your eyes, and you're yelling at people to get out of your way. You can feel a cramp shooting down your calf. You're completely out of breath. And then the final boarding call. It's now or never. If you don't make your flight, you're stuck in a strange city, and that job interview you've worked so hard to secure, and really need financially, is in danger of slipping away. Oh, and this is the last flight out. Do you give up or do you do everything in your power to make that flight?

This is not an implausible scenario. In the moment, everything seems like it could lead to utter failure and in farce, that is death. Our brains and bodies work overtime as we strive to compensate for a disastrous situation. Now, as you were reading that last paragraph, part of you was thinking (albeit from the calm, comfort of your reading place): "This is silly…she could just call the employer and let them know her flight got delayed and she missed her connecting flight? Surely they would understand." Maybe. But where is the humour in that? Farce characters do not have the luxury to think through all of those scenarios.

Such scenarios have all the earmarks of a farce waiting to happen, and speaks to what Whitehall Theatre impresario Brian Rix observed as the thing common to all farces. They all "have the same thread running through them, though they may be presented differently: people with reputations to lose caught in situations where they can lose them" (Arditti 1992). We all worry about our reputations. We worry about how we'll be perceived by others. Reputation defines how we are perceived by society, the amount of respect we are allotted, and the rewards we reap based on public perception. For one to worry about the loss of reputation, however, implies that one has attained a certain outward status. If one has acquired a certain status in society's eye, it usually means they have much more to lose and subsequently may experience a greater downfall. With this in mind, Rix is correct that the potential danger to one's reputation runs through the majority of the farces that appeared onstage in the 19th through the mid-20th century. Whether it's the bourgeois characters from a Feydeau farce, or the wealthy guests and politicians that populate Neil Simon's 1988 play *Rumors*, there is a certain glee in watching privileged characters thrown into a dire situation where they will experience hardship previously unknown to them. They will suffer humiliation and face exposure in the public eye. Ironically, their worst night is probably a luxury for many of us. We *wish* that was the worst night of our lives! It seems, however, we need something stronger to struggle with. Another word that encompasses more than one's reputation. 'Status' becomes a catchword as it references not only one's class status, but also one's status in a marriage, social sphere, or workplace. Status can encompass both an inward and an outward loss.

The words 'reputation' and 'status' carry potent weight and are on the line in farce. However, both can be attributed to something more resonant to our contemporary audiences. In surveying the types of farces being written in the 21st century, there appears to be a more prominent force fueling these characters.

Failure.

Specifically, the fear of failure.

That might sound ponderous. But, in fact, in a world that often judges people based on levels of success, it is that fear that drives people to take action. To take a stand, to be activists, to make something of themselves. And in the process, take those risks that may require one to look foolish. Looking at a world that is in social, political, and economic upheaval, we see people valiantly struggling not to fail. Failing their loved ones, failing their community, failing their country, and failing themselves. Contemporary farce seeks to address these serious issues using the tropes of the form to disarm audiences.

## *Defining Contemporary Farce*

Playwright Michael Frayn, once wrote:

> One of the funny things about farce is that it seems to defy definition…farce is wonderful when it works and dreadful when it doesn't, and that it's incredibly hard to do. Hard to set up and harder still to sustain.
>
> *(Rix 180)*

In researching an active definition of farce, one observes a pattern of reductive language. Farces are described as 'ridiculous', 'light', 'improbable', 'highly exaggerated', 'cartoonish', 'absolutely absurd', 'broadly stylized', and 'silly'. Words like 'slapstick', 'bedroom' and 'sex' often appear as well. *The Bedford Introduction to Drama* sums up farce as "a short dramatic work that depends on exaggerated, improbable situations, incongruities, coarse language, and horseplay for its comic effect" (Jacobus 1798). Most definitions seem to agree that its sole purpose is to make people laugh and that its chief elements are physical comedy and highly convoluted situations.

Reading these words and phrases together, one senses condescension. That farce is merely a *divertissement*: a light-hearted theatrical endeavour whose singular purpose is to make us laugh at extremely 'ridiculous' behaviour.

Yes, we relish the recognizable and dynamic elements of the genre. Mistaken identities, miscommunications, tongue-twisting language, an actor portraying multiple characters, lightning-fast quick changes, and the razor-sharp timing of characters narrowly missing each other entering and exiting a room, have always been key and expected ingredients to crafting a successful and raucous farce. What will become readily apparent as we journey through our study of contemporary farce is that we must move beyond clichéd ideas and images of the genre and redefine it in contemporary terms.

It's not that slamming doors, witty wordplay, falling trousers, and broad physical comedy are no longer present in contemporary work. The physical nature of farce is what makes it a universally shared genre. The difference is that they are no longer the endgame. Playwrights and productions are finding innovative ways to present farce, often pushing actors' capabilities and designers' concepts. In the adapted works produced by British companies Le Navet Bete and Peepolykus, in collaboration with playwright John Nicholson, small ensembles of actors are tasked with telling epic stories, requiring them to portray anywhere from 5 to 10 different characters each over the course of an evening, with split-second changes in dialects, gender and costumes. In the *Goes Wrong* plays of Mischief Theatre, many of the farcical elements that befall the young actors of the Cornley Polytechnic Institute come in the form of set pieces falling off the wall, furniture collapsing, costume malfunctions and scenic elements being destroyed. And it all has to look 'accidental'.

A good farce is expertly choreographed, yet feels improvisational. It is a high-wire act that dares its performers to fail (fall?). Will the actors pull it off that evening? Will they make that costume quick-change in time? Will the doors open and close when they need to? Will the vomit spew on cue? Watching these acts of virtuosity is a delight of farce.

Beneath this virtuosity lies an urgency directly connected to serious themes. The genre invites brave playwrights who decide to wade into the form, addressing macro issues through the micro world of farce. Instead of pleasantly 'diverting us' for two hours, contemporary playwrights lure us in under the guise of farce and use humour to interrogate our world.

Speaking to this, scholar Eric Weitz observes that

> …the existential zeitgeist and historical horrors of the twentieth century compelled some practitioners to consider it as lit from below. How else to express the seemingly random manipulation of happenstance for maximum misfortune than through the genre of leering nightmare; what more relevant model for the dark arts of anti-communication than farce's natural affinity for deception?
>
> *(Weitz 34)*

Over the last twenty years, in the wake of 9/11, multiple wars, mass shootings, and civil unrest, farce has dared to venture into even darker territory. Farce no longer guarantees an audience a happy ending where everything works out; where problems are smoothed over, misunderstandings cleared up, and all knots untied. Danger is no longer someone getting caught cheating. Danger is the downfall of a family. Danger is the collapse of government. Danger is the threat of actual death. The physical worlds in which these plays are set might be contained within one living room set, but the stakes have ramifications beyond the five or six doors that dominate that set. Contemporary farce is no longer 'diverting us' with laughter. It is reflecting the fractured world around us.

To contextualise the evolution of farce, let us briefly define the differences, historically, among tragedy, comedy, and farce. Generally speaking, tragedies (either classical or modern) are serious dramas regularly featuring characters of note, respect, or accomplishment who fall from 'great heights' because of a fatal or 'tragic' flaw, perhaps pride, jealousy, loyalty, or ambition. Additionally, this flaw intertwines with fate, often leading to the death of one or more of the principal characters, including the protagonist.

Comedy is a broad form of drama that puts an emphasis on eliciting amusement or a warmed heart. It encompasses not only a perceived narrative technique, but also a range of styles: from satire to parody, from vaudeville to stand-up. Comedy focuses on ordinary characters attempting to resolve a problem, ascend their station, bring down 'the man', win their crush, while surmounting a series of escalating events. Comedies can be either situational or character-centred. In the process of the comedy, a character will have learned something about themselves, often going through a transformation. Traditionally, comedies end happily with a celebration, e.g. a wedding, a birth, a promotion.

Farce, as a subgenre of comedy, finds its earliest roots in Greek New Comedy, with Menander being one of the most popular playwrights of the time. New Comedy plays

> are about relatively plausible characters trapped in implausible situations… a standard plot involves a pair of lovers, who, thwarted by a parent, a pimp, or some other blocking character, ultimately find happiness together thanks to the schemes of a cunning slave.
>
> *(Berg and Parker vii)*

New Greek Comedy would give way to Roman Comedy, and the work of Plautus and Terence. Plautus exulted in bawdy jokes, wordplay, and sight gags. It is in his plays that we see the seeds of vaudeville, burlesque, and musical hall. Terence, on the other hand, wrote tightly-plotted comedies that were situation-based. His plays focused on domestic relationships involving parents, children, spouses, and siblings. It is in the work of Terence that we find the kernels of the modern 'sitcom'. As we look at farce's theatrical lineage beyond Greek and Roman comedy, the footprint of those early works would inspire early mediaeval English and French farces, the *Commedia dell'arte* troupes of 16th-century Italy, the plots and stock characters appearing in plays by Shakespeare and Molière, the playwrights of the Restoration and Georgian periods, leading to the 19th-century work of French dramatists Eugene Labiche and Georges Feydeau. They would, in turn, lay the groundwork for the modern farces that populated the 20th century. All of which brings us to contemporary farce.

So what is contemporary farce?

Contemporary farce actively combines narrative elements of comedy and tragedy and filters them through the tropes of farce. Marked by plays written in the 21st century, contemporary farce is defined by serious, even tragic stories contained within a comedic structure, where characters must persevere, with irrational fortitude and physical dexterity, to find order in a world spiralling into chaos.

**The 'Four Ps' of Farce**

Surveying work from the last 20 years, one sees a story pattern emerging. We can call this a 'Four P Story Arc' applicable to farce, allowing us to delineate its specific stages:

- Passion
- Persistence
- Panic
- Preservation

*Passion*

When we think about the singular demand for a character in a farce, we always come back to 'passion'. Characters passionately *want* something, and will stop at nothing to get it. In her book *What's the Story*, Anne Bogart posits that "[p]assion is engendered not by feeling or emotion, but rather by action. Taking a risk or hazarding one's life for moral or political choices creates the kind of heat that generates passion" (Bogart 16). It might be something they pursue like money (Bialystock and Bloom in Mel Brooks' *The Producers*), revenge (Paige, the cheated wife in Moira Buffini's *Dinner*), freedom (Dexter, the Roman servant in Phil Porter's *Vice Versa*), or food (Francis Henshall, the very hungry 'one man serving two guvnors' in Richard Bean's *One Man, Two Guvnors*). It might be something they need to conceal, like a tryst or someone else's secret (Robert protecting Bernard, his philandering friend, in *Boeing-Boeing*). The characters might be committed to a political or social agenda (Padraic in Martin McDonagh's *The Lieutenant of Inishmore*), or to exposing one (The Maniac in Dario Fo's *Accidental Death of an Anarchist*). Or simply, they want to put on a good show (the cast of *The Play That Goes Wrong*). In a farce, obtaining one's objective rises to absurd levels of need. This level of passion is important because it is what fuels the character's desire over the course of the play, and the character will stop at nothing to achieve it. Oftentimes, passion begets another form: obsession. Obsession sees a character so entranced that they will go to ridiculous lengths to avoid failure. Actor Jill Paice sums it up this way:

> As an actor, you must be willing to risk NOT being funny. You must consider yourself a TRUE actor, one with deep and desperate needs. Farce becomes funny not because you are landing a joke but because everything is SO important to your character. You must be willing to play high stakes and you must let them feel as real as your need to cram onto the subway at rush hour. Farce is all elbows and tears and true belief in what your character needs to accomplish.
>
> *(Paice 2020)*

In the words of playwright John Mortimer, "farce is tragedy played at 1000 revolutions a minute" (Arditti 1992). The needs and wants of characters in farce require as much passion, and are equally as important, as those in a tragedy. Characters' goals may not be as weighty as winning a war or curing cancer, but to the characters in a farce, they are life and death.

### *Persistence*

No matter how many obstacles are thrown at a character, they must *persist* in the pursuit of their passion/obsession. Even as their world is thrown into greater chaos. Boston-based director Jim Petosa says the essence of farce lies in a character's single-minded pursuit of a singular objective. This statement perfectly encapsulates how farce characters approach their challenges. Characters hide in closets, don ridiculous outfits, and make up outrageous stories not to consciously make us laugh. They engage in these outrageous activities: persisting in their quest, believing it is the most logical and truthful thing to do 'in the moment.' We must believe there is no alternative for the character.

Farce is about watching people with no sense of peripheral vision. We can liken it to horse racing. The blinkers that are worn by horses keep them from being distracted by their competitors or surroundings. The target is the finish line and they must keep their eyes up and straight ahead. Likewise, characters in a farce are so committed to their objective or 'target', that their blinkers leave them unable to see all possibilities. It's at these precise moments that characters engage in split-second decisions, resulting in lying, hiding in closets, pretending to be others, even risking their lives. Characters become so focused on their objectives, they may mis-hear or completely miss important information, resulting in even more problems and complications. Yet, they must persevere. The last thing they want is to fail. No matter how irrational the action taken is, the character believes "this choice will get me out of this situation." In a farce though, it usually leads to…

## Panic

Keeping the stakes high and the tension taut in farce is imperative. Stakes create pressure. Pressure forces choices. Choices reveal character. Playwright Michael Frayn sums it up this way,

> The action of farce is propelled by panic, with characters lying to save face, which compounds their troubles since they now have to deal not only with the original problem but also the lie and hence they behave even more bizarrely.
>
> *(Arditti 1992)*

Further to that, in his book *Stage Directions*, Frayn writes that when panic sets in, "characters lose the ability to control their destinies or even to recognise their own best interests…characters are reduced by their passions to the level of blind and inflexible machines" (Frayn 170).

Characters in a comedy do not know they are in a comedy. One of the best pieces of directorial advice you can offer an actor performing in a farce is to play the situation as if they're in a tragedy. No matter how absurd the situation becomes, judgement cannot enter into the equation. Farceurs should

> play the absurdity of their characters with a straight face – after all, this is what some members of their audience do outside the theatre. Besides, people do not always see other people for who they are, but see substitutions for them, people they want or would prefer to be…
>
> *(Bevis 45)*

Farce depends on its characters to make big impulsive choices; to think and act fast in the face of potential disaster. And there is *always* potential disaster lurking behind a door or around a corner. This allows the comedy to escalate. No matter how frivolous the situation, those life and death stakes propel the action forward with gusto. If done well, we are kept guessing as to what happens next; excitedly anticipating the next disaster and how characters will extract themselves from it. In drama, we dread disaster. In farce, we delight in being taken to the brink of disaster. As the gears of the plot mesh, and characters are forced to take more risks, panic morphs into hysteria, and we can feel the screws of the play's action tightening. It is also at this point in the play – a place of utter crisis – where plot threads converge, the rhythm of the play accelerates, and we land in full-blown bedlam with little resolution in sight.

What's critical, though, is that the choices characters make, no matter how ludicrous or unbelievable, emerge from the truth of the situation. We often judge the actions and reactions of characters as extreme. Maybe they are. Maybe not. Think about the lengths you would go to for something you are passionate about.

Indeed, "comic characters find a welcome home in farce because farce can make delusion seem lucid" (Bevis 45).

### Preservation

Inevitably, panic leads to an attempt at preservation and hopefully survival (literal or metaphorical!). As the play reaches its chaotic zenith, our characters must make crucial decisions. Do they confess their lies, admit defeat and take their comeuppance, or throw that figurative 'Hail Mary' pass that once and for all puts an end to the proceedings and allows them to escape unscathed? Often by the end of a farce, characters have done everything in their power to preserve not only their existence but their dignity, and have come out on the other side having restored order to their world.

Prior to the 21st century, farces usually ended up happily, with everything working itself out and all the right people ending up together. Today we're more likely to see farces end with characters and/or audiences left with unresolved feelings, as evidenced in plays like Thomas Bradshaw's *Intimacy*, Anthony Neilson's *The Lying Kind*, or Yasmina Reza's *God of Carnage*.

—

### The 'Mechanics' of Farce

A good play asks the classic Passover question: "Why is this night different from all other nights?" Something in the lives of the characters is different from yesterday, and the day before, and so on. Different enough to create high drama. For farce to take off, the difference between 'this night and all other nights' is that this is, in the words of writer and director Jonathan Lynn, "the worst day of your life" (Billington 2013). It must be for the piece to build, spiral out of control and result in potential tragedy. For the characters in a farce, as previously mentioned, the stakes are life and death. Farce sees its characters racing or pitted against time or a deadline, forcing them to think on their feet. Whether it's accomplishing a task before someone returns, or doing everything in their power to get rid of someone in order to 'buy time' or 'hide the evidence', we are always waiting for the metaphorical (or depending on the play, literal) bomb to go off.

This usually results in a 'pressure-cooker' situation, where one main story plays out over the course of 24 hours or less, restricting its characters to one onstage location. Doors become important because they trap people, sequester people, and also keep the outside world at bay. When characters leave a room, they potentially leave themselves open to trouble. Doors lead to pleasure or pain. A well-designed farce set can feel like a labyrinthine nightmare to the characters.

Interestingly enough, we have seen some contemporary farces dare to do away with doors, or any kind of realistic setting. Instead, emphasis is placed on absurd character pursuits (Marius Von Mayerburg's *The Ugly One*), an actor's ability to morph into multiple characters in a heartbeat (Patrick Barlow's *The 39 Steps*), or forging a unique camaraderie with the audience (Ben Ashenden and Alex Owen's *The Comeback*). In these pieces, it's less about the solidity of doors and more about the act of entering and exiting a space. What does a character bring into a room, and what do they take with them when they leave? And how do these two actions complicate the proceedings? The physical opening, closing, and slamming of doors can produce a choreographed euphoria. At its root, however, it is the energy produced with every coming and going.

We tend not to find as many subplots in farce simply because the one main action becomes so convoluted, that adding too many extra layers to the story can actually dampen its impact. In drama, a 'sub-' or secondary plot often complements, mirrors, or augments the main action. In farce, we find characters getting swept up by the main action, resulting in new complications splintering off from the original problem. A rare example of farce that does the opposite of this would be Larry David's HBO comedy *Curb Your Enthusiasm*, where petty choices splinter off, creating major problems.

Recently, the Aristotelian unities of time, place, and action, which have defined the majority of farces over the years, have given way to interesting experiments. John Guare's *A Free Man of Color* spans years. Richard Bean's *One Man, Two Guvnors* takes place in a variety of settings. James Graham's play *The Culture* features three different intersecting plots. Even without the building steam of the 'pressure-cooker', more and more playwrights are finding unique ways to corral the farcical energy in the storytelling, with the reversals or upheavals in form often deepening the thematic ideas.

## Structure and Farce

Farces tend to start slowly with fewer laughs. This is intentional on the playwright's part. Farces may have a longer 'wind-up' because they are predominantly driven by plot and situation. For later payoffs, the playwright must take more time to clearly introduce the characters, their relationships and potential conflicts. As the play moves forward, if we are not clear about who is doing what to whom at any given moment, we may lose the thread of the action and the humour of the circumstances.

One of the thrills of farce is watching how the characters 'unknot' themselves from the improbable situation in which they find themselves entangled. A problem is presented to the protagonist throwing their life out of balance. The remainder of the play sees one or more characters helping or hindering the protagonist in solving this initial problem. Inevitably, their attempts result in reversals of fortune and added problems. Audiences delight in the plot complications.

The playwright is planting what we can call theatrical landmines. These are plot points carefully orchestrated to 'blow up' later on. Audiences pick up on these and recognise that a character's lie, or an unexpected revelation will come back to haunt the story.

For example, in Marc Camoletti's *Boeing-Boeing*, Bernard has structured his trysts with three different stewardesses based on their predictable airline schedules. Up to this point, his carefully crafted calendar ensures the three women will never cross paths. When the American stewardess reveals early in the play that the new Boeing airplane model is *faster*, audiences quickly hear the potential wrench being thrown into Bernard's gears.

Secondly, if the action of the play is pitched too high at the start, the farce has nowhere to go. A well-constructed farce requires patience on the part of the audience. Part of the fun is the anticipation. We want to watch the farce unfold and then unravel.

To help with this, especially in situational comedy, farce structure may incorporate three key ingredients: repetition, inversion, and interference. Repetition, be it in dialogue or action, plays on audience expectation and investment in the snowballing of plot. In Dario Fo's modern one-act farce, *Non tutti i ladri vengono nuocere* ("The Virtuous Burglar"), the word 'misunderstanding' is tossed off casually at the beginning of the play by a philandering husband. By the time we get to the end of the play, and multiple 'misunderstandings' have played out, the word is invoked repeatedly as a desperate defence of morality by the four cheating spouses, and an exhausted Burglar who has reluctantly been caught up in their cover-up. From an action perspective, repetition may find its form in multiple characters donning the same disguise, hiding under a similar piece of furniture, or, as in the case of *One Man, Two Guvnors*, the repeated violence inflicted upon Alfie, the decrepit waiter, and his recurring tumbles down the stairs.

Inversion is an important tool playwrights use for comic effect. The playwright upends audience expectations by "reverse[ing] the situation and invert[ing] roles" (Bergson 51) that are understood by audiences to be societal norms. In *The Virtuous Burglar*, the Burglar is our hero and stands out as a beacon of virtue amidst the two entitled bourgeois couples. Another stark example would be in Joe Penhall's *Birthday*, where husband Ed is on the cusp of giving birth after his wife Lisa is no longer able to conceive.

The third ingredient heightening the comedic plot is what Bergson calls "the reciprocal interference of series [where]…a situation is invariably comic when it belongs simultaneously to two altogether independent series of events and is capable of being interpreted in two entirely different meanings at the same time" (Bergson 52). This is on full display in Act 2 of *Ken Ludwig's A Comedy of Tenors*, where characters believe they are engaging with volatile opera singer Tito Merelli, when they are actually speaking to (or making out with) his *doppelgänger*, bellhop Beppo. Beppo's innocuous responses and actions not only confuse Tito when he is confronted with a conversation he never had, but also lands him in hot water with his loved ones. These cross-wired conversations and actions are standard fare in farce, and, as we will see, not only produce comic complications, but in some cases lead to unexpected violence.

A well-constructed farce is like a roller coaster. We strap ourselves in for the show. We are slowly pulled up a steep incline with the playwright planting landmines of plot and character. Anticipation builds. We finally reach the top and the accelerated drop begins a ride where we endure the twists and turns of the plot, until we finally come to the end, with heart rate and order restored to 'normal'.

## Character and Farce

As we have noted, the writing of a farce requires the precision of a clockmaker. It's not surprising that words like mathematical, scientific, and musical are also used as descriptors of farce. Farce scripts require meticulous attention to detail, excellent comic timing, and an innate ability to play well with others.

Producing a farce is like conducting a musical score. Look at Act II of Michael Frayn's *Noises Off* on the page and see how the play echoes a musical score. An expert ensemble of actors is required to pull off a farce and, more importantly, they have to be 'in tune' with one another. Every character has a 'line of music' – through physical action or text – that they are responsible for executing.

One character carries the 'melody line' of the plot and two others offer a form of harmony (even if it's a dissonant sound!). When two pieces of action are happening on different parts of the stage at the same time – it's a form of point/counterpoint. Staging a farce requires the director to sculpt moments of fortissimo and moments of pianissimo. Rhythm changes are necessary to maintain surprise and stay ahead of the audience. And because the entire ensemble is integral to the execution of farce, actors have to determine who needs to 'sing out' and who needs to 'back-up'. When do you 'riff' and when do you embrace the silence or 'rest?' This equates roughly to recognising in both the overall arc of the play and in individual moments, who the 'set-up person' is and who delivers the punchline. Who is the one trying to restore order, and who is there to upset the social order? Each character is equally important to the overall story. It is up to the actors to understand their role in the score/script, so no one obscures the action or tips the scales of the play and we lose the thread of the plot.

As previously mentioned, because of its emphasis on plot, characters in farce are rarely allotted the time to fully develop, preventing them from achieving a well-roundedness. Instead, we are often met with characters who have inherited traits from classical comedies, in particular that of the *Commedia dell'arte* – the scheming Arlecchino, the lecherous/miserly Pantalone, the Young Lovers, and the sassy servant, Columbina. In some ways, these recognizable types offer a disarming familiarity, and situate the audience almost immediately. This character evolution is patently evident in the contemporary stock roles of the naive adult-child (Bertie Wooster in *Jeeves and Wooster in Perfect Nonsense*), the blustering know-it-all (Ester in *Waiting for Waiting for Godot*), and the secretive young lovers (Mimi and Carlo in *Ken Ludwig's A Comedy of Tenors*).

Characters themselves rarely evolve or change. Growing a conscience or suddenly undergoing a huge political or spiritual shift is an infrequent occurrence, unless employed as a tactic. This is why we tune in each week to our favourite television sitcom. Characters are established for their unique traits and personalities and we want to see how these traits land characters in uncomfortable situations and how they will survive to see another day. Think about sitcom characters like Julia Louis-Dreyfus' 'Selina Meyer' in *Veep* or Matt LeBlanc's 'Joey' from *Friends*. Selina is an ambitious, yet self-centred political narcissist. Joey is the loveable, not-too bright ladies' man. We accept these characters for who they are and *want* to see them get into trouble, knowing there is pleasure in watching them get out of it. It's not to say they don't have surprising moments that reveal nuance. In fact, those moments are important. Selina recognizes a moment of hubris; admitting she made a mistake in the way she handled a political situation. Joey is given the opportunity to show flashes of insight that surprise everyone. Sitcoms require this so that characters never grow stale. These reversals in character logic humanise them in a way that fascinates us. What the writers are careful not to do is let these moments transform the characters entirely. We don't want to see Selina become a sentimental political pushover. We don't want to see Joey bask in his brilliance and become consciously aware of it. Those things would tilt what are carefully crafted ensemble dynamics, where the characters have been designed to complement, and counter, each other. This is the same in theatrical farce. You would think that after surviving major trials, characters would have learned lessons or be more attuned to perils. They simply do not have the wherewithal to do that. Most likely, if we were to revisit these characters after the curtain falls, we'd find many of them making the same mistakes or becoming enmeshed in similarly compromising situations.

Farce scripts can be seen as blueprints that are skeletal. The playwright has given us a well-crafted plot, clear character goals, and a physical playground allowing ample opportunity for considerable stage business. Together, these provide a huge catalyst for one of the most telling aspects of the genre…

**Physical Comedy & Comedic Violence in Farce**

In musical theatre, when characters can't speak their thoughts anymore, they sing. Farce is similar. When characters can no longer talk their way into or out of a situation, they will respond with a bold physical choice that erupts from their body. They hide behind a door or eat a letter (quite literally, eat a letter). When confronted with the possibility of being 'caught', the best decision in that moment might be to take on a new role or pretend to be someone else; possibly even donning the clothes and appearance of someone of the opposite sex. Physical comedy is a character's logical corporeal response to a spiralling situation.

Performers of farce are athletes. They run, jump, slide, shake, fall, and crawl. Farce is physical. Very physical. It requires stamina, concentration and focus. Even in moments of stillness, there is a physical specificity and commitment that energises the space. One of the true pleasures of watching farce is witnessing actors at the top of their game performing with a virtuosity that can only be seen to be believed. And whether we're watching one character trying to talk their way out of hot water, or witnessing the dexterous abilities of actors switching characters with lightning-fast speed, it thrills us in the same way as when we are watching death-defying acts at the circus. As stated previously, the characters in farce always seem to be on the *brink* of death – metaphorical or literal. And for this reason, the characters in a farce will do everything in their power to survive the day.

The physical body is an important element of farce. Because "there's no time", as Mortimer notes, characters in a farce do not have the luxury to get overly philosophical. Farce vibrates in the scenic container of the space and the body. Mouths and bodies are working faster than their brains. Instead of adapting logically to the circumstances, characters engage in what French philosopher Henri Bergson describes as "mechanical inelasticity" where comedy is borne out of an inability to "[shape] our conduct in accordance with the reality which is present" (Bergson 13).

Because there is no time to think, the farce body must act on impulse. If characters wait for the brain to work out the rational response to a moment, the energy and fun of farce would be derailed. Instead, the body leads the way and the actions follow. The farce body expresses itself in strange and unpredictable ways. For this reason, the 'unthinking farce body' engages in and sustains numerous acts of pain and violence. Characters trip over furniture, are slapped in the face, kicked in the groin, and fall down stairs. They shove people out of the way, push them through doors, and knock them over the head to shut them up. These actions are not designed to produce laughs (even if they elicit laughter from the audience). The laughs are a by-product of watching a character struggle to escape failure under time constraints, in a high-stakes moment. The more momentum a farce picks up in its telling, the greater the chance a character will suffer physically in the process. The threat of pain in farce becomes inevitable.

**Language and Farce**

With farce putting an emphasis on the physical body, language is often dismissed as secondary. In the words of playwright John Mortimer, "comedy [has] to do with people saying funny lines. In farce, after the first ten minutes there's no time to make jokes because [the characters are] so busy running around; the laughs come from character and situation" (Arditti 1992).

Farce may not be language-driven, but it does showcase witty repartee and dialogue. Characters are rarely given long monologues or prone to speechifying – unless it's set up as a character trait. There is not enough time amidst the action for a character to pause for an emotional breakthrough. It can be argued that language in farce functions similarly to irrational physical actions. Verbal responses are kinesthetically the result of the mouth moving faster than the brain, in the pressure of the moment. As a result, characters in farce are always improvising stories and arguments that have not been well-thought-out, causing further trouble.

Depending on the character, speed can elicit wit. Insults, puns, and double entendres are trademarks in farce. Language itself can become a form of self-defence for characters and wielded as a weapon. Audiences love to see characters think on their feet and when they're being called out or questioned, we want to see where this leads. And as we started this section, when talking is not enough, sometimes you have to run, hide, and pray you won't be exposed!

All of this provides the aforementioned blueprint in which actors, directors, and designers must fill in the world between the lines with ingenuity and imagination.

### Themes and Farce

The question remains: does contemporary farce have more on its mind than the conventional 'bedroom' or 'sex' farces that were popular in Europe in the mid-late 19th century and early 20th century? Yes! Granted, we still see tried-and-true plot conventions and set-ups on a regular basis. Mistaken identities, missed connections, and misinterpreted letters and messages remain farce de rigueur. Playwrights are still asking their characters to wrestle with adultery, jealousy, and hypocrisy. However, contemporary farce casts a wider net when it comes to subject matter. Instead of simply filling a need for escapist entertainment, contemporary playwrights consciously employ the conceits and constructs of farce to examine family dynamics, gender and identity, class, race, political agendas, culture, and theatre itself. We are invited to laugh, but, increasingly, contemporary laughs come with discomfort.

Farce has always dealt with uncomfortable subjects and themes. It is the Seven Deadly Sins writ large and unabashedly across the stage. These 'sins' are then filtered through complex plots that revolve around basic human needs: from power to sex; from food to money. These are needs that we all identify with, and when given the opportunity to see a character unabashedly act out base impulses to satisfy these needs, we experience a certain adrenaline rush, a vicarious feeling of understanding or horror or recognition. In the words of theatre essayist Eric Bentley, people who enjoy farce

…are shielded by delicious darkness and seated in warm security…[enjoying] the privilege of being totally passive while on stage our most treasured unmentionable wishes are fulfilled before our eyes by the most violently active human beings that ever sprang from the human imagination.

*(Bentley 229)*

There is also a great deal of voyeuristic pleasure in watching people suffer at the hands of others; brought to the precipice of death only to 'live to see another day'.

Until the second half of the 20th century, save for a handful of plays by the likes of Alfred Jarry (*Ubu Roi*), and the absurdist/tragi-farces of Eugene Ionesco, Samuel Beckett, and Thornton Wilder (*The Skin of Our Teeth*), farce has not been labelled as dark, edgy, or experimental. The sins remain the same, the stories in which these sins are now wrapped have taken on an immediacy, even danger. The farce worlds that contemporary playwrights are presenting feel more perilous. They are infusing their farces with vicious satire. Parody has greater urgency.

Products of their time, many farces that once elicited laughs based on racial, gender, or sexual stereotypes are recognised as inappropriate and unacceptable. Instead, playwrights are pushing the envelope, playing off and exploding those stereotypes; consciously asking us to take a look at our biases, flaws, and foibles through a 21st-century lens.

Farce is angrier, more pointed and willing to break the rules. Marriages break up. People die. Worlds are left in disarray. The play might offer a 'happy ending' for the characters, but we are often left unsettled.

## The Five Doors to Contemporary Farce

To help anchor our discussion on contemporary farce, we will specifically focus on plays written since 2000 and significant revivals of classic or forgotten works. In the process, we will see patterns emerge from an anthropological perspective. The types of stories and thematic ideas being treated within the farce construct are edgier, challenging, and virtuosic; unafraid to upend or play with comedic expectation in order to provoke discussion through laughter.

These observations lead to the following:
The Five Doors to Contemporary Farce:

1) Domestic Farce
2) Social Farce
3) Political Farce
4) Cultural Farce
5) Backstage Farce

These 'doors' are designed to offer readers, practitioners, and audiences an entrance to viewing contemporary farce. Contemporary farce is no longer content to offer an entertaining night out. Its laughter is now drawing on 'hot-button' contemporary issues, often steeped in domestic, social, and political commentary.

Laughter remains at the heart of the work. It might be tinged with pain and our smiles might be a little forced, but we still laugh. In certain instances, we may laugh so hard we cry. Farce offers us an outlet to purge and experience a form of catharsis. The laughter today may even be more needed. Our contemporary world continues to endure war, economic collapse, terrorist attacks, school shootings, police brutality, racism, homophobia, sexual harassment, and, most recently, a crippling pandemic. Farce can help us understand and move through the chaos. Farce teaches us what it takes to survive in a world gone mad. Sometimes it's uproarious and uncontrollable, sometimes it's sweet, and sometimes the comedy is as dark as night.

As we enter our five doors, exploring plays and playwrights that have embraced, subverted, upended, and expanded the genre, we will observe how contemporary farce, through its experiments in form, theme, and character, announces itself as a 'legitimate' theatrical entity demanding our attention.

Welcome to the art of serious laughter.

## Works Cited

Arditti, Michael. "An Anatomy of Farce." *Michael Arditti*, 9 Sept. 1992, https://michaelarditti.com/non-fiction/an-anatomy-of-farce/

Bentley, Eric. *The Life of the Drama*. Applause, 1991.

Bergson, Henri. *Laughter: An Essay on the Meaning of the Comic* (Translated by Cloudesley Brereton and Fred Rothwell). Book Jungle, 2007.

Bevis, Matthew. *Comedy: A Very Short Introduction*. Oxford University Press, 2012.

Billington, Michael. "Forget Hatchet-Faced Critics – Farce Is the Quintessence of Theatre." *Guardian*, 2013, https://www.theguardian.com/stage/2013/sep/05/defence-farce-theatre-trend

Bogart, Anne. *What's the Story*. Routledge, 2014.

Frayn, Michael. *Stage Directions: Writing on Theatre 1970–2008*. Faber & Faber, 2008.

Jacobus, Lee A. *The Bedford Introduction to Drama* (Fifth Edition). Bedford/St. Martin's, 2005.

Paice, Jill. Personal Interview. 20 Aug. 2020.

Parker, Douglas, and Berg, Deena (Translators). *Plautus & Terence: Five Comedies*. Hackett Publishing Co., 1999.

Rix, Brian. *Life in the Farce Lane, or Tragedy with Its Trousers Down: The A to C (Aristophanes to Cooney) of Farce*. Andre Deutsch, 1995.

Weitz, Eric. *Theatre & Laughter*. Red Globe Press, 2016.

# 1
# DOMESTIC FARCE

To define contemporary domestic farce, we must contextualise what this type of farce has looked like historically. Behind this door we find a host of bedroom or 'sex' farces featuring characters doing everything in their power to hide, protect, even juggle, their or someone else's indiscretions. In his book *Farce: A History from Aristophanes to Woody Allen*, Albert Bermel refers to these as 'popular farces' that "[confine] themselves for the most part to living rooms and bedrooms [and that] inescapably concentrate on those time-hallowed twin themes, adultery and cuckoldry – that is, adultery unconsummated and cuckoldry feared" (Bermel 240). Indeed, one could argue that the theme of adultery is the defining feature of most farces up through the 20th century. In the words of playwright Michael Frayn, "The bare minimum of farce is usually three people – two people discovered in a compromising situation by a third …" (Moseley 133). The key words there are 'bare minimum'. An exquisitely executed farce may double, even triple the number of people caught in compromising positions. These plays feature a protagonist – often male – who is caught up in one of the following situations:

1) They are carrying on an affair and trying to hide it from their spouse or another partner (e.g. Ray Cooney's *Run for Your Wife*).
2) They are stuck in a loveless/static marriage or relationship, and a new potential suitor, or a romantic partner from their past, shows up igniting old feelings, thereby complicating matters with the current partner (e.g. Peter Shaffer's *Black Comedy*, Brian Friel's *The Communication Cord*).

DOI: 10.4324/9780429268809-3

3) They inadvertently get caught up in the hijinks of a friend or loved one and must help that person i) hide a sexual indiscretion, ii) extract them from a potentially explosive domestic situation or iii) help their friend unite with the person they're meant to be with. In the process, this character often finds themselves forced to make ethically or morally questionable choices. (e.g. Marc Camoletti's *Boeing-Boeing*).

The words 'bedroom' and 'sex' have often been invoked to describe these farces because the plots revolve around characters jumping in and out of beds. The bedroom, that most intimate of places, becomes a place of potential danger. It is a place where indiscretions threaten to literally or metaphorically soil the marriage bed and rip a relationship apart. The taboo of adultery is both fascinating and uncomfortable. By spending an evening in the presence of adulterers, liars, and cheaters, an audience can live vicariously from the comfort and safety of its theatre seats. Set in a seemingly innocuous urban American home or a London flat, we watch fictional characters to whom we have no personal attachment, act on their sexual impulses. This may include craving a younger, more beautiful object of affection, living out that secret life of adventure, or simply finding alternate ways not to drown in the doldrums of marital and familial responsibilities. Instead, we watch characters obsess over their heart's desire; hiding, seeking, and doing everything in their power to obtain a coveted prize. Of course it's a farce, so nothing goes according to plan. We revel in the havoc onstage, watching with glee and laughter as a play's domestic world is turned upside down. As obstacles mount, more questions arise: Will this person 'get away with it'? Will they be able to lie and improvise their way out of a spiralling situation? Will they return to their loved ones unscathed with no one the wiser to their scheming, plotting and cover-ups? Will their loved ones leave?

The general result of the traditional bedroom or sex farce was that the main adulterer or schemer in question either got away with their infidelities (oftentimes by pure luck or chance) or made a conscious decision to forego their illicit affair and return to their loved one with a greater appreciation for what they have in the marriage. On the odd occasion, a character's indiscretions were exposed or prompted a 'confession', but the fallout never seemed to be of consequence. Part of the joy of these modern farces is that a moral barometer is rarely employed. Playwrights are not interested in passing judgement on their characters' behaviour. They are more interested in the behaviour itself and watching how characters extricate themselves from an ever-mounting situation of ridiculousness. Buried beneath the farcical tropes of these modern bedroom farces are satirical explorations of privilege. We may argue, however, that these writers are plumbing the middle and upper class as targets because there is more fun to be had at the expense of the 'haves' who can afford to be taken down a peg, rather than the 'have-nots' who are trying to squeak by. For this reason we rarely see farces about the homeless, the poor, or the destitute.

Audiences are more inclined to see those who seem to have it all, fall from their privileged perch. Mind you, the target audiences of these farces were of a similar class background: those able to afford a Broadway or West End production. So, in some ways, watching a character 'get away with it' might be life-affirming.

As we move into the 21st century, the 'bedroom farce' label has lost traction. Instead, playwrights are finding further comic possibilities in domestic and social situations, where a shared understanding of what is customarily appropriate and what is not, exists among a group of like-minded people. In his essay "Laughter", French philosopher Henri Bergson says,

> To understand laughter, we must put it back into its natural environment, which is society, and above all must we determine the utility of its function, which is a social one…Laughter must answer to certain requirements of life in common. It must have a social signification.
>
> *(Bergson 12)*

Generally, laughter in farce was mined from adulterous situations, or characters bucking conventional domestic 'rules' for carnal pleasure. Now, laughter emerges as families wrestle with moral conundrums and self-preservation.

Let's take a closer look at the word 'domestic'. 'Domestic' on its own conjures images of 'home life', 'chores', and 'family BBQs'. There is a sense of tranquillity and calm. A way of living that indicates one's wild days are behind them. From the outside, a domestic existence appears balanced and ordered. The domestic farce label seems more appropriate because it is concerned with upheaval in the family. Domestic farce exposes the unhappiness of one or more parts of the household. Characters in a domestic farce are no longer satisfied with their home life. As characters are introduced to us we quickly become aware that the well-polished silver is quite tarnished. These characters are looking for love, acceptance, respect, and a sense of belonging – things they are not getting from their families or loved ones. In certain scenarios, their behaviour is a cry for help, a need to have more control over their life. What prevents this from spilling over into serious drama is the comical and often-irrational decisions these family members make in their search for change, landing them in spiralling chaos. More and more, contemporary farceurs are looking at how to exploit families in the middle of social upheaval for laughs. Domestic farces remind us that all is not greener on the other side of the homemaking fence.

## Domestic Farce in the 21st Century

The traditional bedroom farce that populated stages during the late 19th and 20th centuries began to wane at the turn of the 21st century. With the millennium ushering in the catastrophic events of 9/11 and its military aftermath, the #MeToo movement calling out misogynistic behaviour, civil unrest invoking people to stand up and protest, and a divisive political landscape amid a Covid-19-ravaged world, familial pain is palpable. The sex farce now seems frivolous. Laughter does not come in the guise of adultery. With so many more pressing issues dominating the world, few contemporary playwrights are interested in watching privileged characters (especially white men) get away with adultery or other acts that defy the domestic order, especially at the expense of a put-upon wife or 'naive mistress'. It's not that the bedroom farce has gone away. Rather, playwrights have relegated it to the role of plot complication rather than being the driving force in the action. Farcical laughter in the domestic farce is born out of recognisable and relatable situations. Parents trying to protect their children. Children trying to assert independence from their parents. Siblings navigating their complicated bonds. We see characters wrestling with midlife crises, growing old, and trying to remain relevant or useful. The *breakdown* of domesticity is what drives domestic farces in the 21st century. Humour emerges from a sense of familial fragility. This fragility is compounded by fear. A fear of loss, a fear of being wrong, a fear of being seen as past one's prime or irrelevant. When we meet characters in a domestic farce, these elements are ready to erupt, finding the primacy of its humour in the potential implosion of family.

We all understand the complicated nature of families. In farce, we laugh at their pain because there is familiarity. We are catching family members not only at their most ridiculous, but also at their most vulnerable. Fear and fragility pervade contemporary domestic farce. In the past, no matter how dire the situation, farce characters on the precipice of disaster were all but assured that everything would work out in the end. In contemporary domestic farce, endings aren't always 'happy' or even satisfactory.

In this chapter, we will examine the evolution of domestic farce, citing specific examples from 20th-century European and North American theatre. This will lead us to look at selected 21st-century works by contemporary playwrights, focusing on how they have embraced and played with the genre.

**Rire Domestique: French Domestic Farce**

Before we look at contemporary examples of domestic farce, we must look to the past and recognise the grandfathers of modern and contemporary farce: Eugène Labiche (*An Italian Straw Hat*) and Georges Feydeau (*A Flea in Her Ear*). These two Frenchmen, in addition to the lesser-known playwrights Maurice Hennequin, Henri Meilhac and Louis Halevy, would not only pave the way for many of the domestic farces surveyed in this chapter, but also create a structural template that has been and is still used today by many of our 20th- and 21st-century farceurs. Cleverly combining two of the most popular French theatrical forms from the 19th century, the 'well-made' play and the satirical 'vaudeville', Labiche would create and Feydeau later master what we might refer to now as the 'well-made' farce. Often derided for its formulaic and two-dimensionality, the 'well-made' play

> depended on a tightly-organised plot in which the entire action was motivated by some secret involving the main character, a secret revealed only gradually as the play proceeded, until by the final curtain full knowledge had completely changed everyone's lives – for the worse in a 'well-made' melodrama, for the better in a 'well-made' farce.
>
> *(McLeish ix)*

Other narrative elements and devices that defined the 'well-made' play (and would find their way into the subsequent 'well-made' farces) included previously disguised characters being unmasked, letters revealing withheld information falling into the hands of the wrong person, and expertly timed entrances and exits resulting in characters narrowly missing one another.

The 'well-made' play was designed to be seen by audiences for its serious (melo)drama, even with its clearcut heroes and villains. Yet looking at the aforementioned structural elements, it is not hard to see how farce as we know it today evolved from the form. The above tropes, to varying degrees, have been adapted (and subverted by) playwrights such as Joe Orton, Dario Fo, Ken Ludwig, Richard Bean, Martin McDonagh, Selina Fillinger and Deborah Salem Smith.

Vaudevilles or 'boulevard comedies', on the other hand, were strictly comic pleasures for 19th-century French audiences. Filled with stock characters, slapstick, and familiar songs, vaudevilles were heavy on plot and comic situations. These theatrical soufflés poked gentle fun at the bourgeoisie.

By combining the two forms, Labiche and Feydeau could craft a well-structured and entertaining farce, built on the recognisable conventions of the 'well-made' play, and use it to effectively satirise "bourgeois morality and convention" (McLeish xii). The expert plotting and seemingly organic cause and effect of action and dialogue never gave way to preaching or 'moralising'. Yet amidst the hilarity of the work, a playwright like Feydeau could explore more serious issues. For example, the "status of women: their equality with men and their 'power' within society and especially within marriage and the household" (McLeish xiii). It is his female characters that actually drive the action and expose the male characters for their obtuse behaviour. Feydeau's treatment and empowerment of his female characters carries over into the French farces of the 20th and 21st centuries. They are not easily manipulated puppets at the hands of bumbling male protagonists. Feydeau's mastery of the conventions of the well-made play – not to mention his audience's familiarity with the form – allowed him to ironise and parody both it and its component parts, to deal easily and farcically with subjects which, handled by serious dramatists at the same period, evoked howls of outrage and embarrassment.

*(McLeish xiii)*

Content aside, what contemporary farce owes to Feydeau is his precision in farce construction. A strong admirer of farce and specifically Feydeau's work, actor/writer John Cleese says

a perfect farce script is like clockwork: the writer winds it up by carefully establishing credible premises, and then lets the whole thing unwind, with inevitable but startling logic. My heart always goes back to…Feydeau, the best of a crop of farce writers who kept Paris amused during the belle epoque era.

*(Cleese 2017)*

It is the work of Feydeau and his contemporaries that have paved the way for farce, and specifically domestic farce that we see today.

### *Marc Camoletti:* **Boeing-Boeing *(1960)***

In 2007, a long-forgotten Parisian farce that had premiered in Paris forty years prior, took London, and subsequently Broadway, by storm. After decades of being relegated to the farce remainder bin, a revival of Marc Camoletti's *Boeing-Boeing* (English translation by Beverly Cross and Francis Evans) opened in the West End, charming audiences, surprising critics, and receiving two Olivier Award nominations. This traditional 'bedroom farce', complete with six doors, was dusted off and given a 'Swingin' Sixties' polish and shine. What could've been an antiquated revival not only became a smash hit, but also reminded audiences that there is joy to be mined from a well-crafted domestic farce, when viewed through the right theatrical lens.

The plot of *Boeing-Boeing* has a very simple and recognisable premise, allowing for myriad complications: one person trying to protect a secret/indiscretion which we learn about at the top of the play. Bernard, an architect and Parisian bachelor (an American living abroad in the Broadway revival), is secretly engaged to three different airline stewardesses (American, Italian and German), whom he has been effectively juggling with a well-oiled scheduling system that is dependent on their respective flight itineraries. When two of them announce to him their airlines are upgrading to the much faster 'Boeing' jet, the timetable system Bernard has been relying on (nay, obsessing over) is completely upended. Over the course of approximately twelve hours, mayhem ensues as Bernard tries to keep his three 'fiancées' from discovering one another.

To complicate matters, his old college friend, the comparatively inexperienced Robert, arrives unexpectedly at Bernard's apartment in Paris, and unwittingly becomes caught up in the deception plot to maintain the secret. With the help of Bernard's put-upon French maid Berthe, the two men attempt to prevent Bernard's triumvirate of fiancées from discovering one another and in the process possibly find the person they're actually meant to be with.

How did this "creaky French comedy…[which] had no earthly right to be as funny as it is", (Brantley 2008), and that no one had been producing, find a second life on stage, and become one of the 21st century's most popular farces? The answer lies in a chance encounter with the play's film adaptation, the talents of a 'go-for-broke' acting ensemble, and a thematic refocusing that uses the container of a domestic sex farce to examine how the more one tries to control a situation, the likelier it will lead to chaos.

A few years prior, director Matthew Warchus had seen the play's 1965 film adaptation on television. Upon further investigation, Warchus discovered it had been a play and having

> never had the chance to do any contemporary farce…I was very eager to direct it. There's something very simple and pure about it, almost like Plautus. I think enough time has passed for it to no longer be considered out of date and to move into the genre of a classic.
>
> *(Koenig 2007)*

Camoletti's *Boeing-Boeing* originally premiered in 1960 and ran for an astonishing 19 years in Paris. When the play first opened, it was described as a "young, fresh vaudeville, without a shadow of vulgarity" (Capon 61) and it was said that "Camoletti did not leave three minutes go by without either introducing a new character or imagining a retort that brings out laughter" (Gauthier 61).

Two years later, it opened in London and was met with similar commercial acclaim, running for seven years. Despite negative critical response, what was it about the play that endeared itself to the public and made it so popular, especially in Europe and the UK? In a 2007 article for the *Independent*, Rhoda Koenig says that the public's fascination with *Boeing-Boeing* was because

> England was a different place. Censorship of the theatre was still in force, and offstage, too, the country had more in common with the financially and morally straitened Fifties than with a decade soon to be a synonym for sensual indulgence. When few people had set foot in an aeroplane, stewardesses were seen as glamorous and sophisticated - playgoers of 1962 no doubt agreed with Bernard that such girls were the crème de la crème because "apart from being beautiful, they have to be healthy, good at cooking, good at nursing, witty, wise and friendly.
>
> *(Koenig 2007)*

**32** Domestic Farce

One gets the sense that the original West End production of *Boeing-Boeing* provided British audiences with a story in which they could indulge their inner 'naughtiness' and live vicariously, through the bad behaviour of its male protagonists, but also through siding with the 'take charge' attitudes of the three airline stewardesses and even Berthe:

> The girls may be shacking up with Bernard, but this daring behaviour is indulged because each believes she's his fiancée; the sexual turnabout at the end is both logically and emotionally inexplicable to anyone born since the play's premiere. Back then a man of marriageable age who, like Robert, says he doesn't know much about kissing was seen as a figure of affectionate fun, not someone in need of a psychoanalyst.
>
> *(Koenig 2007)*

Since the 1960s,

> there have been broader social changes than those wrought by prosperity and sex. It is no longer possible for decent people to dismiss someone of a different race or gender as not quite real. Part of this is increased worldliness. Women are no longer assumed to be interested only in fashion and babies. Presented with the situation of a man deceiving three women, who today would not think of the cruelty and heartbreak?
>
> *(Koenig 2007)*

With its ties to Feydeau and Labiche, *Boeing-Boeing* exemplifies not only the classic thematic tropes found in those 19th-century farces, but what would become recurring subjects in Camoletti's work: secrets, misunderstandings, sex, and relationships. His play is structured with the same tight precision found in the work of his predecessors. Whether or not the reference is intentional, in the play, not only does the character Bernard describe the beauty of his timetable system, but even Camoletti himself seems to be articulating the essence of writing farce through Bernard:

> Bernard: "Pure mathematics. Everything designed, organised, regulated and working to the precise second. The earth revolves on its axis and my fiancées wheel above the earth. One this way. One that. One towards the sun. One towards the moon. And eventually they all, in turn, come home to me. It's geometrical, my dear Robert. So precise as to be poetic".
>
> *(Camoletti 19)*

*Boeing-Boeing* had not been produced in London or New York since the 1960s. In 2007, the play was revived in London to commercial success and critical acclaim, before ultimately transferring to Broadway. In his review of the

West End production Michael Billington notes that this revival has been "buffed up, re-polished, and given the kind of dream cast which the National Theatre used to devote to Feydeau" (Billington 2007). He also observes that Warchus "…[presented] real people rather than mechanical objects" and that credit should be given to Mark Rylance for a "farce performance in which innocence is corrupted by experience" (Billington 2007). Of note, he says "the peculiar joy of the evening lies in a perfectly controlled, geometrically planned disorder, confirming farce is the quintessence of theatre" (Billington 2007).

It's easy to see why the lens of the play needed to be shifted. Viewed through a 21st-century lens, the play seems to straddle a 1950s conservative view of women that borders on misogyny. Bernard is having his multinational cake and eating it too. The trick is how to balance those two forces. With its conservative 1950s roots, Warchus believes that the play clearly combats claims of sexism by saying

> …if you look at it from the girls' points of view, all three of them get what they want, and love wins out in the end. The audience has got to feel the pressure the characters are under, with everything getting faster and faster. I think they'll identify with that. We all keep trying to cram more and more things into the same number of hours. Sex is the MacGuffin here. The play is really about someone believing [Robert] can control everything.

In order to prevent the play from devolving into 'camp' or parody. Warchus shares that the company "…play[s] it in earnest rather than spoofing it. It's all about situation and truth: That's what creates the extreme tension and agony and, thus, the hilarity" (Benedict 2008).

Over the course of a fifty-year career, Camoletti wrote 40 plays that have been translated into approximately 18 languages and performed in over 55 countries. At a time when the boulevard farces of Feydeau were waning in popularity, Camoletti drew inspiration from the structure and craftsmanship of those classic 19th-century farces, dropping both recognisable stock characters and a swinging' 1960s mentality into a long-held French theatrical tradition, with *Boeing-Boeing* being one of his most popular concoctions.

### *Yasmina Reza:* God of Carnage *(2008)*

In her work Yasmina Reza regularly indicts the middle class for their bourgeois hypocrisy. Her plays, which include *Conversations After a Burial, Life x 3, Art* "…explore relationships at breaking point with humour that is savage and devastating" (Glynn 262).

Yet none of those works approach the unhinged physical manifestations that bubble to the surface in Reza's dark satirical farce *God of Carnage*. By the end of the play, the gloves are off and the unfiltered impulses of each of the characters rise to the surface.

From her Tony Award-winning play *Art* to her experiment with form in *Life x 3*, there is a throughline in her work that seeks to expose those who, on the surface, appear to have everything one would need to ensure happiness: money, status, privilege. Underneath all of that lurks discontent and unhappiness. "Reza foregrounds how violence simmers under the fragile surface of social conventions" (Glynn 262).

As audience members Reza invites us to bear witness to a domestic world unravelling. French academic Denis Guenoun offers "that Reza's plays delight the reader [and the audience] because she writes about lives in crisis, and she presents a world in which the future is uncertain." (Giguere 8). Describing the kernel of inspiration for the play, author and dramaturg Amanda Giguere says Reza witnessed

> a playground fight…on her kids' playground, and she knew these parents were having it out. And she thought, oh, that's kind of interesting. When parents start to parent other kids, that could really be a good source for a play…the deeply recognizable-ness is probably where the humour is coming from, as opposed to starting with humour.
>
> *(Giguere 2020)*

Premiering in Switzerland in 2006 and then in the West End in 2008, Reza's *God of Carnage* (with an English translation by British playwright Christopher Hampton) takes place in the Parisian living room of Veronique and Michel Vallon. As the lights come up we find Veronique (a writer), Michel (who sells domestic hardware) and their guests Alain Reille, a lawyer, and his wife Annette, who is in wealth management, in mid-conversation. They are discussing a playground 'incident' involving their two 11-year-old sons, Ferdinand Reille and Bruno Vallon. A fight has resulted in Bruno getting hit in the face by a stick-wielding Ferdinand, and losing a tooth. What begins as a cordial debate about teaching their sons the consequences of childish behaviour quickly devolves into unruly adult behaviour. Over the course of an afternoon filled with coffee, wine, and French pastries, these four adults lose all sense of decorum. Pride, hubris, and clashing personalities reveal individual arrogance and biases. Deep-rooted marital cracks that have never been discussed clearly, let alone publicly acknowledged, bubble to the surface. As allegiances change throughout the evening, much like schoolyard friendships, all four parents take on animalistic qualities, a survival of the fittest. By the end we are unsure whether any of these marriages will survive.

The farce that emerges in the play is a result of the two sets of parents putting their pride and reputations before their children's best interests. In the process, we watch this ordered and insulated world dissolve into a messy domestic landscape; a classroom overrun by a group of overindulged preschoolers. The physical manifestation of chaos in the Vallons' living room echoes the 'unsaid' turbulence marking the homelife of these two couples.

At first glance, it might not seem readily apparent, but *God of Carnage* is a microcosmic rendering of society on the verge of collapse. Premiering two decades ago in Switzerland, Reza's play feels even more relevant today as we increasingly observe grown adults engage in hateful and narcissistic discourse and violence. Like the four parents in *God of Carnage*, societal behaviour seems to be disintegrating as more and more adults engage in primal schoolyard behaviour, complete with taunting, tantrums, and tears. In her book *The Plays of Yasmina Reza on the English and American Stage*, Giguere's thematic summary of the play could be applied to contemporary society:

> Their meeting, which is initially laced with politeness, quickly spirals out of control. The playground fight between the boys becomes a catalyst for both sets of parents to reveal their own inherent cruelty, savagery, and selfishness. The play brings up themes of savagery versus civilization, personal responsibility, parenting and global relations as Reza peels away the layers of these four characters to reveal their atrocious cores.
> *(Giguere 117)*

It's important to note that Reza's work never gets bogged down in intellectual ideology. About her writing, she has said: "I'm not cerebral…I never theorise about human nature. My work is visceral and subjective. I'm interested in the banal, unguarded moments and the hairline fractures in a character that let the light through" (Thurman 2009).

The living room becomes a domestic playground where expensive rugs and prized travel books are stand-ins for treasured toys and bragging rights. The home, which should be a place of sanctity, becomes a battleground with a home team and visitors.

Adhering to the unities of time, place and action, Giguere is reminded of an old college professor's advice that

> the tighter [the action] the smaller the boxing ring. We don't want to see a boxing match where the parameters are a field because we want [it] tightly focused…let's zoom in on this one situation and then let's push these people to their limits. I think that's probably what [her plays are] tapping into.
> *(Giguere 2020)*

In a moment of irony, Annette says "An insult is a kind of assault…he wouldn't have [hit Bruno] without a reason" (Reza 34). She goes on to say "Ferdinand was insulted and he reacted. If I'm attacked, I defend myself, especially if I find myself alone confronted by a gang" (Reza 36). As language deteriorates over the course of the play, giving way to taunts, insults, and profanity, the urgency of the play's pace drives the characters to speak from a sense of preservation and survival. They are all obsessed with being good parents, and only they know what's right for their children. However, it's clear that they're primarily concerned with keeping their dignity and reputation intact. The play spirals out of control with spouses chasing and hitting one another, handbags being hurled, tulips being shredded, and cell phones being extinguished in a vase of water.

Experiencing Reza's plays, the laughter elicited helps us understand viscerally what happens when we not only lose control within our own world but also lose sight of our peripheral world.

*God of Carnage* may not contain the robust physical comedy and classic plot contrivances and mechanisms that define the work of her fellow French dramatists. But the engine of French farce is on full display as we watch these four characters go to extremes in language and behaviour, as they become the children they are defending.

Playing out in 'real time' over the course of approximately 90 minutes, the play forgoes the traditional farce 'box set' design of multiple doors and instead lands the four characters in the middle of a room Reza describes as "A living room. No realism. Nothing superfluous" (Reza 2). Entrances and exits are made, but the formality of doors is gone. The "violence in *God of Carnage* is particularly traumatic and scandalous as it takes place in a realistic domestic setting" (Glynn 267).

The production's original director, Matthew Warchus, expertly manoeuvred the four characters around the set, with changing allegiances being reflected in ever-evolving triangular patterns. The play moves quickly, which is integral to the visceral aspect of the farce. Reza gives her characters no chance to pause. She pushes them to the brink, where not only their language but also their bodies seem to break down. The bile that is spewed becomes literal when Annette projectile vomits all over Veronica's prized travel books. This moment is simultaneously both horrifying and hilarious, enhanced by the subsequent action when Michel attempts to clean the damaged books with water, sponge, and a blow-dryer.

Reza may not have set out to write farce, though critics have referred to her work as such. Alice Jones, writing for *The Independent* about the 2008 West End production, observed: "What begins as an agonisingly polite discussion over espresso, rapidly deteriorates into a farcically awful, rum-fired slanging match" (Jones 2008). In his *New York Times* review of the Broadway iteration in 2008, Ben Brantley said

> *God of Carnage* follows the formula (think of it as slapstick with a slide rule) of taking three or four smug, upper-middle-class characters and stripping them, with algebraic precision, to their lonely, frightened ids. In this instance farce trumps formula, and *God of Carnage* is the richer for it.
> 
> *(Brantley 2008)*

It's interesting to hear Reza speak about her work with a clear reluctance to label her plays as comedies. In an interview with *The Guardian*, she said

> Laughter is very dangerous. The way people laugh changes the way you see a play. A very profound play may seem very light. My plays have always been described as comedy but I think they're tragedy. They are funny tragedy, but they are tragedy. Maybe it's a new genre.
>
> *(Day 2012)*

Whether or not Reza would consider her work farce, her own description of it being 'funny tragedy' offers us insight into the material. The rhythm and speed of the writing propels the play and Reza lands us in a forum for farce. Her characters are not caricatures. These are 'real' people defending their point of view and going to great lengths to do that. These are not characters we side with either. The truth is, we want to see these four people get their comeuppance.

The last line of the play is very telling. With the four parents standing in chaos of their own making, there is a long silence, which is followed by Michel simply saying "What do we know?" (Reza 67). This statement is apropos. Clearly what they thought they knew, and who they thought they were, has been completely shattered.

**Farce and Chips: British Domestic Farce**

> Farce has always been regarded in this country [Britain], in fact everywhere, as rather downmarket, popular entertainment…When I first started writing farces, interviewers would ask me, "Why do you do farces? Why don't you write about life as it is?" and I couldn't understand what their lives must be like. I mean it seems to me that everyday life has a very strong tendency towards farce, that is to say, things go wrong. And they go wrong often in a very complex and logically constructed way – one disaster leads to another, and the combination of two disasters leads to a third disaster, which is the essence of classical farce: disaster building upon itself.
>
> *(Moseley 109)*

Michael Frayn's quote encapsulates the majority of the domestic British farces that populated 20th-century stages. Descendants of the structurally complex farces of Labiche and Feydeau, or those of British playwrights like Brandon Thomas (*Charley's Aunt*) or Arthur Wing Pinero (*The Magistrate*, *Dandy Dick*, and *The Schoolmistress*) took up the gauntlet and piled on those disasters. The Aldwych Theatre farces of the 1920s and 1930s by Ben Travers featured puns, sexual innuendoes and stock characters like "the hen-pecked husband, the lecherous man-about-town…the comic charlady, the nagging wife, and the comic foreigner" (Smith 65). In Travers' work, we see not only "excellent craftsmanship and sense of structure" in his farces (Smith 67), but also a farce playwright unafraid to take risks and insert an underlying darkness in the work; foreshadowing a direction that playwrights like Joe Orton, Martin McDonagh, and Enda Walsh would explore. The Whitehall Theatre farces of the 1950s and 1960s carried on the Aldwych tradition. They were often set in either domestic settings or military locales. The brainchild of actor-manager Brian Rix and playwrights like John Chapman (*Dry Rot, Simple Spymen*), Colin Morris (*Reluctant Heroes*), Tony Hilton and Ray Cooney (*One for the Pot*), the farces were not only performed at the Whitehall but also toured to various venues around the UK and Ireland. In the spirit of, and rooted in, the touring troupes that characterised the *commedia dell'arte*, audiences throughout the UK could experience a uniquely evolving British sensibility in farce.

Throughout the 20th century, British playwrights began taking structural risks with domestic farce, which led to more serious themes emerging. Playwrights like Peter Shaffer, Alan Bennett, Alan Ayckbourn, Michael Frayn, and Peter Barnes waded into the farce pool in their own unique ways, playing within and off of the conventions of farce.

In 1965, British playwright Peter Shaffer (later to pen *Amadeus*) paved the way for subverting the farce form by pulling off his own subversive trick. His one-act farce *Black Comedy*, set in a British flat, begins in complete darkness. In a theatrical coup, the audience soon comes to realise that when the characters are enveloped in darkness their world is 'fully lit'. When the stage becomes 'actually lit', the ensemble attempts to carry on their obsessive actions as if they were in 'darkness.' At certain points throughout the play, matches are struck, flashlights are turned on, and candles are lit. In these brief moments, the stage lights in the space dim to varying degrees, letting us know that the space is being illuminated.

Shaffer was inspired by "an excerpt from a [Peking Opera] play called *Where Three Roads Meet*" (Cooke and Page 33). Referred to as 'Duel of the Dark Room', Shaffer described the scene as follows:

> It is supposed to be pitch darkness, except it is all done in brilliant light, light so ferocious that it almost suggests darkness. The warrior gropes for his sword and challenges the intruder…Real swords. The effect on the audience was extraordinary, because it was wildly funny and wildly dangerous as well, so that they were caught between two emotions of alarm and delight.
> *(Cooke and Page 33)*

One could dismiss the 'light reversal' as a gimmick, but what it does is escalate the proceedings from conventional domestic farce to a virtuosic display of physical comedy. Shaffer, who was aware of this possibility, remarked: "The reversal of light and dark was not in itself a sufficiently sustaining idea…what was needed was a reason for one of the people to keep the others in the dark.

From this necessity arose the actual plot..." (Cook and Page 34). In this farce, under the cover of light, everyone is literally in the dark.

Much has been written about Alan Ayckbourn, one of Britain's great comic writers. The author of approximately 90 full-length plays, Ayckbourn's work often takes a darkly comic view of marriage, love, sex, and loneliness, and he has described comedy and farce as "tragedies that have been interrupted" (Page 6). Between 1972 and 2009 Ayckbourn was the Artistic Director of the Stephen Joseph Theatre, a theatre well-known for its 'in-the-round' configuration, which provided inspiration for Ayckbourn the playwright on multiple occasions. Specifically in relation to farce, Ayckbourn is "substituting for the multiple doors of traditional farce – denied him by in-the-round staging for which his work is first conceived – his own kind of dimensional multiplicity" (ibid.). This would lead him to take more formal risks in his work. Although he has written only a few 'pure' farces, the ones he has written often play with space and time.

The visual world of his plays has impacted greatly on Ayckbourn's writing and how the action unfolds. In his farce *How the Other Half Loves* (1969), the "superimposed composite set – half the sofa and half the dining table belong to one family, half to another – contributes enormously to the storytelling and, incidentally, brings about fifty percent of the laughs." (Ayckbourn 35). This not only allowed for cross-conversation/split scenes to take place, but also set the stage for a "brilliantly experimental narrative device which allow[ed] us to see two dinner parties, which actually happen at different times and in different places, onstage together" (Allen 122). Unable to build a three-storey set in the Stephen Joseph Theatre's 'in-the-round' space, Ayckbourn's 1979 farce *Taking Steps* did away with stairs completely and embraced the parameters of the space "where three floors are all contained on the same level with the cast running up and down imaginary stairs" (Ayckbourn 35). In both plays, the physical design of the homes directly connect the dramatic themes or action of each play. In *How the Other Half Lives*, the two halves of each home represent the "sad and disintegrating lives of the families that inhabit it" (Bull 143). The house in *Taking Steps*

> becomes a character in the farce: a gaunt, ghostly, doomy, looming Victorian pile...in which the audience can see people trying to make their ineffectual escape down imaginary flights of stairs and in other separate crises can erupt a few feet away from each other.
>
> *(Bull 143)*

*Bedroom Farce*, Ayckbourn's 1975 play, takes place in three different bedrooms, initially setting the audience up for a traditional bedroom farce. Instead, our expectations are upended when the "boudoir ceases to be...the locus of illicit sexual mischief and becomes instead the place where licit relationships are sorely tested" (Page 41). The couples in each of the bedrooms are connected by blood or friendship either to one another or a fourth couple. The farcical comedy Ayckbourn has crafted finds the bedroom a vulnerable place for his characters, where sexual and marital problems are exposed.

Written almost 30 years apart, Ayckbourn's 1973 play *The Norman Conquests* and his 1999 play *House & Garden* are two domestic farces that meditate on love and marriage. Each offers its audiences two unique theatrical events, contributing to a cumulative farcical experience. The triptych of plays that comprise *The Norman Conquest* (*Living Room*, *Table Manners*, and *Round and Round the Garden*) take place in three different locales (a living room, dining room, and garden) at a Sussex country house over the course of a weekend. Stand-alone plays in their own right, when they are produced as an event, audiences have the opportunity to actually see the offstage life of these characters, as we are already privy to where they are coming from and where they are going. Knowing what has transpired in the other plays leads to more laughter and greater emotional weight. *The Norman Conquests* are each presented separately at different performances.

Upping the structural stakes of *The Norman Conquests*, *House & Garden* offers two separate plays taking place between 8:00 a.m. and 6:00 p.m. at a country house. Originally designed to be performed *simultaneously* in two different theatres, the casts run back and forth between a sitting room in the house, and the lower meadow of the house's garden. Once again, audiences can take in the two plays at separate performances and gleefully discover what happens when characters leave one space and enter another. Although *Garden* is considered the more 'farcical' of the two plays, the dramatic awareness of what has occurred in the 'other space' adds to the richness of the experience.

Among the other modern British playwrights who have played with the domestic farce form are Alan Bennett and Peter Barnes.

Alan Bennett's 1973 'sex farce' *Habeas Corpus*, was an

> attempt to write farce without the paraphernalia of farce, hiding places, multiple exits and umpteen doors. Trousers fall, it is true, but in an instantaneous way. I wrote it without any idea how it could be staged and rehearsals began with just four bentwood chairs. The big revolution occurred after two weeks rehearsal when the director, Richard Eyre, decided we could manage with three.
>
> *(Bennett 17)*

Bennett distilled the domestic farce to its essence. Upper-class characters with Restoration-like names cross the stage comment on the action with asides to the audience, and fly out of a scene.

Originally presented as part of a trilogy of one-act plays for British television, Peter Barnes' bedroom farce *Not As Bad as They Seem* (1984) is a

Feydeau-esque farce with a twist. A man and a woman are discovered in bed. It is revealed they are having an affair. What the audience soon comes to realise is that both characters are blind. Sefton, the husband of the woman, returns unexpectedly. He, too, is blind but has come home to announce that he thinks he can see again! The stakes are raised with the possibility of the affair being discovered. Echoing elements on display in Shaffer's *Black Comedy*, "there is much physical comedy – some of it slapstick, some of it consciously feeding the audience's sense of superiority, allowing us to see what the characters cannot" (Woolland 167). White canes fly as the three characters navigate to avoid each other in the bedroom, with Judith and Berridge attempting to hide their affair. All three plays that comprise *Nobody Here But Us Chickens* present characters with physical or mental disabilities. Barnes never invites pity for his characters, however, instead exploring "variations on [the] theme of self-delusion and self-perception" (Woolland 167).

### British Domestic Farce in the 21st Century

Comparatively, the kind of domestic farce that populated British stages in the 20th century has waned in the millennium, giving way to more serious family dramas. Gone are the traditional country house farces that were popular settings for 20th-century playwrights. Such a setting was parodied, for example, by Michael Frayn in *Noises Off*. As we'll see in subsequent chapters, British farce pivots, finding acclaim and adoration under the banners of 'Cultural' and 'Backstage' farces.

Two contemporary domestic farces that explore family dynamics in unique ways are Moira Buffini's *Dinner* and Joe Penhall's *Birthday*.

### Moira Buffini: Dinner *(2002)*

In what could be termed a 'revenge farce', Buffini's 2002 *Dinner* serves up a darkly hilarious four-course play. With dollops of satire, this is a comedy of manners 'gone to hell'. Within its opulent dinner party setting, we are introduced to Paige, a woman who has gone all-out to throw her husband Lars a congratulatory party, in order to celebrate the publication of his new self-help book. In fact, Paige has gone to great lengths to use this as an opportunity to humiliate him and more. Unbeknownst to Lars, Paige has discovered the affair he is having with one of the other guests and also his desire to seek a divorce. For Paige, this is a night to reclaim her self-respect and dignity. As dinner progresses, with each course becoming more macabre, the action of the play descends into black farce. Peppered by the arrival of an unexpected guest, who may or may not be a thief, and also a silent waiter who dutifully (and ominously) serves throughout the proceedings, we watch Buffini expose the underbelly of the privileged class.

At one point, as the conversation stalls awkwardly, Paige announces she has planned for this and invites everyone to play a game. Topics have been sealed in envelopes under each of the dinner settings. As the guests contribute to discussions on 'Murder Weapons' and 'Telling the Truth', people are pushed to an uncomfortable brink, revealing secrets and their true colours.

The characters in *Dinner* spar, mocking and insulting one another. Desperate to protect their egos, self-absorption is on full display. Save for one character, everyone lies. By the end of the night, someone dies. The comic darkness that pervades the proceedings connects to Buffini's description of the space. She says "my dramas do not have walls…Dinner is a table surrounded by darkness. That's the stage direction. If you stage the play in a room, you kill it" (Sweet 182).

The lack of naturalism allows the vileness in the play to breathe. The table and those around it float in the ether. As in *God of Carnage*, doors are not necessary for farce to flourish. Once the characters enter the space, they are trapped, held hostage by dinner. The lobsters served for the main course aren't even dead! The guests are given the option to boil their meal themselves or set the lobsters free into the garden. With each course being inedible (Lars rings for pizzas), the numerous drinks imbibed result in the characters becoming less and less guarded. The farce that spirals out in real time over the next 90 minutes, is a truth detector.

Interestingly, Buffini rewrote the ending between its premiere at the National Theatre and its West End debut at the Wyndham Theatre. In the production at the National, Mike the van driver (and the evening's intruder) "dies, a working-class pawn of rich folk's games" (Sierz 171). For the play's 2003 revival in the West End, Buffini has the waiter threaten to kill Lars but Paige calls him off, and instead he appears to assist her in committing suicide. In Buffini's words, "Ultimately, greed eats itself. Paige engineers her pact with the eternal footman" (Sierz 172). We never find out what has caused the marriage to fracture beyond repair. For the purpose of the play, this is irrelevant. In his book *Rewriting the Nation*, Aleks Sierz indicates Buffini is "[suggesting] that crisis is a natural state and that the longer the marriage, the more violent the explosion" (Sierz 172). Not to mention, the darker the comedy.

## *Joe Penhall:* **Birthday *(2012)***

The farce that emerges in Joe Penhall's 2012 play *Birthday* was borne out of anger and frustration following "his wife's horrendous experience when she gave birth to their second child" (Boles 208). Part domestic farce, part satirical attack on the National Health Service (NHS), *Birthday* invites comedic discourse about parenting and fatherhood in the 21st century, perceptions of gender, and what we are willing to sacrifice for family. Penhall's desire to write the play came out of a need "to show my wife that I understood viscerally…the humiliation, degradation, boredom, horror and fear that she'd somehow managed to surf with incredible dignity" (Jones 2012). Penhall, who has called out the shortcomings of the NHS in his more 'serious' plays *Some Voices* and *Blue/Orange*, returns to the medical arena, drawing directly on his and his wife's harrowing experience describing at one point that "…they wouldn't give her an epidural because there was no one there to give her one. It went on for 17 hours and it turned into an emergency. It was dramatic and frightening and farcical" (Boles 208).

Set in an understaffed NHS maternity hospital, married couple Lisa and Ed are anxiously awaiting the arrival of their second child. Following a challenging first pregnancy that left Lisa unable to have children, the couple have opted to participate in a relatively new 'procedure'. As the lights come up, the audience is faced with a surprising gender reversal. Ed, sitting up in the hospital bed, is visibly pregnant and in labour. With the majority of the action spanning the 24 hours leading up to the birth, Ed and Lisa's marriage is tested. Penhall challenges domestic norms, gender roles, and the pangs of parenthood, as the couple navigates a public health system fraying at the edges.

On the surface, the play may strike one as a sketch that quickly extends beyond its due date. There is a certain amount of comedic mileage derived from watching a pregnant man bemoan the struggle of childbirth as his wife looks on with sympathy and bemusement. From time to time, she levels him with phrases that begin with "Wait till they…"or "Wait till you feel…" We experience Ed's 'hormonal' outbursts, watch as he rides the pain of labour, and hear Lisa try to keep him calm and focused. She even offers to 'wank' him when he mentions he's had an erection for almost an hour, at which Ed snaps, "…it's about the furthest thing from my mind! You know how I feel about sex at the moment" (Penhall 21). These kinds of exchanges happen throughout the play and resonate as the audience recognizes the irony in the role reversal.

Building to a farcical close, Act One combines the squeamish and the scary as it is revealed that the umbilical cord is wrapped around the baby's neck. No surgical theatre is available. As Ed's pain intensifies, amid a life-and-death situation, a catheter is inserted, and an IV breaks leaving a bloody mess. As Ed begins to deliver, and the nurse is about to probe him rectally, an operating room opens up and he is promptly wheeled off.

As the pace of the scene increases, so does the level of panic. The biological reversal remains laugh-inducing because we know this is not medically believable. The image of this hysterical man, doing everything in his power to protect himself and his unborn child, is funny. We laugh, perhaps horrified, at Ed's increasingly dire situation. It also points up the fact that if Lisa was in Ed's position, we would not be laughing at her pain.

Penhall is a smart writer. Amidst the comic chaos in the 'paternity' room, he is still able to find emotional weight. Ed's parents haven't seen him since he got pregnant because they think "it's just another of [his] stupid…obsessions"

(Penhall 5). Describing an encounter at the playground with his son Charlie, while six months pregnant, Ed claims the other parents were "looking straight through me as if I'm not there – as if they personally *define* parenthood as if we're the transgressors" (Penhall 10). Audiences draw a direct line to the views many still hold about same-sex partners or any non-heteronormative partnerships raising children.

Although the play is set in a parallel world, this is not speculative or science fiction. These are contemporary messy characters. Ed, for all his whining and fussiness, is a "father who goes the extra distance for his family" (Boles 203). Because of this choice, Lisa is able to have her career and experience being a mother again – even if there is unresolved pain because she is no longer able to bear children. This begs the question based on both their experiences: is trauma worth the ordeal of childbirth?

Penhall has written a domestic farce with social underpinnings. A second-time father when he wrote *Birthday*, Penhall has given us a biting farcical comedy that, in the best sense, is much funnier than passing a kidney stone.

### Farce Americana: Contemporary Domestic Farce in the United States

Domestic farce in America has not had the storied history of the French or the British. If anything, American farce lives equally on stage and screen. In the early part of the 20th century, American theatre audiences found laughter in the variety acts of Vaudeville and later on in Burlesque sketches which parodied social, political, and cultural elements of America. The witty repartee, innuendo, absurdity and even anarchy that comprised these two early American forms would contribute to the farce stylings found in the works of playwrights like Thornton Wilder (*The Skin of Our Teeth* and *The Matchmaker*), and George Kaufman. Kaufman, in particular, would co-write what we now consider classic farces of the genre, partnering with the likes of Morrie Ryskind (*Animal Crackers* and *The Cocoanuts* featuring the Marx Brothers), Edna Ferber (*The Royal Family*) and, most notably, Moss Hart (*The Man Who Came to Dinner, Once in a Lifetime*, and *You Can't Take It With You*). His collaborations with Hart provide the first notable American domestic farce. One can trace the impact of these early 20th-century farceurs on modern playwrights like Neil Simon, John Guare, Christopher Durang, and Richard Greenberg.

### Ken Ludwig's 'Two Tenors'

Recognizing these 20th-century American masters, one would be hard-pressed to find a more prolific playwright of comedy, particularly farce, than Ken Ludwig. Ludwig describes comedy as "edgy in the way that a tragedy is not because it looks at the world from more of an angle. And this is an edgy time in our lives. And that makes this a perfect time for comedy" (Ludwig 2020). With approximately thirty plays under his belt, Ludwig is one of those rare playwrights of comedy whose work is consistently seen all over the world.

One surmises that Ludwig's plays are so popular because they often feature likeable and relatable characters bringing us into their plight with charm and naivete. He gives us people to root for in the story, even as they tie themselves up in farcical knots. Actor Rob McClure, who originated the role of Max in *A Comedy of Tenors*, echoes this, saying "[Ludwig] writes brilliant comedic webs and then creates empathetic characters to untangle them…at breakneck speed"(McClure 2020).

Unlike some of the other domestic farces discussed in this chapter, there is something delightfully old-fashioned about his characters. Frequently focusing on an underdog, Ludwig's plays feature much heart. A Ludwig farce is not mean-spirited. We gleefully watch families make fools of themselves as they struggle to make peace with very human concerns, including self-belief, ageing, watching a child grow older, or reconciling issues of love and commitment. The relationships among spouses, parents, and their children are what allows these pieces to resonate universally with audiences. It's not that his characters aren't driven or ambitious or flawed. They most certainly are. But there is a sweetness to them that does not arise as often in other contemporary farce. His characters care about humanity and, as they strive to 'save the day' or 'right the world', they discover an inner strength. We see this in his domestic farces *Lend Me a Tenor* (West End: 1986; Broadway 1989), *Moon Over Buffalo* (1995, also a Backstage Farce), *The Fox on the Fairway* (2010), *A Comedy of Tenors* (2015), and *The Gods of Comedy* (2020). In addition to the above farces, Ludwig has written 'adventure' or 'mystery' plays drawn from literary classics like *Robin Hood*, *The Three Musketeers*, or *Treasure Island*, not to mention the worlds of Agatha Christie (*Murder on the Orient Express*) and Sherlock Holmes (*The Game's Afoot*, *Baskerville*, and most recently *Moriarty*). Whether it's a farce, a mystery, or an adventure, by the end of his plays, order has been restored. All that was askew in the world has been righted, very much in the tradition of classic comedy, where audiences *are* given a 'happy ending.' It is no surprise to hear Ludwig say that:

> …comedy is just so cathartic when it's triumphant…a type of literature where everything gets thrown up into the air, into a sense of chaos, but comes back and locks itself together like a jigsaw puzzle…[it] restores a sense of order to society and gives it a meaning that is sensible, that is explicable…And that's one of its greatest attributes. That's why it's so beautiful and that's why it inspires us.
> 
> *(Ludwig 2020)*

The influences of playwrights like Sheridan, Feydeau, Wodehouse, Coward, Wilder, Travers, and, most dear to his heart, William Shakespeare, haunt Ludwig farces with affection. Unsurprisingly, Ludwig was a classics scholar in school.

Alongside Michael Frayn's *Noises Off*, Ludwig's play *Lend Me a Tenor* has been cited as one of the great farces of the late 20th century. Predominantly a domestic farce set against the cultural backdrop of the opera world, Ludwig's hotel suite-set play has the clockwork precision of Feydeau, the doubling contrivances of Shakespeare, and the madcap antics of the Marx Brothers.

From its opening lines, the play lands us in the middle of a burgeoning artistic disaster. Set in 1934, the Cleveland Opera Company is set to present their production of *I Pagliacci* featuring the great Italian tenor Tito Mirelli (aka *Il Stupendo*). At the top of the play, we find a distressed Max (assistant to Henry Saunders, who is the Company's General Manager and also the father of his girlfriend Maggie) in an agitated state because Mirelli is two hours late for the dress rehearsal. The production is scheduled to open that night. When Mirelli finally arrives, chaos ensues as he is accidentally administered a double dose of tranquilisers. Believing him dead, Saunders and Max must improvise a solution so that the evening's performance can go on. Max, an aspiring opera singer himself, puts on Tito's clown costume and white make-up, going on in place of Tito. A 'not dead' Tito then wakes up, realises he is late for the performance, and dons a second clown costume and make-up. Soon, two clowns are running around the hotel suite, wreaking havoc, and inadvertently finding themselves in bed with two women who think they are each cavorting with *Il Stupendo*. Among the disguises and mistaken identities, an apoplectic General Manager, a star-struck ingenue, a fiery Italian wife, a diva soprano, a singing bellhop, and six doors, Max somehow manages to iron out all of the plot wrinkles. In the end, *Lend Me a Tenor* is about "finding yourself within yourself and not letting yourself get stopped when you know for certain what resides in your heart" (Ludwig xvii). As Max discovers a new-found confidence in both his professional and personal voice, he proves not only to himself but also to Maggie what it means to take those leaps of faith. Trust in yourself and others will follow.

It should be noted that in 2019, Ludwig revised his original script, substituting *I Pagliacci* in place of *Otello* as the opera being produced within the farce. As the cultural landscape has shifted over the years, the long-held operatic 'tradition' of having white tenors donning blackface to play the title role has thankfully been dispensed with. Although the play's original use of the convention was designed as a plot contrivance and complication, seeing white actors don blackface now leaves us uncomfortable and distracted. Amazingly, almost every aspect of the farce remains the same with Ludwig sacrificing little of the play's original text and stage business (including a comic bit where a bunch of makeup rubs off on Maggie after she kisses Max).

Although *Lend Me a Tenor* is a modern farce, its revival on Broadway in 2010 prompted Ludwig to contemplate a unique and rare occurrence in the theatre: a contemporary farce sequel. *A Comedy of Tenors* offered Ludwig the opportunity to ponder the lives of his characters post-*Lend Me a Tenor*:

Where would Max – dogsbody and aspiring opera star – be? Would he be singing for a living? Would Max and his girlfriend Maggie be married? What about the world famous opera star Tito Merelli and his wildcat wife Maria? Would they still be together?

*(Ludwig 2020)*

Written almost thirty years later, Ken Ludwig's *A Comedy of Tenors* sheds light on these questions, offering audiences the chance to revisit some old friends in a semi-new setting. We are in a hotel suite(!) in Paris at the Faubourg Ritz. The year is 1936, two years after the events of *Lend Me a Tenor*. Producer Henry Saunders is bringing together three of the world's great tenors to perform a concert at the Olympic Stadium. *Il Stupendo* himself, Tito Merelli, will be performing with the famous Swedish tenor Jussi Bjorling, and Max (now a respected tenor in his own right, married to Saunders' daughter Maggie, who is stateside about to give birth to their first child).

Tito and his wife Maria (once again) have arrived late, and are still squabbling, mostly about their daughter, Mimi. Unbeknownst to her parents, Mimi, an aspiring actress, is in Paris auditioning for a movie. She also happens to be secretly dating Carlo Nucci, a young American hot-shot tenor whom Tito actively dislikes – mostly because he's more popular than Tito.

Complications ensue when Bjorling quits the concert after learning his mother has died. Then, after overhearing and misinterpreting a conversation Maria is having with Carlo in the hotel room, Tito accuses Maria of having an affair. Maria is outraged at the accusation and they both ask for a divorce. When Saunders introduces Carlo Nucci as Bjorling's replacement, Tito recognises him as the man whom he believes is the one having an affair with Maria, and tries to strangle him. Tito quits the concert leaving Saunders and Max with "One Tenor" instead of "The Three Tenors".

Tipping a hat to Feydeau's *A Flea In Her Ear* and Shakespeare's *The Comedy of Errors*, Ludwig introduces a new character at the end of Act 1 – a bellhop named Beppo. Beppo, who happens to look exactly like Tito (and is played by the same actor in a virtuoso portrayal), also turns out to be an excellent opera singer, becoming a wildcard solution for Saunders and Max. They hire Beppo to 'stand in' as 'Tito' (as Max did in *Tenor*) for the concert and he is overjoyed. For the first time in his life, Beppo is living a dream he thought would never be realised. Of course, the path to the concert isn't easy. Matters become even more convoluted when Tito's former paramour, the famous Russian soprano Tatiana Racon, finds out Tito is in town and decides to pay his hotel suite a visit. Beppo, who has shaved his moustache and is wearing one of Tito's dressing gowns, soon has everyone believing he is an enlightened Tito, embracing Carlo as Mimi's boyfriend, ravishing Maria in one room with a long-forgotten passion, and making love to Tatiana in the other room. When Tito finally returns to the hotel suite (after having walked out), more miscommunications and mix-ups ensue with Beppo and Tito emerging from various doors and speaking and acting in contradictory ways with the other characters. Max, who is on edge himself because he is unable to be at Maggie's bedside for the birth of their first child, remains Saunders' faithful assistant, figuring out what has transpired and once again, saves the day. In the end, all are reconciled, Carlo and Mimi get married (and find out they are going to be parents themselves) and the concert takes place, now re-named "The Four Tenors and the Soprano".

If *Lend Me a Tenor* focused on believing in yourself, cherishing the ones you love, and "the encouragement of youth by their natural heroes" (Ludwig xvii), *A Comedy of Tenors* was an opportunity for Ludwig, "to write about things I cared about…fatherhood…art and how do you be an artist and juggle the rest of your life?" (Ludwig 2020). All of the characters seem to be wrestling with the artist's struggle of balancing one's professional and personal lives. In addition, Ludwig interrogates through farce the complicated feelings that arise as one comes face to face with ageing and remaining relevant, as both artists and parents. This time around, Tito and Maria are struggling with the prospect that their baby girl is growing up and may not need them anymore.

Although Ludwig has referred to *A Comedy of Tenors* as a sequel, it was important to him that the play "be totally independent of the first, and that the theatergoer does not need to know anything at all about *Lend Me A Tenor* in order to enjoy *A Comedy of Tenors*" (Ludwig 79). From an event standpoint, however, there is something unique about watching actors revisit roles in two different plays. For example, we've seen theatre companies produce *Hamlet* and Stoppard's *Rosencrantz and Guildenstern are Dead* with the same actors reprising their roles in each show. It's rare though to see them recreate roles within the same world, let alone in two farces. In 2013, the Paper Mill Playhouse produced *Lend Me a Tenor* with a talented ensemble of Broadway stalwarts. Four years later, Paper Mill reunited the majority of the cast to play their same roles for *A Comedy of Tenors*. Both productions received critical and commercial acclaim.

In 2010, *Lend Me a Tenor* was adapted as a musical by Peter Sham and Brad Carroll. Most recently, the Alley Theatre premiered *Lend Me a Soprano* (2022), a new version by Ludwig that keeps the original structure but gender-reverses the characters of Max, Saunders, Mirelli, Maria, Diana, and Maggie.

### *Deborah Salem Smith:* Faithful Cheaters *(2017)*

In general, contemporary domestic farce in America has taken a backseat to both social and political farces. When families are featured, more so in social farces, we find issues of race, gender, and sexuality upending familial dynamics and subsequently driving the action. Similarly, we have not seen many female American playwrights take up the domestic farce gauntlet.

Despite that, Deborah Salem Smith's 2017 farce *Faithful Cheaters* offers both a laugh-out-loud and reflective meditation on marriage, fidelity, commitment, and honesty.

Over the course of a July weekend, at Sonoma, a once-upscale, now-derelict beach property in Michigan, Poppy and Theo are trying to rekindle the spark in their marriage. Workaholics who have not been paying much attention to one another, the two have decided to purchase the property as a second home to which they can retreat. They have brought along Poppy's mothers, Nance and Marion, whom they hope will help them invest in Sonoma. As the play progresses, we find out that Poppy had a one-night stand with the property's realtor, who also turns out to be the boy Poppy had lost her virginity to in high school. Meanwhile Theo, a scientist, has been developing a nose spray for fidelity and enlists her mother, Nance, also a scientist, for help. Unfortunately, Theo lost his research funding and took $60,000 from the couple's savings without telling Poppy.

The play proceeds with the requisite mix of "spit takes…bawdy humor, mistaken identity, double entendres, slapstick, a bear costume, and multiple malapropisms…". There are three significant aspects to Salem Smith's play that demand recognition: the adultery committed by Poppy, the portrayal of a same-sex couple where their sexuality is not a dependent plot point, and an ending that leaves the audience in an uncertain place.

When it comes to infidelity, farce history has shown us it is usually the man in the relationship that is the adulterer. In this instance, however, Poppy is the one who has cheated. A physician who is feeling disconnected and lonely in her marriage, is looking for excitement and spontaneity in her life. Although no one is excusing her behaviour, including her mothers, Salem Smith crafts a contemporary situation that acknowledges women are as prone to cheating as men. Poppy regrets what she did. It is clear that she still loves Theo. But her words betray dissatisfaction and a fractured relationship: "I've been lonely…*I* was being carefree…I felt young again" (Smith 16). We watch Poppy as she conceals her indiscretion, but also comes to recognise not only what's missing in her marriage but also what she has with Theo. Salem Smith keeps the farce light, however, never letting it get bogged down in heavy sexual or gender politics.

The inclusion of Marion and Nance not only as a married same-sex couple but also as an older and sexually active married couple is important because we rarely see an LGBTQ+ couple portrayed without affectation in farce. In older farces, gay characters tended to be instruments of ridicule and contrivance (e.g. heterosexual men 'pretending to be gay' to fool people into thinking they are not adulterers). In *Faithful Cheaters*, Smith allows Marion and Nance's relationship to be completely natural, rather than being used as a plot mechanism. She sees this as a responsibility, that

> …when I had kids…I wanted to be careful about what types of characters I was putting on stage because my kids are being raised by two women. As a younger writer pitching stories, I had sometimes fallen into the trap of telling stories not inclusive enough of my own identity. It's easy to slip into that in different ways because once you put it on stage, others think you have politicized the story. And then I was like, what if I say it doesn't? What if it's just a lovely fact of the world?
>
> *(Smith 2022)*

Although both Poppy and Theo have made mistakes, Salem Smith has given us two characters we want to see reunite. We recognise their flaws, and know that they have work to do. Salem Smith does not give us an easy ending. An invitation to vote is offered and everyone but Nance votes either to 'Forgive' or 'Divorce'. Alone on the beach at the end of the play, staring at a beautiful sunset, the couple is left to sort out what happens next.

While expressing immense joy for the genre, Smith wanted to explore the question:

> …can a play [still] end after great fun, in a moment of consequence? Can all the hijinx and the misunderstandings and the painful human experiences turned into comedy still ultimately amount into a sort of quiet reckoning.
>
> *(Smith 2020)*

### Feckin' Farce: Irish Domestic Farce

For all its rich literary history, modern Irish farces have been few and far between.

Two of these rare farces criticise contemporary Ireland's mythologising and idolatry of the past.

*The Patrick Pearse Motel* (1971) by Hugh Leonard (*Da*) "is a Feydeau-esque bedroom farce, mocking the new Catholic middle-class aspirations to wealth and taste" (Pine 165). Leonard's play "offers a satirical view of the Irish bourgeoisie and the values they espouse. Moreover, he suggests that the Irish are willing to use their national heritage for economic, rather than moral or spiritual gain" (Pine 166). Business partners Dermod and Fintan are opening a motel using the name of Irish patriot Patrick Pearse to draw guests. "The men's need to put commercial concerns first and their marriages second is a mockery of their supposed Catholic and Republican morals" (Pine 165).

Another play, Brian Friel's 1982 domestic farce *The Communication Cord*, satirises the sentimental romanticism of rural origins typified in the reproduction peasant cottage in modern Ballybeg where the play is set...the disguises, cross-purposes and mistaken identities typical of farce, enhanced by characters who are assumed only to be able to speak French or German, creates an anarchic theatrical Babel.

*(Grene 100)*

Another writer, Martin McDonagh (who is discussed further in the chapter on Political Farce), like Labiche and Feydeau, draws on elements of the well-made play and filters them through an Irish gothic sensibility. McDonagh overtly flirts with black farce throughout his work, riding the line between comedy and horror, especially in the domestic-infused Leenane trilogy. However, no other contemporary Irish playwright has endeavoured to tackle family dynamics with as much farcical verve as Enda Walsh.

### *Enda Walsh:* The Walworth Farce *(2006)*

Born in Dublin in 1967, Enda Walsh has made a name for himself as one of the foremost contemporary Irish playwrights currently writing for the theatre. A true experimentalist, Walsh has written over 20 original plays, adaptations, and books for musicals.

Walsh's 2006 play *The Walworth Farce* was an experiment in form for the playwright. In a 2009 interview with former Guthrie Theatre Artistic Director Joe Dowling and writer Fintan O'Toole, Walsh discusses his lack of knowledge of the genre, having never been exposed to it as a child. Growing up,

> [the Irish] don't have a tradition of farce, and I really didn't read any...I was interested in Irish theatre and that was about it. So I actually had to...learn the constructs of [it.]. I just got in there and learned it...and it's quite liberating – writing within a mechanism as tight and rigid as that.
> *(Interview between Joe Dowling and Enda Walsh; in Walker Arts Center 2009)*

What Walsh has crafted is a dark domestic 'very Irish' farce that both embraces and subverts recognisable tropes of the genre. Walsh refers to the play as 'very Irish' because it is "about a shared family story where a person visiting will somehow force the truth out of that uncertain history'" (Pilny 85). Walsh uses the farce form to parody the longstanding traditions of Irish storytelling. The play "caricatures the stereotypical notion of the Irish as a nation of storytellers and that involves one of the most improbable yarns ever told..." (Pilny 95–96). It also offers up its own subtle discourse about Irish citizens who emigrate from Ireland, by "[telling] a typical story of the diasporic experience of Irish migrant workers in London who feel uprooted in the foreign city and are engrossed in nostalgic memories of the Emerald Isle" (Pilny 95).

*The Walworth Farce* takes place in a run-down council flat, located on Walworth Road in the Elephant and Castle area of South London. For years, fifty-year-old Dinny and his two sons Blake, 25, and Sean, 24, have been performing a 'play' every day on an endless loop that depicts their last day in Cork City, Ireland. Dinny, who plays an idealised version of himself, also functions as the 'production's' director. Sean plays all of the male-identifying characters, and Blake portrays all of the female-identifying characters in the story, donning a variety of coloured wigs. The two brothers also portray sadistic versions of their adolescent selves. With the action taking place in the flat's living room, kitchen and bedroom, for an invisible audience, the theatre audience comes to learn about the death of Dinny's mother and Dinny's subsequent murder of both his brother, Paddy, and sister-in-law, Vera.

Sean is the only one of them to ever leave the flat. His job is to go down the street to the local Tesco and pick-up 'props' for the day's performance. On this particular day, after distractedly chatting with Hayley, who is black and one of Tesco's grocers, he accidentally takes home someone else's shopping bag. This mistake not only leads to adverse tension among the three men but causes multiple interruptions to the 'performance.' A roasted chicken is 'replaced' by a sausage; sandwiches are made out of Ryvita crackers instead of white sliced bread. For Dinny, these mistakes are unconscionable. One senses that Sean's error, which has never happened before, causes Dinny 'the director' to lose control of the story. The grocery mix-up, however, leads to an even bigger interruption when Hayley shows up at the end of Act 1 to return Sean's groceries. The comically shaggy, yet slightly sad farce permeating the first half of the play becomes much more sinister as Hayley is 'incorporated' into the performance. For Dinny, finishing the story his way is an obsession. Keeping the outside world from intruding on this obsession is imperative. But Hayley's presence and what she represents stirs something in Sean, leading to more than the 'scripted' number of deaths.

The play showcases the overtly performative nature of farce in a self-aware manner. The existential and circular nature of the work is played for laughs and the grotesque. The characters are caught in a theatrical loop, which echoes the work of Samuel Beckett. The brothers effect quick costume changes in front of us, while running in and out of two poorly constructed wardrobes. Blake, who portrays his mother Maureen, his Aunt Vera, Eileen, the wife of a neighbour, and eventually Hayley, must puppet the character wigs in order to carry on conversations between the women. Walsh seems to be honouring the inherent theatricality and highwire act of farce, calling attention to the 'inner mechanics' of the performance. When scenes are interrupted, Dinny insists that they be performed again. When Sean and Blake become distracted or are taken 'out' of the scene, Dinny feeds them their lines. Missing or malfunctioning props abound. It should also be noted that aside from the front door, all of the doors in the apartment have been removed, leaving only frames. There is no privacy in this domestic setting. Walsh seems to be having fun with our own grasp of the form being one that often features doors – by removing them.

Walsh has said that the idea for the play "was effectively about the relationship between me and my [three] brothers…" (Dowling 2009). "I like family stories with characters who we find monstrous or grotesque but who we then begin to like" (Zinoman 2008). The play uses the comedic conventions of farce to disarm and invite the audience to explore how the stories we tell ourselves and our loved ones repeatedly – in order to shield all from the harsh truths of the world – after a while become the truth. Walsh enjoys "exploring the creation of identity, family, and community through language and storytelling. His strange dramatic worlds are inhabited by dysfunctional characters who… [create] their own myths that structure and limit their lives" (Fitzpatrick 439). Dinny crafts a whole new story which denies the double murder he actually committed, a murder over an inheritance dispute. Dinny re-writes the narrative surrounding the true events in Cork City, absurdly casting himself as innocent, in fact, a hero in his own story. (Even going as far to christen himself a brain surgeon.) Fleeing Cork City into self-imposed exile, Dinny and subsequently the two boys (like many characters in Walsh's plays) "opt to avoid the rest of the world, [and] bury themselves in fictions to hide from the grief and pain of life" (Fitzpatrick 443).

Their passionate commitment to replaying the farce day in and day out becomes a way for these three characters to "engage in storytelling obsessively, not as a means of advancing plot but rather to come to terms with some trauma" (Lonergan 250). For Dinny, the execution of the story may subconsciously be to deny the truth of what happened; on a juvenile, yet obsessive level, however, it is to win the 'acting trophy' which is awarded at the end of every 'performance'. Predictably, Dinny has always been the recipient.

Although not said overtly, we know that Blake and Sean arrived at Dinny's apartment when they were four and five years old. Sent at the behest of their mother, this would mean that they have been living with Dinny for approximately 20 years. This begs the question: how long have they been acting out this revised narrative? We know that they are suspicious of the outside world and have clearly been brainwashed to believe that leaving the apartment would make them vulnerable to an environment populated by zombies in a horror film:

> Dinny: And then the people. They come out from the houses and shops and they're after you. Their skin, it falls to the ground and them bodies running you down and wanting to tear you to shreds.
>
> *(Walsh 31)*

The only thing they know, the thing that has defined their world and identities for the last twenty years, *is* the performance of the farce. The two boys are at the mercy of their short-tempered father. Dinny has "denied his sons 'diasporic identity' by keeping them at home 'and only grants them the substantial identities as children or as performers'" (Pilny 96). A commentary on Irish migration to London, the irony is that the brothers aren't even given the opportunity to forge a new identity. Instead, they need to keep replaying this domestic story because it's the only thing they have been allowed to know. It gives them purpose and keeps them in good stead with their temperamental father. It is clear that Sean wants to leave. He just doesn't know how. By the end, the home becomes a stage for domestic destruction.

The play closes with Hayley escaping and four people dead (Paddy, Vera, Dinny and Blake). At first we think Sean is going to break the cycle and leave. Instead, he resets the house for the 'top of the show' and proceeds to reenact the main action of Act 1 in two minutes. Sean proceeds to…

> [Stage Direction]: … [fire] a look towards the front door…picks up HALEY'S coat and puts it on, he lifts up her bag and places it on his shoulder. He takes a plastic Tesco bag from the ground and holds it. He turns his back to us and stands at the door. He's applying something to his face…SEAN turns. He's covered his face in DINNY's brown shoe polish. He's making HALEY'S entrance.
>
> *(Walsh 85)*

There is something haunting about this final image. Instead of fleeing the premises, Sean decides to stay and rewrite the story from the moment Haley enters the apartment. By rewriting the story, he is using farce to reclaim an identity and craft a new narrative. Peter Crawley writes "that is the tragedy of Walsh's comic play, the exhausting, depleting consequence of living a lie" (Crawley 2015).

**A Few More Contemporary Domestic Farces**

Remi de Vos' three-character French farce *Till Death* (2006) has subtle echoes of Feydeau. Madeline's elderly mother has been cremated. Madeline's estranged son, Simon, has come home for his grandmother's funeral. The seeds of farce are planted when Madeline warns Simon not to drop his grandmother's urn. Madeline also tells Simon that his old school crush, Anne, will be coming by to pay her respects. What follows is a broken urn, an improvised engagement, a snowball of lies, and an unexpectedly sweet reconciliation.

Written in 1994, and receiving a West End revival in 2016, Terry Johnson's *Dead Funny* is a domestic farce that explores marital neglect. Eleanor's biological clock is ticking, but her husband Richard seems more interested in his position as Chair of the Dead Funny Society, a group dedicated to dead comic icons of classic British comedy. Lisa and Nick, also members of the Society, are parents to a newborn, which has exposed the cracks in the relationship. The recent death of Benny Hill brings together the members of the Society (including their closeted neighbour, Brian) to celebrate Hill's life and recreate old routines. As the evening goes on, however, comic sketches give way to hurtful revelations and farcical spectacle (including an old-fashioned pie fight) as we laugh and watch with horror and sadness at the disintegration of these two marriages.

American playwright Sandy Rustin's 2014 farce, *The Cottage*, is an ode to Noël Coward, with a contemporary twist. Set squarely in 1923, Rustin filters the story through a decidedly feminist lens. The play opens with Sylvia and Beau having spent the night making love. They are not married to one another (although they are related by marriage). The two have been carrying on this affair for a while, meeting once a year up at the family cottage. On this day, however, Sylvia has decided she no longer wants to sneak around. Instead of hiding her infidelity, she wants to expose the affair to both her husband and her lover's wife. After both her husband and her very pregnant sister-in-law arrive, they are soon joined by Beau's *other* lover, Deidre, and her homicidal husband Richard. Secrets are revealed, more infidelities emerge, and murder is threatened. With its witty repartee and ample opportunity for physical comedy, Rustin effectively gives us a drawing room, Coward-esque farce that empowers her lead female character to make an individual choice that is squarely connected to her emotional happiness; a unique trait for a young female character of that period. Rustin says that

> ...as an adult, I had the benefit of seeing that much of Coward's work did little to promote the wisdom, strength, and independence of women. So, I made it my mission to infuse this Coward-inspired play with a boost of the feminist energy I had found in myself as a performer and writer. I challenged myself to write a period piece bedroom farce in a Coward style, with a modern eye toward feminism. And that's how *The Cottage* was born!
> 
> *(Rustin 2020)*

*The Cottage* made its Broadway debut in July of 2023. Reviewing the production for *Entertainment Weekly*, Emlyn Travis described the play as "a sensational, feminist twist on a classic British period drama...delivering comedy gold while simultaneously encouraging theatergoers to consider the roles love, sex, and societal expectations play in our lives" (Travis 2023).

The Danish playwright Line Knutzon's macabre *HÅNDVÆRKERNE* ("The Builders", 2008), is a domestic revenge farce that capitalises on every new homeowner's worst nightmare. Jonathan and Alice are a young married couple who have recently purchased a country home. Unfortunately, they find themselves at the mercy of a manipulative foreman, and a group of lazy builders who are not only drawing out the renovations unnecessarily but also bilking the young couple for more money. When Jonathan catches one of the builders taking a nap in their bedroom, an altercation ensues, resulting in a fatal fall down a flight of stairs. Reporting this 'accident' would only bring about more delays (and, of course, legal issues), so the decision is made to store the body in the cellar...after Alice has taken care of it with a chainsaw. Soon, each of the five builders meets with a progressively gruesome death (à la *The Ladykillers*) and, in the process, not only do they get the house they dreamed of, but Jonathan and Alice also rediscover their passion for one another. *The Builders* is "a farce proving how a combination of lifestyle dreams and cowboy builders can turn an ordinary middle-class couple into serial killers" (Embassy of Denmark 20).

In 2012, Irish playwright Mark Cantan's award-winning *Jezebel* was commissioned and premiered by Rough Magic Theatre Company. This unique three-hander stands out for a couple of reasons. The triangular farce that emerges among the three characters Robin, Alan, and Jezebel does not play out as one might expect. We meet Robin and Alan at the beginning of the play: He is a statistics analyst; she writes motivational books and offers positivity lectures. What was originally a business meeting set up by a mutual friend, leads to a date which then leads to six months of sexual bliss. At the six-month mark, the two find themselves in a 'rut' and propose adding a third person to their bedroom activities. Enter Jezebel, a lonely artist looking for companionship, whom Alan and Robin pick up at a bar.

Following their one-night threesome, one could surmise a few directions in which the farce might have gone. Perhaps Alan and Jezebel continue to see one another, unbeknownst to Robin. Or perhaps Robin and Jezebel begin to see one another, unbeknownst to Alan. Perhaps both Robin and Alan begin to see Jezebel, and try to hide their respective indiscretions. Cantan takes the farce in a different direction, with both women discovering they are pregnant. Alan is informed by both, but in an effort to find the right moment, hesitates to share the news with either of the women. This leads to a series of misunderstandings, including one very funny phone call where the two women, each believing Alan has shared their happy news, end up in an explosive argument where they mistakenly believe their baby is going to be kept (or taken) from them.

Of note, adultery never enters into the mix, and, instead, given the unique circumstances, the arrival of both babies strengthens the bond shared by the three characters.

Cantan allows the action to move seamlessly from scene to scene with 'doorless' energy. Instead, he intersperses direct address with the dialogue, giving us the chance to hear the inner thoughts and observations of all three characters, and evoking images of mockumentary television shows like *The Office* and *Modern Family* (not surprisingly, the 1980s American sitcom, *Three's Company*, is invoked too). It would be a disservice, however, to dismiss the play as a frivolous exercise in misunderstandings and miscommunication. In fact,

> there are some serious observations here about love and loneliness in our busy modern world. Jezebel belies her name and is a lonely, warm-hearted girl who looks for romance in the wrong places; Robin and Alan are too uptight to embrace the possibility that love and perfection might not reside together; and the whole piece takes a sceptical look at the principles of internet dating.
>
> *(Hemming 2014)*

*Jezebel* feels like a domestic farce for the new millennium. It is an 'against-type' sex farce where happiness is not tied to carnal behaviour or desire, but the sincere possibility of failing one's partner or self.

Scrutinising what differentiates the contemporary domestic farce from the modern 'bedroom', 'cottage', or 'sex' farces that dominated the first half of the 20th century, a couple of crucial observations come into focus. The contemporary playwright's willingness to expose familial fragility by allowing unresolved, fractured relationships to bubble to the surface and crack open under farcical pressure, is refreshing and admirable. These plays position its characters in situations where they are forced to confront hard, unacknowledged truths about domestic pain and unhappiness. By the end of these plays, the domestic world inhabited by the characters has been turned upside down. Relationships break apart, are revaluated, or mended. The literal and metaphorical 'mess' that is made of the household is indicative of the struggle the characters must endure, and how they must persist to preserve their relationships, save face, and not fail their loved ones.

## Works Cited

Allen, Paul. *Alan Ayckbourn: Grinning at the Edge*. Continuum, 2002.
Ayckbourn, Alan. *The Crafty Art of Playmaking*. Palgrave Macmillian, 2002.
Ayckbourn, Alan. *House & Garden*. Faber and Faber, 2000.
Ayckbourn, Alan. *How the Other Half Loves*. Samuel French, 1972.
Ayckbourn, Alan. *The Norman Conquests*. Grove Press, 1975.
Ayckbourn, Alan. *Taking Steps - A Farce*. Samuel French, 1981.
Barnes, Peter. *Plays: 2*. Methuen Drama, 1996.
Benedict, David. "Variety." *Variety*, 25 Apr. 2008, variety.com/2008/legit/news/broadway-digs-up-boeing-farce-1117984684
Bennett, Alan. *Plays 1*. Faber and Faber, 1996.
Bergson, Henri. *Laughter: An Essay on the Meaning of the Comic* (Translated by Cloudesley Brereton and Fred Rothwell). Book Jungle, 2007.
Bermel, Albert. *Farce: A History from Aristophanes to Woody Allen*. Southern Illinois University Press, 1990.

Billington, Michael. "Boeing-Boeing." *The Guardian*, 26 Mar. 2020, www.theguardian.com/stage/2007/feb/16/theatre2

Boles, William C. "Joe Penhall's Fatherhood Plays: Escaping the Influence of Sam Shepard and the Lad." *After In-Yer-Face Theatre* (Edited by William C. Boles). Palgrave Macmillan, 2020, 203–208.

Brantley, Ben. "Boeing-Boeing - Review - Theater." *The New York Times*, 8 May 2008, www.nytimes.com/2008/05/05/theater/reviews/05boei.html

Brantley, Ben. "Yasmina Reza's Living Room Rumble, at Bernard Jacobs Theater." *The New York Times*, 23 Mar. 2009, www.nytimes.com/2009/03/23/theater/reviews/23carn.html

Buffini, Moira. *Dinner*. Faber and Faber, 2002.

Bull, John. *Stage Right*. Macmillan, 1994.

Cantan, Mark. *Jezebel*. Playdead Press, 2014.

Camoletti, Marc. *Boeing-Boeing* (Translated by Beverly Cross and Francis Evans). Samuel French, 2013

Camoletti, Marc. *Don't Dress for Dinner* (Adapted by Robin Hawdon). Samuel French, 1992.

Cleese, John. "John Cleese: How to Write the Perfect Farce." *The Guardian*, 26 Mar. 2020, www.theguardian.com/stage/2017/feb/17/john-cleese-farce-bang-bang-fawlty-towers-rat-manuel-feydeau

Capon, M (Combat), and Gauthier, J.J. (Le Figaro) "World Premières." *Institute International Du Theatre*, Dec. 1960.

Cooke, Virginia, and Page, Malcolm (Compiled by). *File on Shaffer*. Methuen, 1987.

Cooney, Ray. *Run for Your Wife*. Samuel French, 1984.

Crawley, Peter. "Gleeson Family Values Put to the Test in This Fantastical Farce." *The Irish Times*, 15 Jan. 2015, www.irishtimes.com/culture/stage/gleeson-family-values-put-to-the-test-in-this-fantastical-farce-1.2067075

Day, Elizabeth. "Yasmina Reza: 'There's No Point in Writing Theatre if It's Not Accessible'." *The Guardian*, 26 Mar. 2020, www.theguardian.com/stage/2012/jan/22/yasmina-reza-interview-carnage-polanski

De Vos, Remi. "Till Death." *The Oberon Anthology of Contemporary French Plays* (Edited and Translated by Chris Campbell). Oberon Books, 2017.

Embassy of Denmark in the UK. "New Danish Drama. Twenty-Two Playwrights." *Issuu*, 16 Sept. 2015, issuu.com/embassyofdenmarkintheuk/docs/new_danish_drama_twenty-two_playwri

Feydeau, Georges. *Plays: 1* (Translated with an Introduction by Kenneth McLeish). Methuen Drama, 2001.

Fitzpatrick, Lisa. "Enda Walsh." *The Methuen Drama Guide to Contemporary Irish Playwrights* (Edited by Martin Middeke and Peter Paul Schnierer). Methuen Drama, 2010.

Friel, Brian. *Collected Plays 3*. Faber and Faber, 2016.

Gieselmann, David. *The Pigeons* (Translation by Maja Zade). Unpublished manuscript, 2009.

Giguere, Amanda. Personal Interview. 30 Jun. 2020.

Giguere, Amanda. *The Plays of Yasmina Reza on the English and American Stage*. McFarland & Company, Inc., 2010.

Glynn, Dominic. "Yasmina Reza and Florian Zeller: The Art of Success." *Contemporary European Playwrights* (Edited by Maria M. Delgado, Bryce Lease and Dan Rebellato). Routledge, 2020.

Grene, Nicholas. "Brian Friel." *The Methuen Drama Guide to Contemporary Irish Playwrights* (Edited by Martin Middeke and Peter Paul Schnierer). Methuen Drama, 2010.
Hemming, Sarah. "Jezebel, Soho Theatre, London – Review." *Financial Times*, 17 Aug. 2014, www.ft.com/content/d9c66dc4-246e-11e4-be8e-00144feabdc0
Innes, Christopher. *Modern British Drama: The Twentieth Century*. Cambridge University Press, 2002.
Johnson, Terry. *Dead Funny*. Bloomsbury Methuen Drama, 2016.
Jones, Alice. "God of Carnage, Gielgud Theatre, London | the Independent." *The Independent*, 27 Mar. 2008, www.independent.co.uk/arts-entertainment/theatre-dance/reviews/god-of-carnage-gielgud-theatre-london-801139.html
Jones, Alice. "Guess Who's Having a Baby: Joe Penhall's New Play, Birthday, Tackles Childbirth – With a Twist | the Independent." *The Independent*, 28 Jun. 2012, www.independent.co.uk/arts-entertainment/theatre-dance/features/guess-who-s-having-a-baby-joe-penhall-s-new-play-birthday-tackles-childbirth-with-a-twist-7893600.html
Knutzon, Line. *HÅNDVÆRKERNE* ("The Builders"). Unpublished manuscript, 2008.
Koenig, Rhoda. "Boeing Boeing: What a Farce! | the Independent." *The Independent*, 18 Jan. 2007, www.independent.co.uk/arts-entertainment/theatre-dance/features/boeing-boeing-what-a-farce-432628.html
Labiche, Eugene. *An Italian Straw Hat* (Translated and Introduced by Kenneth McLeish). Nick Hern Books, 1996.
Leonard, Hugh. *The Patrick Pearse Hotel*. Samuel French, 1971.
Lonergan, Patrick. "Enda Walsh and Martin McDonagh: Reimagining Irish Theatre." *Contemporary European Playwrights* (Edited by Maria M. Delgado, Bryce Lease and Dan Rebellato). Routledge, 2020, 244–260.
Ludwig, Ken. *Ken Ludwig's A Comedy of Tenors*. Samuel French, 2016.
Ludwig, Ken. *Ken Ludwig's The Fox on the Fairway*. Samuel French, 2011.
Ludwig, Ken. *Ken Ludwig's Lend Me a Tenor* (Revised Edition). Samuel French, 2019.
Ludwig, Ken. *Lend Me a Tenor and Other Plays*. Smith and Krauss, 2010.
Ludwig, Ken. Personal Interview. 1 Jul. 2020a.
Ludwig, Ken. "Revisiting the Tenors — Ken Ludwig." *Ken Ludwig*, Jul. 2020b, www.kenludwig.com/posts/revisiting-the-tenors
Mason, Jeffrey D. *Wisecracks: The Farces of George S. Kaufman*. UMI Research Press, 1988.
McClure, Rob. Email Interview. 10 Jul. 2020.
Moseley, Merritt. *Understanding Michael Frayn*. University of South Carolina, 2006.
O'Brien, Larry. "BroadwayWorld Rhode Island Awards December 5th Standings; NEWSIES Leads Best Musical!" *BroadwayWorld.com*, 5 Dec. 2023, www.broadwayworld.com/rhode-island/article/BWW-Review-FAITHFUL-CHEATERS-at-Trinity-Repertory-Company-20170427
Page, Malcolm (Compiled by). *File on Ayckbourn*. Methuen, 1989.
Parenteau, Amelia. "In Review: Contemporary French Plays." *The Mercurian*, 8 Nov. 2018, the-mercurian.com/2018/05/10/in-review-contemporary-french-plays
Penhall, Joe. *Birthday*. Methuen Drama, 2012.
Pilny, Ondrej. *The Grotesque in Contemporary Anglophone Drama*. Palgrave Macmillan, 2016.
Pine, Emilie. "Hugh Leonard." *The Methuen Drama Guide to Contemporary Irish Playwrights* (Edited by Martin Middeke and Peter Paul Schnierer). Methuen Drama, 2010.

Pronko, Leonard C. *Eugène Labiche and Georges Feydeau*. Macmillan Press, 1982.
Reza, Yasmina. *The God of Carnage* (Translated by Christopher Hampton). Faber and Faber, 2009.
Rustin, Sandy. Email Interview, 2020.
Rustin, Sandy. *The Cottage*. Dramatists Play Service, 2023.
Shaffer, Peter. *Black Comedy*. Samuel French, 1967.
Sierz, Aleks. *Rewriting the Nation*. Methuen Drama, 2011.
Smith, Deborah Salem. Personal Interview. 4 Nov. 2022.
Smith, Leslie. *Modern British Farce*. Barnes & Noble Books, 1989, pp. 65–67.
Sweet, Jeffrey. *What Playwrights Talk about When They Talk about Writing*. Yale University Press, 2017.
Thomas, James. *Script Analysis* (Fifth Edition). Focal Press, 2013.
Thurman, Judith. "Nowhere Woman." *The New Yorker*, 9 Mar. 2009, www.newyorker.com/magazine/2009/03/16/nowhere-woman
Travis, Emlyn. "*The Cottage* Review: Jason Alexander's Broadway Directorial Debut Is a Knock-knock-knockout." *EW.com*, 25 Jul. 2023, ew.com/theater/theater-reviews/the-cottage-review-broadway-jason-alexander
Walker Art Center. "In Conversation: Joe Dowling and Enda Walsh." *YouTube*, 25 May 2010, www.youtube.com/watch?v=BCJdK-U1Q-4
Walsh, Enda. *The Walworth Farce*. Nick Hern Books, 2007.
Woolland, Brian. *Dark Attractions: The Theatre of Peter Barnes*. Methuen, 2004.
Zinoman, Jason. "Mr. Normal's Dysfunctional Irish Families." *The New York Times*, 2 Apr. 2008, www.nytimes.com/2008/04/06/theater/06zino.html

# 2
## SOCIAL FARCE

The farces behind our second door are coloured by social (often satirical) commentary. These plays thrust their characters into increasingly heightened situations forcing them to confront social biases when it comes to issues of identity, gender, class, and race.

Contemporary playwrights comment on the hypocrisy found within these social categories and wrap them in circumstances where farce highlights the issues being explored. In most examples throughout this chapter, farce underscores character fragility and highlights the absurdity of traditional social constructs. The farce in many of these socially-pointed plays borders on grotesquerie.

Most of these farces carry elements of satire. Many start out as satire and descend into farce. A select few transform into something darker and ultimately serious.

For this reason it seems important to define satire, and how social farce intersects with it. On the subject of satire, Andrew Stott writes that "satire aims to denounce folly and vice and to urge ethical and political reform through the subjection of ideas to humorous analysis" (Stott 156). For scholar Eric Weitz, "satire is now seen broadly as a free-ranging mode of artistic attack, usually against some real or perceived orthodoxy in thought or practice" (Weitz 184). Reading these, one is struck by an aggressive vocabulary, employing words like 'to denounce', and 'artistic attack.' Satire is incisive, sharp, and subtle. It seeks to take down its subjects with a comedic razor.

Social farces, on the other hand, explode the constructs that define an individual character, a cultural group, or an entire community. The entrenched beliefs characters hold are tested when their irrational responses expose a deep-rooted and recognisable pain infecting society. We cannot make a hard and fast distinction between the two as mutually exclusive. In many of the pieces we will examine, satire and farce not only co-exist, but interweave for optimal impact.

The first section of this chapter puts an emphasis on Farce and Identity. Farces often land characters in situations where they are forced to question, change or, forego their identity and gender. What does it mean to be male, female, or non-binary? What is the changing notion of social constructs as they connect to these gender roles? In an effort to extract themselves from precarious situations, characters may willfully or unintentionally lose their identity and gain a new one. Similarly, taking on new guises can play havoc with notions of sexuality. How does changing one's identity further confuse or liberate a character? Where are characters left when they no longer know who they are? The plays discussed in this section each consider the fluidity of identity and how that can be both a blessing and a curse.

The second section focuses on Farce and Class, and how characters are defined by their societal and economic standing. In these works a fear of *losing* both their social standing and reputation dictates character behaviour. These are characters who have everything, yet seemingly remain insulated from the harsh realities of the world around them. For all the wealth and power they carry, a lack of awareness renders them inert and/or useless in the face of catastrophe. On the other hand, farces that focus on working-class characters see them struggling to get by. Their actions are borne out of desperation to improve their status or simply keep their heads above water and stay out of trouble. In some cases, even if their actions are illegal, it is with the belief that the world owes them something. They have self-justification. Their modus operandi may be illogical, but they recognise that in order to survive, they must make something of themselves. They are rising up against a world that is keeping them down. These characters come armed with good intentions but do not have the money, resources, or connections to dig themselves out of difficulty.

The last section in this chapter surveys a selection of contemporary farces exploring what it means to be the social 'other.' Written by a cohort of racially and ethnically diverse playwrights, the satirical farces in this section interrogate racism, cultural appropriation, and societal constraints that threaten to quash progress.

## *Joe Orton*: Farceur of Misrule

If Labiche and Feydeau are the 'grandfathers of contemporary farce', laying the groundwork for domestic farce, the late British playwright Joe Orton can be seen as the mischievous and outspoken uncle of societal farce. The one who understands the rules of farce enough to joyfully break them. Orton admired the mechanical logic of Feydeau's farces, and he himself extolled the virtues of the mathematical precision he took in the writing of his plays. In putting his own spin on the genre though, the socially provocative Orton was able to:

> ...marry terror and elation in his highly stylized theatrical idiom. Violating social and familial pieties, farce's pandemonium created the panic Orton wanted in laughter. In tragedy, character is fate; in farce where characterization is minimized and action emphasized, mischief is fate.
>
> *(Lahr 186)*

It is not surprising that when examining works of contemporary farce, Joe Orton's name surfaces frequently. Wielding comedy as a weapon, Orton was unafraid to open a dialogue about identity and sexuality, and in the process offend the masses, upset those in authority positions, and speak the words often thought but seldom uttered. In a very short period of time, Orton established himself as one of the most daring playwrights of the 1960s. He sought to redefine the boundaries of farce – especially at a time when the work of classical farceurs like Noël Coward, Ben Travers, Brian Rix, and Terence Rattigan were experiencing a resurgence in London. Unlike those playwrights, the laughter in Orton's plays was borne out of despair, isolation, and the violence of modern British life. Orton's work stands out because it lives between horror and tragedy.

In his final two plays, *Loot* and *What the Butler Saw*, farce allowed Orton to "make a spectacle of [social] disintegration. He showed man dummying up a destiny in a world by making panic look like reason" (Lahr/Orton 7) With farce, Orton could flaunt those aspects of life people chose to forget or ignore. For Orton, there is no moral high ground. Everyone is culpable and capable of acts, bordering on the nightmarish. Orton's plays, especially *Loot* and *Butler*, "embody a mocking response to a contemporary world, a response which, seeing laughter as a 'serious business', uses humour as a weapon" (Smith 120). To jump into the 'Ortonesque' fray, a term that "refers to work characterised by a similarly dark yet farcical cynicism" (Glosbe Definition), is to see the world through the lens of a playwright for whom the stage world was a playground to expose the hypocrisy of authority figures, offer views on sexuality, and bring to task the medical industry, government, and law enforcement. Orton's view of the world was one that skewed to the side of chaos, a world where a lack of order was a means to highlight the two-facedness of those who considered themselves the 'moral right.' Characters in Orton's plays do not feel guilt or shame, and neither do they apologise for their actions. They are not punished for their transgressions. Instead, farce is a way to release man's basest desires and wishes. The boundless, the Dionysian, the unfettered.

## Loot (1966)

In his 1966 play *Loot*, Orton's farcical treatment of taboo topics brings about all kinds of fated mischief. At the top of the play, we find out that Hal and Dennis have robbed a bank. Feeling the heat of the police, they hide the money in the coffin of Hal's recently deceased mother, which is lying in a room in the McLeavy house before being taken to its final resting place. Mrs. McLeavy, however, is not in the coffin. In order to make room for the stolen 'loot', Hal and Dennis remove her corpse and stuff it upside down in a wardrobe. Meanwhile, Fay, Mrs. McLeavy's nurse, informs Mr. McLeavy that immediately before she died, Mrs. McLeavy changed her will, leaving the majority of her estate to Fay. Although it's only been three days since her death, Fay (a seven-time black widow who murdered Mrs. McLeavy) proposes marriage to Mr. McLeavy. If they marry, the money could be transferred into a joint account, and he would be eligible for Fay's inheritance. Complicating matters is the arrival of Inspector Truscott, with the aim of capturing the bank robbers. As Hal, Dennis and Fay manoeuvre both the stolen money and Mrs. McLeavy's body, they eventually enter into a pact with Truscott whereby a cut of the money ensures nothing comes of the investigation and no police report gets filed.

The play, which fuses black comedy with farce, takes a rebellious approach to hypocrisy, calling out institutions and sacrosanct traditions. Its

> attitude towards death and bereavement, piety and the Roman Catholic church, and towards authority in general and the police in particular [known to target and entrap homosexuals at the time], [is] clearly intended by Orton to shock conventional opinion and to encourage a sense of moral anarchy.
> *(Mayne xviii)*

Orton's treatment of death – with an eye for the macabre – invited writer Andrew Mayne to label *Loot* a 'deathroom farce' (Mayne 100). Glass eyes roll around on the floor, false teeth are used as castanets, and a corpse is manhandled.

Although it is not explicitly stated in the text, we can infer from their interactions that Hal and Dennis are lovers. Like Nance and Marion in Deborah Salem Smith's *Faithful Cheaters*, the presentation of Hal and Dennis' relationship is straightforward and incidental, not tied to the mechanics of the plot. For a man who was openly gay at a time when homosexuality still suffered under the threat of prosecution, Orton would live long enough to see the passage of the 1967 Sexual Offences Act (No. 2), but not to feel its full impact on London society. Ironically, Orton remained quite silent on matters of homosexual reform. Instead he was "working to explode the very definition of 'homosexual'" (Coppa 89). Neither Orton nor his characters were defined by any stereotypical notion of the times as to what was meant by 'queer', 'gay', 'straight', etc. Orton himself was working class, masculine, and literary, and happened to be homosexual. In discussing the characters of Hal and Dennis, Orton said:

> I don't want there to be anything queer or camp or odd about [their relationship]. Americans see homosexuality in terms of fag and drag. This isn't my vision of the universal brotherhood. They must be perfectly ordinary boys who happen to be fucking each other. Nothing could be more natural. I won't have the Great American Queer brought into it.
>
> *(Smith 126)*

### *What the Butler Saw* (1969)

Within the first fifteen minutes, we are pulled into the play thinking we are watching your average 'titillating' British sex farce. *What the Butler Saw* follows Dr. Prentice, a respected psychiatrist, whose world is upended after a misguided attempt to seduce Geraldine, a young woman who he is interviewing for a secretary position. To conceal his indiscretion from both his wife and Dr. Rance, a visiting fellow psychiatrist, Prentice concocts multiple stories, manipulates three different people (including a police sergeant) into switching clothes and identities, and compounds the situation by never telling the truth. Ironically, it is this indiscretion, along with the mayhem that follows, that leads not only to order being restored, but also to an unexpected family reunion. John Lahr provides a succinct metaphor for the action of the play: "Orton [feeds] his characters into farce's fun machine and makes them bleed" (Lahr 260).

Orton pushes the aggression of the physical and emotional violence, subjecting his characters to anguish, and leading them to question their own identity, even reality. The would-be secretary Geraldine is certified insane (twice!), drugged, has her hair cut to 'within an inch of the scalp', and is straitjacketed, and forced to give up her identity. Where the act of 'undressing' and putting on another's clothes in a conventional farce is often a simple plot device, Orton pushes the convention even farther. Here, in the process of dressing and undressing, characters completely lose their self-respect, and are forced to fight for their identity, even their existence. Scenic Designer Jeremy Barnett observes that "Power dynamics are fundamentally a part of farce. And then stripping – literally stripping and also figuratively stripping – away those power dynamics, [creates] role reversals. And that's a big part of *What the Butler Saw"* (Barnett 2020). Orton seems to be using the 'mistaken identity' convention as a way of breaking down gender designation. Girls become boys. Boys become girls. Men put on women's clothing. Orton seems to be saying that very little separates us sexually, and it is reductive to simply label us heterosexual/homosexual/bisexual etc. Instead, we are all sexual beings. Orton expertly uses farce as a vehicle to emphasise this in *What the Butler Saw*. His play is energized "with all possible varieties of sexual behaviour: buggery, necrophilia, lesbianism, exhibitionism, hermaphroditism, rape, sadomasochism, fetishism, transvestism, nymphomania, and the triumphant incest which crowns the mock-Wildean recognition scene" (Charney 101–102).

British director Sean Foley, who helmed a 2013 West End revival of *What the Butler Saw*, sees Orton's final work as

> a deeply shocking and subversive play, masquerading as a farce. In a lot of farce, taboos are tackled. People have argued that the best subjects for comedy are death and sex. And in farce, you always have sex and you very often have death, which really gets people laughing. Farce does deal, though some would say in a very light way, with very deep themes.
>
> *(Lawson 2013)*

In this work the line between sanity and insanity is completely erased. This 'innocent' Edwardian Peep Show called *What the Butler Saw* goes from titillating and voyeuristic to uncomfortable and implicating. We are no longer bearing witness to a failed seduction. We are complicit in acts of violence. Innocent characters are injected, scalped, assaulted, drugged, and shot. It becomes clear: those who run the madhouse are just as mad as those who live there.

Order is eventually restored with Orton tying up loose ends by cleverly employing and parodying Oscar Wilde's 'handbag' *ex machina* at the end of *The Importance of Being Earnest*.

The ending of the play is a happy one, if not unsettling. Dr. Prentice is absolved of his sexual indiscretion with Geraldine. Dr. Prentice and Mrs. Prentice are reconciled. And the Prentices discover they are the proud parents of Geraldine and the bellhop Nick (who has engaged in illicit behaviour with Mrs. Prentice and had planned to blackmail her). Everything has been resolved, incestuous behaviour aside.

Beyond the machine-like plotting driving the play, Orton uses language in a very precise way. His characters speak in epigrams throughout. The wit echoes the work of Oscar Wilde, and is used both offensively and defensively by characters. Language becomes a mode of deflection and denial. It does not reveal character; rather, it prevents us from becoming emotionally involved with these people.

> *Prentice:* My wife said breast-feeding would spoil her shape. Though, from what I remember, it would've been improved from a little nibbling…She's an example of in-breeding among the lobelia-growing classes. A failure in eugenics, combined with a taste for alcohol and sexual intercourse, makes it most undesirable for her to become a mother.

> *Mrs. Prentice:* I hardly ever have sexual intercourse.
> *Prentice:* You were born with your legs apart. They'll send you to the grave in a Y-shaped coffin.
>
> *(Orton 15)*

As in *Loot*, Orton seeks to shatter sexual taboos and institutional barriers. Director John Tillinger, who has directed multiple plays by Orton, sees *What the Butler Saw* as

> …a blistering treatise of a playwright raging against the culture that had marginalised him – not only for his homosexuality, but also for his impoverished roots in [the] working-class neighbourhood of Leicester, England. The farce skewers the societal pillars of marriage, sexuality, politics and medicine as its bourgeois characters indulge in bribery, blackmail, adultery, incest and rape.
>
> *(Pfefferman 2014)*

Since its premiere in 1969, major productions of *What the Butler Saw* have been few and far between. Although it has been met with its fair share of plaudits and derision, when viewed through a contemporary lens the play still offers a potent commentary. For many, time has dated Orton's play, neutering its shock value. Yet society's attitudes towards the above themes remain palpable. The emergence of the #MeToo movement has brought squarely into focus the uncomfortable debate about the onstage treatment of rape. Discussing what she sees as Orton's "savage satire on rape", scholar Emma Parker writes, "…by making sexual assault widespread and routine throughout the play, Orton derides a society that professes to regard rape as repugnant but refuses to take it seriously as a crime" (Parker 2019). It's important to underscore the fact that Orton is not being flippant in his treatment of rape. Instead, he "uses laughter not to trivialise rape – but to deflate the power of rapists and rape myths. The persistence of these myths indicates that, rather than being dated and redundant, his comedy remains sadly relevant today" (Parker 2019).

Australian director Danielle Maas, who directed a gender-reversed production of *What the Butler Saw* for the New Theatre in Sydney, believes *What the Butler Saw* still speaks to audiences today, observing

> …Orton is nowhere more ruthless than in his final play in his furious damnation of gendered hypocrisy, social conservatism, and sexual repression as a solution to queerness and the patriarchal abuse of power. Given the world we live in today, the thing I find most shocking is that there's still a great deal of misunderstanding and miscommunication regarding mental illness; we still live in a world that's xenophobic, racist, sexist, misogynist, homophobic, transphobic, violent, prejudiced and politically incorrect. That's not to

say we haven't made institutional changes and advancements in intellectual discourse in the last fifty years, but I don't think we can look at the state of our world right now and not be appalled by the lack of empathy and wisdom within it. Yes, we should take these things seriously. Yes, we should be angry. Yes, we should create change. But to choose to satirise that which beholdens us to pain and trauma by laughing is to choose life, hope, catharsis and empowerment.

*(Maas 2020)*

Joe Orton's death at 34, at the hands of his lover, Kenneth Halliwell, robbed the theatre not only of a playwright hitting his prime, but also of a bold, dangerous theatrical voice unafraid to infuse the genre of farce with a social conscience and macabre sense of humour. The prankster-ish presence of this 'Farceur of Misrule' is felt throughout this book as contemporary playwrights find ways to laugh at the pressing issues of the day.

## Farce and Identity

In a post-Orton world, playwrights began to address themes of identity, gender, and sexuality through farce in wide-ranging stories. Some filter these themes through classical farce structure and elements. Others dare to explore these themes by broadening the parameters of farce, sometimes veering into heightened states of absurdity.

### *Jean Poiret:* La Cage aux Folles *(1973)*

In 1973, the French playwright and actor Jean Poiret wrote the wildly popular farce *La Cage aux Folles* ("The Cage of Madwomen"). A social farce wrapped inside a domestic story, Georges, the owner of an infamous drag club in Saint Tropez, and his long-time lover Albin (aka Zaza – star of 'La Cage aux Folles') find their world turned upside down when Georges' son Laurent announces that he is getting married and has invited his fiancée and her ultraconservative parents over for dinner. Complications ensue as Georges and Albin try to figure out how to help Laurent without compromising their relationship, ideals, and sexual identities. Poiret's play "was heralded as groundbreaking at the time for foregrounding not only a gay relationship but a gay family set-up" (Wicker 2020). As a domestic farce, the play interrogates the parent–child relationship, and paints an honest portrait of a loving gay couple. It also addresses ageing and coming to terms with the changing nature of our domestic relationships. As a social farce, the play is about acceptance, gay pride, celebration of diversity, and reminds us that a loving family need not follow any social template.

*La Cage aux Folles*, in its various iterations and adaptations (musical, cinematic and a recent 2020 English language adaptation by Simon Callow), resonates today because, even though we have come a long way in recognizing, celebrating, and normalizing LGBTQ+ rights – including the legalization of gay marriage – bigotry and homophobia continue to exist as narrow-minded views of love and non-traditional families foment hate. Despite forward progress, many legitimately fear the reversal of individual rights. Through farce, we may educate those too blind to see their moral shortcomings.

### *Sabina Berman:* The Agony of Ecstasy *(1985)*

Sabina Berman is considered "Mexico's foremost female dramatist and, gender aside…one of Mexico's most prolific and commercially successful playwrights" (Bixler xxi). Berman's 1985 *El suplicio del placer* ("The Agony of Ecstasy") is a trilogy of three short one-act plays, each featuring a male and female character simply referred to as 'He' and 'She.' These three quarrel farces which put an emphasis on the verbal by-play between the male and female characters, juxtapose pleasure and pain to examine identity, gender, and sexuality.

In *El bigote* ("The Mustache"), a false moustache is shared between a husband and wife, whom Berman describes as looking "astonishingly alike" (Berman 1). The mustache becomes a transformative object for both of them. For 'He', donning the moustache transforms him from a meek, apologetic "effeminate man…into a suave, debonair Don Juan…who carries out a series of sexual conquests" (Versényi xiv). On the other hand, 'She', who is described as a "masculine woman", applies the mustache when "her confidence and strength leave her and she needs to ward off suitors." Their individual genders bleed into one another and they become so in tune, one is not sure where the feminine starts and the masculine stops.

*La casa chica* ("The Love Nest") focuses on a businessman intent on asserting dominance over the identities of the women in his life, including his wife, daughter, and mistress. Ultimately, we see power resides with these women.

The couple in *La pistola* ("The Pistol") are in a marriage appearing to be on the brink of collapse. One night 'He' brings home a package containing a pistol, claiming it's for self-protection after a friend had his house burgled. The gun becomes a source of theatrical tension, farcical gamesmanship, and ambiguous questions about their relationship.

In her book *The Politics of Farce in Contemporary Spanish American Theatre*, Priscilla Melendez discusses how "Spanish American farce fulfills a consciously ambiguous role, exaggerating and showing the grotesque side of reality misleading the spectator, and ultimately proposing that even the most serious social and artistic issues avoid prescriptive and fixed solutions" (Melendez 90). These tensions elicit laughter and a sense of unease.

## *Terrence McNally:* The Ritz *(1975)*

Terrence McNally's 1975 farce, *The Ritz*, is unique among farces for a couple of reasons: the setting is a men's bathhouse in New York City, and the majority of the play is populated by out and proud gay characters. The seed of the play "was born during the 1970s sexual revolution, an era of liberation extravagantly celebrated at the Continental Baths, a gay New York bathhouse where unknowns Bette Midler, Barry Manilow, Wayland Flowers, and others once performed for a towel-clad audience" (Outtraveler Staff 2007). In his review of the 2007 Broadway revival, *New York Times* critic Ben Brantley reflected on the original production, noting that *The Ritz*

> arrived on Broadway at a moment when gay culture seemed to embody the most advanced evolution of the sexual revolution. Heterosexual theatregoers who never made it to Plato's Retreat or wife-swapping parties could dip a vicarious toe into baths where you went to get dirty.
>
> *(Brantley 2007)*

To capture this voyeuristic spirit, McNally wanted audiences to feel a constant motion of activity throughout the bathhouse as the play went on. In his stage directions introducing *The Ritz*, McNally paints us a vivid picture:

> The main thing we see are doors. Doors and doors and doors. Each door has a number. Outside of these doors are corridors. Lots and lots of corridors. Filling these corridors are lots and lots of men. One of the most important aspects of the production is this sense of men endlessly prowling the corridors outside the numbered doors…Most of them are dressed alike; i.e. they are wearing bathrobes…
>
> *(McNally 272)*

With an abundance of men wandering in and out of rooms, the audience sees both who and what may lie on the other side of those doors, and is left imagining that to which they are not privy.

Set in 1975, between a post-Stonewall/pre-AIDS era, the basic plot finds the Cleveland Sanitation Executive Gaetano (Guy) Proclo hiding out at 'The Ritz' after his dying father-in-law puts a hit out on him. Thinking this is the best place to elude his hitman brother-in-law Carmine (who turns out to be the owner of The Ritz), the 'very straight' and 'in over his head' Guy is not only mistaken for a gay man by everyone in the bathhouse, but inadvertently becomes an object of affection for one of the patrons. Added to the mix, The Ritz's in-house resident (and talent-free) entertainer, Googie Gomez, mistakes Guy for a Broadway producer. He, in turn, mistakes her for a man. A unique facet of this farce is its multiple subplots leading to a host of comic coincidences, mistaken identities, and Guy in a dress. As he sets the farce wheels in motion, McNally ratchets up the pace and the multitude of doors become the source of "Keystone Kop-like chase scenes" (Wolfe 84). By the play's end, McNally expertly ties up the multiple plot strands into a satisfying finale.

The Ritz, like the woods in *A Midsummer Night's Dream* or the Forest of Arden in *As You Like It*, becomes a location of liberation, providing the characters a place where they can indulge their sexual tastes and not be judged.

McNally, who referred to the play as "a sex farce, my tribute to Feydeau…" (Outtraveler Staff 2007), goes on to say

> I always wanted to write in that style, and it's the only play I've done that way…I've often wondered why I never wrote another one [farce]. I think part of the reason was that it was just so much work. Farces are really fine-tuned. They are like Swiss watches.
>
> *(Outtraveler Staff 2007)*

When he was asked about reviving the play, McNally said "…There was a time at the height of the AIDS crisis that I would not have allowed a revival… but I think we're ready to see it again" (Outtraveler Staff 2007). However, the play's 2007 revival was met with mixed responses, and even McNally himself referred to the play as a period piece and no longer shocking. Yet, with its frank depiction of gay sexuality, one has to view the play in context, admiring what McNally was crafting at the time. Employing the mechanisms of farce, McNally was able to disarm his Broadway audience and invite them into a heightened level of understanding and acceptance.

### *Marius Von Mayenburg:* The Ugly One *(2007)*

The German playwright Marius von Mayenburg's 2007 play *The Ugly One* (translation by Maja Zade) is a four-character satirical farce that poses thematic questions about the nature and commodification of beauty and identity. Lette, an engineer, has invented a high-voltage connector 'plug' that he looks forward to demonstrating at an upcoming trade fair. When Scheffler, his boss, tells him they are sending Karlmann, Lette's assistant in his place, Lette is shocked. The reason? Scheffler says, "[your] face is unacceptable…we can't stand the sight of you…You can't sell anything with that face" (Mayenburg 8). Lette is stunned. When he confronts his wife Fanny with this information, she lovingly confirms this sentiment: "Sweetheart…I thought you knew. I've always admired you for coping so well" (Mayenburg 10).

Lette seeks out a specialist to secure a new face. The specialist, also named Scheffler, is reluctant, believing this would require him to build an entirely new face for Lette. The operation proceeds and after Lette's new face is revealed (much to his horror), the response from everyone else is the complete opposite.

The world is taken with Lette and his new face. He is empowered and finds a confidence that he never knew. Scheffler, the Boss, does an about-face and extols his virtues, sending him to the trade fair. Lette and his face are celebrated. Women and men throw themselves at him, causing a rift in his marriage. Unfortunately, the virtues ascribed to this new face do not last. When Karlmann decides to get Lette's identical face, he too begins to reap the rewards. Soon, more and more people are 'purchasing' Lette's face. As the play careens towards the end, "the play borders on existential farce when Lette suddenly finds his perfect looks replicated by almost everyone around him, and he finds not just his face but his life being usurped" (Isherwood 2012). In the process, Lette loses his wife, his job, and his uniqueness. The only thing he and those with his face seem to gain is a narcissistic infatuation. By the end of the play even the plastic surgeon, who has run off with his nurse (also named Fanny), wants Lette's face. Now, his creation is what he wishes to become.

Discussing *The Ugly One* in *Contemporary European Playwrights*, Peter M. Boenisch says "Subjectivity becomes just one more thing available for order from a catalogue, making us, eventually, all faceless and interchangeable" (Boenisch 139).

It is important to note that according to Mayerburg's stage direction, the actor portraying Lette "should look normal and not wear make-up to make him look ugly…You shouldn't be able to see any changes in the actors' faces after the operation" (Mayerburg 2). By doing this, the production does not project what it defines as ugly and beautiful. The irony is that the same face which was previously deemed ugly takes on beauty once Lette has gone in for the operation. The commodification of the face – the idea that he has purchased a new one – seems to change everyone's mind. Beauty is a capitalistic result.

Aside from the actor playing Lette, the other actors all play characters with the same name: Fanny, Karlmann, and Scheffler. This contributes to the farce by landing us in a play world not unlike one created by Ionesco. Scenes bleed into one another with dexterity. One minute Lette is speaking with Scheffler, when instantaneously a line from that scene dovetails into a completely different scene with Fanny. This 70-minute play moves with alarming speed, and calls for an agile display of ensemble work. The actors must navigate variations on their multiple characters without letting them devolve into cartoons. Characters morph with a simple costume piece or a physical adjustment. Reading the play, one sees a dizzying fluidity. Lette's life becomes a farcical whirlwind as he moves from one scenario to the next – be it professional or personal. His new face helps Lette assert himself in a way he never has before, giving him not only confidence, but arrogance. Yet, no sooner does this face give him a new identity, than that unique identity fades. Discussing Mayerburg and how his work and those of his contemporaries reflect a changing Europe, Boenisch says it reflect[s] a search for, and an exploration of, identity and place in the drastically shifting European cultural formation of the present – which, since 1989, and even more so since the financial crisis of 2008 and its manifold political and socio-cultural repercussions, has been characterized by an encompassing dislocation and disorientation…

*(Boenisch 145)*

Dislocation and disorientation are two words that define the experience of watching *The Ugly One*. As Lette's world spins out of control, and he becomes 'dislocated' from his work and married life, the sheer speed at which the play moves leaves the audience disoriented.

### *Nell Benjamin:* The Explorer's Club *(2013)*

There's nothing like watching a play about female empowerment – especially when the female points out the follies of a bunch of boorish males. Strong females asserting their identities in a 'man's world' or who are expected to live up to society's expectations, runs through the work of American playwright, lyricist, and composer Nell Benjamin (*Mean Girls the Musical, Legally Blonde the Musical*). Her 2013 farce *The Explorer's Club* may not be set in a high school, but the gender politics feels very familiar.

The year is 1879, London. The setting is the prestigious 'Explorer's Club', a place where renowned explorers gather to share their exploits and regale each other with their adventures, discoveries…and get pissed drunk. It's also a boy's club about to be infiltrated.

When Lucius Fretway, the Club's acting president, announces he wants to admit a woman into the ranks of membership, the men strenuously object. Enter Phyllida Spotte-Hume, a smart, witty, and 'beautiful' explorer. She bursts into the club having discovered a lost city. Accompanying her is Luigi, a denizen of this lost city. Luigi is blue, tattooed, feathered, and wears knickers. He is also a member of the NaKong Tribe of the Lost City of Pahatlabong.

On a surface level, Luigi could easily be treated as an object of ridicule, laughed at for his 'uncultured', even 'savage' behaviour. Instead, it is Luigi with whom we share a laugh, at the expense of the pompous, narrow-minded male explorers.

Benjamin sets up a classic 'fish-out-of-water' scenario, where not only is Luigi the 'outsider', but so is Phyllida. Benjamin uses Luigi as a comic foil, highlighting his quasi-indigenous presence and simultaneously deflating long-held attitudes regarding the appropriateness of colonialism. Then, using Phyllida, she scrutinises 'traditional' gender disparities.

In addition to having to prove herself worthy for membership in the eyes of the 'Old Boys' Club', we find several other roadblocks in Phyllida's path. These include a group of aggrieved Irish insurrectionists, Luigi's slap of the Queen, the possibility of war, the impending colonisation of Pahatlabong, the unexpected arrival of Phyllida's twin sister, and a protective pet cobra named Rosie. Clearly, all the ingredients for a riotous farce have been established.

Benjamin's historical farce, however, has much more purpose on its mind. Its Victorian setting assumes a lack of respect or acknowledgement of women's roles in society. Women were expected to be home, look after children, and attend to their husbands who spent time drinking, smoking cigars, and often frequenting brothels. Rights afforded to women were few, and having a woman insert herself into this fraternity would have been shocking. Although the men are reluctant to vote her in, their hypocrisy is patent as they objectify Phyllida and cannot take her seriously as an explorer.

*The Explorer's Club* is a social farce exposing gender parity and inequity. The explorers face losing their club and, recognising Phyllida's significant contributions, decide to offer her membership. Benjamin said she wrote the play

> because in the Victorian era in which the play is set, [explorers] were like rock stars. Newspapers would pay for their stories and even send them out to make discoveries, the same way papers now will pay for some celebrity's wedding or baby photos. The story of a woman trying to break into their ranks is very fraught because she not only wants to be a scientist but she also wants to be a rock star. I thought that would be the toughest group for her to break into.
>
> *(Benjamin 2013)*

By framing this social issue within a farce structure, Benjamin believes

> if you can get an audience to laugh at unreasonable people, then you can get them to feel the right thing – to feel like those guys are ridiculous and should be mocked, not indulged or followed. I feel that a play like *The Explorers Club* can change your mind...
>
> *(Benjamin 2013)*

The play explores what it means for women to be knocking on the doors of 'clubs' and not to get in. Benjamin uses *The Explorer's Club* to explore what it means to be a woman trying to make it in a man's world. She has spoken of being patronised and mistreated in various work situations. Only in the last few years, with the rise of the #MeToo and #TimesUP movements, have we seen a real shift in exposing misogyny and sexism in the workplace. The title *The Explorer's Club* takes on multiple meanings. It not only refers to exploring the world external to the club, but also explores the internal social workings of the club. It should be noted, too, that the Royal Society – the explorers' club upon which the play is modelled – did not admit their first woman until 1981.

At play's end, the men have learned a lot from Phyllida. She has proven herself their equal. She is a role model who has earned everything: notoriety, respect, love, and membership.

**Farce and Class**

*Bourgeois Farce*

Neil Simon: Rumors *(1990) and The Dinner Party (2002)*

After almost 30 years in the theatre, with 22 plays and musicals under his belt at the time, one of America's most popular commercial playwrights decided to write a 'pure' farce.

The late Neil Simon, long known for crafting humanistic, character-driven comedies – often inspired by his own life – found himself going through a divorce and mourning the loss of his son-in-law. He felt he needed to write something laugh-out-loud funny. What resulted was his 1988 farce, *Rumors*.

*Rumors* is set in the present day (i.e. 1988) and takes place over the course of a few hours. The action of the play follows four couples who have been invited over to the Deputy Mayor's home, in Sneden's Landing, NY (now known as the Palisades) to help him and his wife Myra celebrate their tenth anniversary. When lawyer Ken and his wife Chris arrive, they discover that nothing has been prepared: the kitchen staff is nowhere to be seen, Myra is missing, and the Deputy Mayor has shot himself. As the guests are gradually let in on the situation, they must figure out what happened and how to deal with it (and protect themselves) before rumours start to fly, putting reputations and political careers in jeopardy. Soon, the police show up, but not for the obvious reason. This miscommunication leads the four couples to mount an unnecessary cover-up that quickly unravels, almost implicating them in a criminal situation. Doors are slammed, closets are entered, stairs are mounted, backs go out, necks spasm, and a priceless crystal is dropped in a toilet. And just when it looks like everything has worked out in the end, and our four couples have escaped unscathed, a voice is heard that catches them all by surprise.

For 'Doc' Simon, this was new territory:

It's unlike anything I've ever written…There are so many more obligations. It's relentless in its needs for plot twists, and to keep the comedy going… And I rarely use plot. I use character development. In all other stories, the characters just seem to move to the next place, as life would have them move. But in the plot in a farce, you move them. The writer's in control all the way.

*(Rothstein 1988)*

Simon learned a great deal from working on *Rumors*. In his autobiography *Memoirs*, Simon offers up words of wisdom to those brave enough to take on the genre. A short list of dictums that includes the need for speed, mounting minor problems that escalate into a major catastrophe, and make it damn funny, he also writes,

> [t]his is not a steadfast rule, but farces, historically speaking, are about rich people and never about poor people. Poor people have enough trouble without getting caught in a farce. Rich people, on the other hand, deserve what's coming to them. Watching them squirm gets howls from the audience.
> 
> *(Simon 557)*

Simon would revisit farce in his 2000 play *The Dinner Party*. A domestic farce with social undertones, Simon's play finds three men of means meeting serendipitously at a Paris restaurant, all thinking they have been invited by their divorce lawyer (who represented all of them). Soon each of their ex-wives unexpectedly shows up, causing havoc. While they all wait for their host to arrive, numerous cocktails are imbibed, and unexpected flirtations occur, while old arguments are rehashed.

Simon sets up the first half of the play with the promise of a French farce about marriage and divorce, with the second half taking a more sobering dramatic tone, verging on melancholy. After their 'real' host is revealed, and the agenda is shared, attempts are made to understand and accept where their marriages went wrong. Although the play hints at the *possibility* that two of the couples may reconcile, one also comes away from the proceedings feeling that being alone is sometimes the better option.

In an interview with the *New York Times*, Simon discussed how his own divorce influenced his writing of the play. He "had the concept of creating a farce up to a certain point, and then instead of continuing the farce, to make a turn to where it becomes quite serious. I wanted to break the concept that farces can never get real, even for a minute" (Rothstein 2000).

## *John Guare: Six Degrees of Separation (1990) and A Free Man of Color (2010)*

John Guare's vast body of work includes *The House of Blue Leaves*, *Marco Polo Sings a Solo*, *Four Baboons Adoring the Sun*, *A Free Man of Color*, and the award-winning musical adaptation of *Two Gentlemen of Verona*. In 1990, Lincoln Center premiered what many consider to be Guare's most popular and acclaimed work, *Six Degrees of Separation*. Revived for Broadway in 2017, this 90-minute social satire/farce moves at a breathless pace, examining white upper-class privilege, race as a social construct, the family constellation, and the tenuousness of the American Dream.

The play opens with Louisa (Ouisa) and Flanders (Flan) Kittredge running onstage in a state of distress. Wearing dressing robes and speaking in panicked agitation, we glean from them that something has occurred which puts their lives in jeopardy. Moments later, Ouisa and Flan remove their robes revealing dinner outfits, and we are now in their Upper East Side apartment, the night before.

The Kittredges, who are heavily involved in the art world, frequent wealthy social circles. This evening they are dining with their friend Geoffrey, who is visiting from South Africa. Geoffrey owns a gold mine and the Kittredges hope he'll stake them with two million dollars for a Cézanne painting that has recently come on the market. Flan, an art dealer, plans to buy the painting, resell it to a group of Japanese investors for ten million, and, in the process, net the three of them a substantial profit. Before they can all leave for dinner, a stranger appears at their apartment door. Bleeding, and claiming he is a friend of the Kittredge children from Harvard, Paul shares with them that he was mugged in Central Park and didn't know where else to go. Once it becomes clear that they won't be making their reservation, Paul insists on cooking the trio dinner as a thank you for taking care of him. As the evening wears on, Paul ingratiates himself, charming the Kittredges with his intelligence, enthusiasm, and philosophical ideas about *Catcher in the Rye* and the imagination. He also reveals that he is in town visiting his father, the actor Sidney Poitier. Paul's presence has a marked effect on Geoffrey, who agrees to put up the two million dollars. The Kittredges, who are also taken with Paul, invite him to stay for the night.

The next morning, Ouisa and Flan discover to their horror that Paul has brought a male prostitute back to their apartment. Aghast, they kick the hustler out (after a comical set piece involving a chase around the apartment) and ask Paul to leave. A familiar strain of dialogue is heard. This is the moment where we first discovered Ouisa and Flan at the top of the play. It emerges that the Kittredges were not the first family to be taken in by Paul, or the last. Yet in none of the situations was anything stolen. Paul may be a con artist, but his desire to infiltrate the homes of the wealthy is rooted in "find[ing] the family he lacks; he is searching for an identity and yearns to be loved, wanted, and appreciated" (Plunka 197). Even though Flan and Ouisa are outraged, we see, especially in Ouisa, that a connection exists between her and Paul that has been absent between her and her own children. Feeling isolated, Paul gives her the opportunity to be the mother she hasn't been for quite some time. Ouisa, and Flan momentarily, give him the respect and friendship he so eagerly seeks.

Guare has Flan and Ouisa breaking the fourth wall, confiding in the audience through direct address. Original director Jerry Zaks had the image of "stories told at a campsite…" and in collaboration with scenic designer Tony Walton, "devised a production scheme whereby the [majority of] the actors s[at] in the front row for the course of the performance, appearing and vanishing, handing up, holding up, and receiving props and costumes as needed" (Guare xi).

The seated characters are all from the Kittredges' domestic or social spheres. The ones who are not present include Paul, the hustler, and the Kittredges' doorman. These 'outsiders' do not get to watch the performance. With this set-up, the audience becomes unwillingly complicit in the proceedings. They are taken with Paul (like the Kittredges) and conflicted by the turn of events.

Floating above the stage is a Kandinsky painting, hovering over the proceedings. The painting is referred to throughout the play. The Kandinsky is two-sided. One side represents geometric order, the other side colourful wildness, possibly a comment on the upper class's two-sidedness: how they want to see themselves (liberal, accepting, open-minded, attentive to the disenfranchised), and who they actually are (not as liberal and open-minded as they'd like us to believe). Like *Habeas Corpus* and *The Ugly One*, *Six Degrees* does not rely on a realistic setting. There are no doors. Big set pieces do not fly in and out. Guare, lamenting a recent production of his, said

> …it's got to move fast…because I just did a production of a play at Yale and the scenery looked pretty as a picture, but it took thirty seconds or a minute to change each scene, and in a farce, that's an eternity.
>
> *(Plunka 186)*

The speed is important because it directly correlates to the panic the characters feel. This panic is tied to urban neuroses and a paranoia that Guare wants to highlight. He does not let his characters off the hook. There is no break in the action. Scenes appear and dissolve through lighting shifts. From the very top, it's as if the characters are on a nightmarish merry-go-round, unable to dismount.

Guare's "brilliant achievement…is a result of his ability to take black comedy to another level, mixing farce and pathos" (Plunka 201). As the play hurtles forward, Flan and Ouisa's ordered life (the geometric side of the Kandinsky) spins into chaos (the colourful wildness of the other side). Ironically, it is the farce in the troubling circumstances that lead to personal epiphanies. For Ouisa, it is a sense of feeling alive again.

Although *Six Degrees of Separation* premiered almost 35 years ago, the themes the play addresses remain resonant, even if it doesn't have quite the same corrosiveness. Yes, we have ventured farther with regards to LGBTQ+ rights and race relations. But perhaps not as far as we'd like to think. In the last few years, we have seen increasing instances of homophobia and racism. There remains a disconnect between social and cultural groups. With the advent of social media, incendiary opinions have a platform to flourish, while allowing people the option of not connecting directly. This need to connect (or disconnect) drives the characters in the play. Connection means being seen, being accepted, being wanted, and being close to celebrity. As the world emerges from the throes of a pandemic, and its forced isolation and omnipresent threat, connection may function also as a paramount need for the audience.

On the surface, the play is

skewering rich, liberal New Yorkers – their insularity, their susceptibility to flattery and the chance of a brush with fame, their hunger to fill the void of their spoiled children's withheld affections…But the play is less about the desecration of a privileged class or the aspirations of outsiders than it is about the realization that nobody really knows anybody, least of all themselves.

*(Rooney 2017)*

Guare, whose work has always contained elements of black comedy and farce, explores the intersectionality of race, class, and politics in his 2010 play, *A Free Man of Color*. It is an epic, sprawling work taking place in a socially permissive New Orleans between 1801 and 1806. The play's central character, Jacques Cornet, our 'free man of color', was "born of a slave…[and] a very rich, very white father" (Guare 7) but buys his freedom and inherits his father's fortune, which includes the services of a slave (or 'administrative assistant') named Cupidon Murmur. Cornet lives a Bacchanalian life. He seduces women, is the envy of men, and presents as a 19th-century fashionista. Guare's story is told through the words of Cornet, who is writing a play about his world right before our eyes. As we see the story play out through the perspective of both Cornet and the city of New Orleans,

> history looks completely different from what was reported along the Eastern seaboard of the United States. The carnivalesque encourages this unusual perspective: seeing the world from the bottom up, privileging the underprivileged, and giving voice to the underrepresented, if only for a moment.
>
> *(Demastes 89)*

Between 1763 and 1801, Louisiana was under Spanish rule. At the time, a person of colour was allowed to live free. In the play, Dr. Toubib, a physician, says New Orleans is "[t]he free-est city in the world. Imagine the unimaginable. Race is a celebration! See the lush palette of skin tones in New Orleans" (Guare 10).

The play features a cast of 40 characters, including historical figures like Napoleon, Thomas Jefferson, and even Georges Feydeau, who won't be born for another 60 years. In a metatheatrical moment, he pops up to reference a farcical playwriting technique being employed by both Cornet and Guare:

> *Feydeau:* There is only one rule of playwriting. Character A says, "My life is perfect as long as Character B does not show up." Knock knock. Enter Character B.
> *Cornet:* My life is perfect.
> *Murmur:* Knock knock.
>
> *(Guare 21)*

Filled with witty wordplay, and a bold theatricality, Guare's play is part history lesson, part Restoration-inspired comedy. With an aggressive nod to *The Country Wife*, Guare borrows two plot elements from Wycherley's play: Cornet, like Harry Horner, pretends to be impotent "to fool the town's cuckolded husbands" (Demastes 90). The arrival of 'country wife' Margery Jolicoeur, who is unhappily married to Cornet's half-brother Pincepousse, provides the second plot element lifted from Wycherley. Cornet ends up seducing Margery. This angers Pincepousse, who Cornet subsequently kills in a duel.

The anarchic energy of farce infusing aspects of the play becomes an apt reflection of the circus of New Orleans society. Perhaps more importantly, "amid the destabilizing effects of the play's buffoonery and comedy, Guare presents injustice and hypocrisy among the ruling classes for what they are" (ibid. 90). The play reels us in with its clever banter, and Cornet's machinations; however, the farcical dealings and ribaldry soon disappear when Spain sells Louisiana back to France, who in turn sells it to the United States. Jacques is betrayed by Murmur and finds himself at the mercy of those he took advantage of along the way. Cornet is sold into slavery, no longer a 'free man of color.' Guare gives Dr. Toubib the last line of the play, a haunting line that reveals the final title of Cornet's opus: *A Free Man of Color or How One Man Became an American* (Guare 69).

## Mike Bartlett: Scandaltown *(2022)*

In spring 2022, British playwright Mike Bartlett had three plays open within a month of one another; a revival of his 2009 play *Cock*, and two new works that draw on the theatrical past to tell contemporary stories: *The 47th*, and *Scandaltown*. *The 47th*, which is written in blank verse (like his 2014 play *King Charles III*), is filled with political intrigue and black comedy that imagines a 2024 US election between former President Donald Trump and Vice-President Kamala Harris.

With *Scandaltown*, Bartlett fashions a *contemporary* Restoration-style social satire/farce, employing all of the delicious elements that characterised the plays of that period. Emerging from years of puritanical rule, the original comedies of the Restoration "show the society's concerted drive towards what had been denied: pleasure and profit. The plays celebrate materialism and sexual license" (Callow 9). One can see the parallels in *Scandaltown*. While in lockdown, Bartlett was reminded of "the subject of those plays – facade and gossip and a corrupt elite in London. Exactly where we are today. The form and the content fit" (Stirling 2022). If the plays of Congreve, Etheredge, Wycherley, and Aphra Behn were licentious responses to a puritanical lockdown, Bartlett offers a orgiastic night of theatre that is a restorative response to being in pandemic lockdown.

Staged at the Lyric Hammersmith – a theatre whose architecture was designed for Restoration drama – *Scandaltown* is set in a post-'plague', hedonistic London where pleasure-seeking and debauchery butts up against generational divides and political ideals. The sheltered Miss Phoebe Virtue hears through the Instagram grapevine that her brother is being corrupted by the evils of London. Disguising herself as a man, she embarks on a mission to save him. A raunchy comedy of manners, Bartlett has a strong ear for the rhythm and cadences of restoration speech, capturing the hallmarks of those 17th-century comedies (double entendres and smutty references) while filtering in contemporary anachronisms that connect to our world. Fashion defines status. Names like Lady Climber, Freddie Peripheral, and Rosalind Double-Budget point up key character traits. Social media is both a lifeline and a weapon. A tweet can make or break a reputation. Everything comes to a head at a 'Netflix Masked Ball' where family secrets are revealed and unexpected sexual awakenings catch the Virtue siblings off-guard.

Actress Rachael Stirling, who played Lady Climber, describes *Scandaltown* as

a great big, sexy, smart, occasionally crass, rock'n'roll piece of theatre…It makes merry of the cross-generational cyber-divide, while never making judgement. It reflects the facade of social media and hypocrisy of politicians, while smiling with real kindness at our shared human folly. It embraces modern life, and gently points out we are all a bit ridiculous to boot.

*(Stirling 2022)*

### *Working-Class Farce*

As Neil Simon mentions, the rich are often fodder for farces because we enjoy watching these characters taken down a peg. We laugh a little easier at the misfortune of those who are in positions of power and wealth. Do we want to laugh at the poor, the downtrodden, or even those of the blue-collar working class? One can argue it depends on the situation. If the 'haves' have everything to lose, the 'have-nots', have nothing to lose. This can result in hilarious scenarios where characters who are merely trying to get by and make something of themselves go to absurd lengths to fulfil their misguided passions. Similarly, we find characters in these farces desperately attempting to escape the demands of a job they hate or a lifestyle they abhor.

Prior to the 21st century, blue-collar farces were few and far between. In the early 'noughties', two Scottish playwrights filtered working-class ennui in comically different ways. *Black Watch* playwright Gregory Burke's first play *Gagarin Way* (2001) is a socio-political black comedy with farcical elements involving an incompetent kidnapping which results in bloodshed. Anthony

Neilson's *The Lying Kind* (2002) is a more traditionally structured farce saturated with Neilson's macabre humour.

### Gregory Burke: Gagarin Way *(2001)*

Set in a Dunfermline factory, in Fife, Scotland, two factory workers, Gary and Eddie, set out to kidnap a Japanese managerial executive, who is visiting from company headquarters. They plan to hold him hostage until he admits that globalisation and capitalism have ruined their working-class mining town… and then kill him, thereby sending a message to their company bosses. Things go awry when Gary reveals to Eddie that the kidnapped executive is in fact not Japanese. The company sent a different managerial executive, a white middle-aged Scotsman named Frank. Gary blames the lack of light and flurry of activity for accidentally kidnapping the wrong person.

The two men, who are on different pages when it comes to their political agendas, find themselves at an impasse, unsure about what to do. Complicating matters is Tom, a political science graduate student, who is moonlighting as a security guard. Tom inadvertently discovers the two men and their hostage, and is promptly knocked unconscious and tied up. Frank proves to be a surprising obstacle, sharing a point of view about his work that none of them expected, throwing a wrench into their plans.

With echoes of Quentin Tarantino's *Reservoir Dogs*, complete with banal banter and existential talk about Sartre, Genet, communism, and socialism, what begins as a kidnapping gone wrong, ends with the play taking a darker turn with pent-up male anger exploding in acts of violence. Eddie and Gary's plan proves faulty, derailing what was supposed to be a momentous political statement for Gary, forcing them to cover up two murders.

Speaking about her 2018 production of *Gagarin Way* at Dundee Rep, director Cora Bissett says that

> you've got two very diametrically opposed people involved in this big act together, for very different reasons. I think one man is doing it for a noble purpose, if misplaced, and the other guy just wants a kick, and then there's the young student character…men at various stages of their life, who really haven't found purpose in any of the places they've been looking and that's very distressing. For me, it's a very fragile play, despite the machismo; just beneath the surface [are] four people who really haven't found much of anything.
>
> *(Taylor 2018)*

Finding the balance in a piece like this, however, can be a challenge. In a separate interview Bissett says

You want audiences to have a good night out. I think they will get that because despite the darkness and the heaviness of the themes it is laugh-out-loud funny. So you have to balance that comedy and not let it override the more serious themes going on. There's a kind of discourse about different political ideologies, capitalism versus communism. That's the core of the play, there's people verbally fighting about ways to live and be…

*(Durkin 2018)*

For local Fife audiences, Burke's characters would resonate as

simultaneously familiar and empathetic; proud, hardworking communist men, driven to extremes from years of working hard and following the dream, only to find themselves in poorly paid and dead-end jobs, living in towns decimated by the end of various industries.

*(Taylor 2018)*

Playing out in real time, the dark farce emerges through Burke's profanely musical text, and the characters' impetuosity and ineptitude.

Beneath the comical machinations of the play, *Gagarin Way* is "…a soul-searching drama about the need for a political identity in changed times. None of the men has the answer; not the old-school revolutionary, not the violent nihilist, not the wishy-washy politics student and not the reluctant global capitalist" (Fisher 2011).

Burke ends the play with a delightful bit of black humour. With two bodies lying on the factory floor, Eddie realises they have to make them 'disappear', and keep quiet about what has transpired. Gary isn't sure he can. Eddie says he has no choice. And that "We better get a move on. We've got tay be back in here in two hours. We dinnay want tay be fucking late" (Burke 92).

*Anthony Neilson:* The Lying Kind *(2002)*

Anthony Neilson is known for his dark, often-twisted works that delve into the human mind. Like Enda Walsh, Neilson had never written a farce before, and his 2002 play, *The Lying Kind*, "was me trying to learn the mechanics of farce…" (Neilson x).

Met with mixed reviews when it premiered, *The Lying Kind* should be reconsidered as an Orton-esque farce that mines taboo laughs from a snowballing situation.

It's Christmas Eve, in an unnamed working-class suburb of Scotland. Police officers Gobbel and Blunt are arguing over who is going to break the bad news to an elderly couple, that their daughter, Carol, was killed in a car accident. A coin toss(!) has resulted in Gobbel being tasked with the duty. What plays out next, in a fairly short Act 1, is akin to a vaudevillian double act. Instead of stepping up and doing their job, the two officers banter about who will ring the bell, whether the shock of the news could potentially kill the elderly parents, and, inexplicably, how they're going to spend their holiday time off.

Added into the mix is Gronya, a nosy Neighbourhood Watch citizen, part of a group called PAPS (Parents Against Paedophile Scum). She shares with the two officers that the group received a tip about a child molester in the area, and accuses the police of protecting the 'paedo' from the group, only to take him elsewhere and dole out their own form of justice. This encounter will come back plot-wise in Act 2.

When Carol's parents, Garson and Balthasar, finally answer the door (and they are *old* old), a mutual misunderstanding ensues. Garson believes the police are there to tell her that Miffy, the couple's dog, is dead. Gobbel confirms this (thinking she's talking about Carol) and Garson collapses into the arms of Balthasar. As the curtain comes down on Act 1, the two officers are left to ponder how she already knew about her daughter.

Once it is revealed that Garson was referring to her dog (following a very funny sequence of cross-talk between Balthasar, Gobbel and Blunt), the two officers decide *not* to tell the couple about the death of their daughter. This withholding of the truth becomes a further complication with the arrival of Shandy, the local vicar. While visiting the police station, he had heard of Carol's death, and he has now come to pay his respects. To protect their lie, Gobbel and Blunt knock Shandy out and hide him in a closet. Havoc ensues with a dog accidentally getting shot, a second woman named Carol showing up at the house, a revelation involving women's undergarments, Gronya serendipitously returning at an inopportune moment to throw out more 'paedo' accusations, and Gobbel and Blunt pretending to be 'strippers.' By the end, with all miscommunications, misunderstandings, and confusion sorted out, Neilson sets the audience up for a happy ending. That is until two final reversals of fortune occur on the last page of the play, pitching the farce into utter blackness – metaphorical and literal.

Neilson has said that

> [*The Lying Kind*] was about how much of a mess you can make when you are trying to be kind, when you are trying not to hurt people. The impulse for the show actually came from a relationship I was in where someone was trying to be kind to me but was hurting me more and more as they did it.
>
> *(Reid 150)*

Although the set-up may be far-fetched, it is within a mode of writing that Neilson became fascinated with in the early 2000s, underlining the potency of comedy: "I have been pursuing an increasingly absurdist agenda. I currently believe that this form plays most fully to the strengths of the medium, allowing me to address serious themes in the most entertaining and accessible way possible…" (Neilson ix). Unlike the overtly corrupt Truscott in *Loot*, Gobbel and Blunt's misguided approach to this situation can be seen as both compassionate and incompetent. Indeed, "[m]uch of the comedy derives…from the incongruous inversion of our expectations about how policemen behave" (Reid 113). The situation presented in *The Lying Kind* may not be realistic, but in current times, with the actions of the police under constant scrutiny for acts of abhorrent behaviour, the farce that Neilson has crafted speaks broadly to a mistrust of those in positions of authority. Gobbel and Blunt's

> cowardice leads to manifold confusions and misunderstanding. They are characterised throughout as both unfit for the particular task at hand, and also for the broader responsibilities of police officers. They lack the basic competence and seriousness. They fail at every turn. Their failures are sometimes outrageous, but always foolish and funny.
>
> *(Reid 111)*

For programming purposes, this taboo-breaking farce, which dares the audience to laugh at the incompetence of the police, the death of a child, the accidental killing of an animal, paedophilia, ageing, and mental illness, one would be hard-pressed to see many regional theatres programming this black comedy at holiday time. Perhaps, however, this is the perfect antidote to the cheeriness of the season, and a reminder that the holidays can be difficult for many.

## Farce and Race

Farce that explores issues of race and racism expands our perspective on the genre. To this point there have been relatively few such farces written, either contemporary or otherwise.

In this final section, we look at a selection of 21$^{st}$-century plays specifically framing issues of race within a comedic narrative. Although these are not 'traditional' farces, they all draw on elements of the genre to highlight the social biases existing between those who identify as white and those of the global majority. The playwrights in this section, all of whom represent a cross-section of the global majority, use farce and satire to challenge their audiences to look inward.

### *David Henry Hwang:* Yellow Face *(2007)*

In 1989, Asian-American playwright David Henry Hwang (*M. Butterfly*) became interested in writing a farce that "would use mistaken racial identity as its comic form" (Boles 74). While searching for an effective plot that would address this issue, a controversy was brewing on Broadway, surrounding the new British musical *Miss Saigon*. Although lauded for his performance, the casting of Welsh actor Jonathan Pryce as the sleazy Eurasian 'Engineer' character, was met with a lot of pushback from both the Actors Equity Association, and the Asian community about this 'colour-blind' casting. Hwang found himself in the middle of the controversy, penning a scathing op-ed in the *New York Times*, which specifically questioned why the production was unable to cast an Asian actor in the role. An agreement was worked out with Actor's Equity and Pryce ended up reprising the role on Broadway (and winning a Tony Award for Best Actor in a Musical). The circumstances surrounding the *Miss Saigon* casting controversy continued to gnaw away at Hwang, and proved to be the catalyst for his new farce *Face Value*.

Taking Luigi Pirandello, Michael Frayn, and Joe Orton as inspiration, Hwang's social-meta farce has particular echoes of Orton's *What the Butler Saw*. In an interview with the *Boston Globe*, Hwang states that everyone in *Face Value* "ends up having to be in a different race than their own by the end" (Boles, p. 75). *Face Value* takes place on the opening night of a new musical called *The Real Fu Manchu*. The lead role of 'Fu Manchu' is cast with a Jewish actor, Bernie Sugarman, who plays the role in yellowface. The farce that follows involves multiple instances of mistaken racial identity, an Asian man donning whiteface to blend in with a predominantly white opening night crowd, various romantic entanglements, white supremacists attempting to kidnap Bernie (whom they believe to be Asian), and finally, in an effort to rescue Sugarman, a host of characters all dressing up as Fu Manchu to confuse the white supremacists. By the end of the play "almost all of the characters end up wearing a different racial mask from their own, resulting in ethnic confusion but also multiracial romantic pairings" (Boles 75).

Unfortunately, *Face Value* was met with critical backlash at its out-of-town tryout in Boston. Revisions did not seem to help the play, and it closed during previews on Broadway. One can see the risks Hwang was taking and applaud how he was attempting to push the trope of mistaken identity to a new place. We have not seen any playwrights attempt this type of farcical storytelling before, complete with a social conscience. Actress Gina Torres, who played the ill-fated play's stage manager, said in a 2020 *New York Times* article, that the reason the play failed had

> more to do with content than with comedy. "It really made you look at the absurdity of color and how we perceive it in human beings, which is, I believe, ultimately what killed us," she said. [Torres] often wonders how it would play today.
>
> *(Soloski 2020)*

Out of the theatrical ashes of *Face Value* (which has never been published) emerged *Yellow Face*, a new play by Hwang, which premiered in 2007. *Yellow*

*Face* mixes mock-documentary, farce, and social satire, to tell a new story inspired not only by the events of *Miss Saigon*, but also by Hwang's own painful experience with *Face Value*'s failure, and "a 'yellow peril' hysteria of sorts that erupted in the political arena at the end of the 1990's" (Rich viii). The mock stage documentary form allows Hwang to re-examine these events in a new light. Additionally, by inserting himself in the play as the central character (named DHH), Hwang is afforded the opportunity to simultaneously make fun of himself while also interrogating in a personal way "a more nuanced and complex portrayal of how race and politics are intertwined. The play is also about the intermingling of fact and fiction, and of reality and fantasy" (Lee 108).

Act One follows DHH's response to the *Miss Saigon* casting controversy and his subsequent role as a spokesperson for the Asian-American theatre community. This experience is turned into *Face Value*. At this point though, reality and fiction co-mingle. In the imagined events surrounding the production of *Face Value*, a white actor named Marcus G. Dalhman is, through a series of miscommunications, mistakenly hired to portray the lead Asian character in DHH's play. When DHH learns the truth, he realises the hypocritical scrutiny he would be under, realising that he must 'save face' or be massacred by the media. Ironically, DHH is unable to fire Marcus for being white, as it would be a violation of anti-discrimination laws, even though he hired him for his race. Instead, DHH uses a small aspect of Marcus' heritage (a partial lineage to Siberia) and crafts a new ethnic identity for him. DHH introduces Marcus at a public event with a group of Asian students as 'Marcus Gee', thereby passing him off as Eurasian. The plan backfires as Marcus embraces his new identity and begins to self-identify with his new Asian-American community, who welcome him with open arms. For Marcus, this acceptance "finally provides him with an authentic sense of identity and connection" (Boles 109), something that he himself has been lacking in his life.

DHH has Marcus let go from *Face Value* (which, like its real-life counterpart, closes in previews); ironically, however, this new sense of identity helps Marcus find work in a production of *The King and I*. His performance as the 'King of Siam' is heralded by critics who refer to Marcus not only as ethnically authentic but as "throw[ing] off the ghost of Yul Brynner and reinvent[ing] the King for our multicultural age" (Hwang 39). DHH has inadvertently contributed to Marcus' rise by essentially crafting a yellow face character – something that he himself has been fighting against on Broadway and, more recently, throughout the *Miss Saigon* casting crisis.

The events surrounding Marcus' ascension leave DHH in a comic spiral as he finds himself questioning his own identity and his place in both the theatre and Asian American communities. As an acclaimed professional playwright, although DHH "is excellent in the job and desires to be an 'Asian American role model', he is increasingly uncomfortable as a spokesperson for Asian American theatre. The play shows DHH set adrift, uncertain where he belongs, yet surrounded by people who expect him to represent his 'community'" (Lee 108).

The farce that spins out in Act One, bleeds into Act Two with Marcus immersing himself fully as Asian American, lecturing DHH on how he isn't there for his community, even dating DHH's ex-girlfriend, who doesn't know Marcus is lying about his ethnicity. As DHH's multiple attempts to unmask Marcus as a fraud fall on deaf ears, he is faced with a growing situation surrounding "his father's involvement in a campaign finance scandal during the re-election of former President Bill Clinton" (Lee 108). Considering Hwang's play as a whole, "the two acts together present different aspects of racial politics in the United States: one is absurd, artificial and farcical, while the other entails dire consequences, including charges of treason" (Lee 108).

The notion of 'face' and what it represents becomes a recurring theme of the play. 'Faces' are appropriated, put on, tarnished, sought after, a source of confusion, and 'saved.' Lecturing DHH about the Chinese concept of "face", Marcus explains that "the face we choose to show the world – reveals who we are," going on to say "Well I've chosen my face. And now I'm becoming the person I've always wanted to be" (Hwang 43). There is something farcical about Marcus christening himself 'Asian,' yet his commitment is unyielding and in this racial proclamation claims to feel liberated. DHH has inadvertently "bestow[ed] upon Marcus an Asian community that is missing from DHH's life" (Boles 109).

At the end of the play, Marcus is outed as 'not Asian' after being tied to the same campaign scandal DHH's father was originally questioned about. DHH realises he needs to 'lose face' and rectify this situation he has created. Agreeing to accompany Marcus on a joint interview, DHH admits to making a mistake, and "tried to conceal [his] blunder by passing him off as a – Siberian Jew" (Hwang 66). In a metatheatrical moment, Marcus 'the character', confronts DHH about why he wrote this play. DHH responds:

> Years ago, I discovered a face – one that I could live better and more fully than anything I'd ever tried. But as the years went by, my face became my mask. And I became just another actor – running around in yellow face. (Pause) That's where you came in. To take words like "Asian" and "American," like "race" and "nation," mess them up so bad no one has any idea what they even mean anymore.
>
> *(Hwang 68–69)*

DHH references being an 'actor.' It is no surprise that Hwang continues to mine the performative-ness of the theatre, as a means to explore social tensions surrounding race and identity. *Yellow Face* is not an 'in-your-face' pressure-cooker farce, filled with slapstick and doors. The play takes place over a sixteen-year period, is filled with a gallery of real and fictional characters and has a structure more akin to Tectonic Theatre's docu-drama *The Laramie Project*. But the situational comedy that comes out of the play highlights the farcical ways we lie to ourselves and craft stories to fulfil personal narratives.

### *Thomas Bradshaw:* Intimacy (2014)

The African American playwright Thomas Bradshaw has a reputation for creating provocative works of theatre that are not for the faint of heart. In an interview with Margo Jefferson for *BOMB* magazine, Jefferson observes

> [i]n a Bradshaw play, no one in the audience gets to sit back in safety and crow over the sins of others. In matters of vanity and perversity, our lust for psychic and social power – in addition to our secret angers: class, race, and gender – are equal-opportunity employers.
>
> *(Jefferson, BOMB magazine, 2009)*

Audiences are often divided about his work with Bradshaw

> elicit[ing] belly laughs from some viewers and disgust from others. Naysayers have called the…playwright's shows…'ugly fantasies' and 'horror shows'… The reactions are due to the fact that Bradshaw, who is black, stages outrageous behavior – including child rape, racially charged sex and modern-day slavery – in casual, conversational ways.
>
> *(Murphy 2014)*

It would be a mistake, however, to simply label Bradshaw as a shock artist.

The laughter that is elicited from Bradshaw's work is situational and in his words, born out of the fact that his characters "pretty much hav[e] no self-awareness and are almost acting on pure id. There is never any subtext in my plays. The characters are always saying exactly what they mean" (Raymond 2022). Bradshaw's description aligns with our notion of the 'single-minded pursuit of a singular objective', and parallels the 'horse blinker' metaphor. His characters have no periphery. Their focus remains out front, responding to the immediacy of the moment, with words and physical actions that feel outrageous. The consequences of these actions are rarely, if ever considered.

Bradshaw's 2014 play *Intimacy* focuses on three families from a wealthy suburb in New Jersey. James and his son Matthew, who are white, live next door to Jerry (who is black), his wife Pat (who is white), and their 18-year-old daughter Janet, who is biracial but looks white. Fred (a contractor), his wife (who works at Walmart), and their 17-year-old daughter Sarah, are Hispanic. Fred is currently employed by James.

All of the characters in the play have some sort of relationship to pornography. Janet, an aspiring actor, has found lucrative employment in the adult industry. Matthew, an aspiring director, discovers his cinematic calling lies in making porn (after watching and videotaping Janet undressing and pleasuring herself one night). His father James, a born-again Christian since his wife was killed in a tragic car accident, masturbates to adult magazines (and inadvertently 'discovers' Janet). Fred masturbates to gay porn while his wife is at work. Sarah, who is secretly dating Matthew, introduces him to 'frottage' (since they have made a pact to wait until prom night to lose their virginity), which becomes the inspiration for Matthew's first film. Jerry and Pat often watch porn together, but can't always talk to one another about their sexual needs. These peccadilloes remain private affairs until the characters are challenged by others to see beauty rather than shame in their sexual predilections. Ironically, porn becomes a conduit for intimate connection between characters, and even liberation of their authentic selves.

For this to happen, Bradshaw pushes political correctness to outrageous places, with characters often responding in ways that are completely opposite of what one might expect. This is what gives Bradshaw's plays their comic vitality and unique voice. Echoing Bradshaw's comments about his characters having no self-awareness, in his review of the New Group's production of *Intimacy*, Ben Brantley observes that Bradshaw's

> characters behave as if the neurological brakes that keep us from acting on our primal impulses – or on the first angry thought that comes into our head – had been surgically removed. And because the consequent behavior is presented so matter-of-factly, Mr. Bradshaw's plays are unsettling in ways that gore fests or sex scenes on multiplex screens usually are not.
>
> *(Brantley 2014)*

Even more unsettling is when we catch ourselves laughing at the things his characters do and say, blushing at their openness.

As in any farce, characters do not ponder what's in front of them for long. They act. Bradshaw's work is messy, profane, and scatological, with racial epithets spewed and bodily fluids flying everywhere. Essentially, Bradshaw's work can definitely be viewed as 'farce of the id.'

In one particular set piece, as they sit down to watch their daughter's porn movie, Pat says to an uncomfortable Jerry, "Stop thinking, 'I'm watching my daughter have sex' and replace that with, 'I'm helping my daughter to further her career'" (Bradshaw 120). Soon they are offering a colour commentary with Pat and Jerry analysing the pros and cons of Janet's technique, eventually giving way to proud parents extolling her orgasm. After Janet walks in on her parents replicating a sexual act from her movie, Bradshaw upends our expectations with Pat and Jerry responding, not in embarrassment to being 'caught in the act', but with parental pride over their daughter's career choice. This is immediately followed by them sitting her down with the video, proceeding to give her notes to improve her performance.

In an interview with scholar Harvey Young, Bradshaw says

> The play really has to do with the normalization of pornography within our society and about class-ism. Part of my hypothesis – and part of my thinking, in general – is how racism doesn't exist in the way that we've traditionally talked about it. It has morphed into classism…Racism is pretty much never talked about in this play. It's…[i]n the atmosphere.
>
> *(Young 2014)*

The atmospheric racism Bradshaw refers to pops up in interactions throughout the play. Jerry assumes, because Fred is Hispanic, that his relatives must be on welfare. James accuses Fred's workers of being "dirty Mexican thieves…" and that, "In Mexico, they get to sit around all day, and sing and play the banjo" (Bradshaw 104). And even though it is never outwardly acknowledged, the brutal beating that James lays on Jerry, after confronting him about his daughter's appearance in *Barely Legal* magazine, reads for a contemporary audience like racial rage, with this white 'Born-Again Christian' beating on this black man. Finally, in a bit of bartering over the replacement of a hot water heater, both Fred and Pat insinuate that Jerry is cheap. The following exchange occurs:

> *Pat:* He's always been that way. You'd think he was a Jew.
> *Fred:* Well, he certainly is trying to Jew me over!
> [*Everyone laughs except for Jerry.*]
> *Jerry:* You know, I might be Jewish. They have those Jews in Ethiopia.
> *Janet:* I'm not sure they have the cheap gene. I mean, they don't have any money to be cheap with.
> [*Everyone laughs.*]
>
> *(Bradshaw 155)*

When asked about these casual slurs at the end of the play, Bradshaw, in an interview with Tim Murphy, said:

> It's portraying people as they actually are. Because I'm a black guy, people will often feel comfortable saying racist things to me as long as they're not about black people. I don't want to generalize, but in wealthy suburbs I have found that people will often feel pretty free to say derogatory things about their Mexican maids and groundsmen. The same exact people who, if someone said the N-word in their presence, would flip out and lecture you. And I've heard way more anti-Jewish sentiment in the Midwest than in New

York or New Jersey, where if you have a problem with Jews, you need to leave. I think that hypocrisy is interesting. We all have ideals, but we're constantly falling short of them and we can't see our own blind spots.

*(Murphy 2014)*

Given the extreme situations that propel *Intimacy*, it seems only fitting that Bradshaw gives the play an Ortonesque 'happy ending.' Matthew invites the other characters to play a role in his 'frottage' porn, with everyone agreeing to participate. Fred helps Matthew discover his bisexuality. Sarah is going off to college and eager to explore polyamorous relationships. And James and Janet get married!

Speaking about this 'happy ending' with Murphy, who mentions it is 'more farcelike' compared to his other plays, Bradshaw admits that he

definitely sought to write this in a lighter tone. Prior plays of mine had an unhappy ending that left audiences in a contemplative mood. With this, I wanted to write a play that mimicked elements of a Shakespearean comedy with a happy ending…

*(Murphy 2014)*

Bradshaw leaves his characters (though not necessarily his audience) in a joyous mood. As the lights fade, a final stage direction indicates Fred takes out a banjo and plays *La Cucaracha* as the cast sings and dances (Bradshaw 155).

### *Nakkiah Lui:* Black is the New White *(2017)*

Australian Aboriginal playwright Nakkiah Lui's 2017 play *Black is the New White* sharply addresses the majority of issues discussed in this chapter. Identity, sexuality, class, and race, are all up for grabs in Lui's play, but she wraps them unapologetically within the blanket of a traditional romantic comedy/farce. Speaking about her work, Lui notes that

[p]olitics is a huge part of my work, but I always think that the things we think of as "political" things, like race, sex, gender and class, they're not political issues, they're human issues because we live them every single day, every single one of us…I like to explore the humane aspect of that, and use laughter as a way to tell stories.

*(Marsh 2019)*

Set during Christmas, Charlotte Gibson, an Aboriginal lawyer, is bringing her boyfriend Francis home to meet her parents for the first time. What Charlotte's family doesn't know is that Francis, who is no longer her boyfriend but now her fiancé, is an unemployed experimental composer…and white. This does not go over well with Charlotte's father Ray, a former champion boxer and politician who has high aspirations for his daughter's future and wants her to marry an Aboriginal man.

Francis's conservative parents have also been invited to celebrate the holiday with Charlotte's family. What neither family knows (outside of Charlotte and Francis) is that Charlotte's Dad and Francis's Dad are longtime political rivals, and enemies on Twitter. Their hostility towards one another knows no bounds, even if it is perceived as utter childishness by everyone else.

The audience is guided throughout the play by an Indigenous Narrator who introduces themself as 'The Spirit of Christmas.' As they omnisciently share character backstory, what follows is an awkward, yet riotous holiday gathering where "[a] Christmas tree falls on top of someone; a food fight breaks out; family members old and new clash; a years-long feud is addressed via, of all things, a dance-off" (Tongue 2017). Lui has cunningly captured in her characters myriad viewpoints that "[stake] out a different and familiar corner of modern Australian identity, but each of them surprises us in different ways" (Marsh 2019). What is most effective is the way Lui sets her characters up with one point of view or perspective, and through plot complications and revelations, force them to reconsider those positions, find the strength to admit their failings, or stand up for themselves. Critic Cassie Tongue observes

> [Lui's] writing, whether devastating or hilarious, has always shown a great deal of accessible humanity and relentless intelligence. In this play and its twinkling take on the romcom form, she throws an erratic but big-hearted spotlight on upper-class entitlement and guilt; black identity and pride (and separatism); sexual repression; women's oppression; the responsibility or consequence of success; and, more broadly, the politics of culture and identity.
>
> *(Tongue 2017)*

Charlotte and her sister argue over racial intersections and what that means for their children. Will they be 'black' or 'white?' Are they still considered 'Aboriginal?' Charlotte's Mom, Joan, interrupts them with her own potent take:

> JOAN: Both of you, stop getting so caught up on Black and White. Race is values, the same as any construct in life. But values aren't people. If you forget about people, your victories can turn into your vices in a heartbeat… Live what you believe in. Keep questioning your privilege and those who have power.
>
> *(Lui 181–182)*

Lui's inspiration for writing the play came from a desire

to present a family of Aboriginal people that hasn't been seen before in the Australian canon – not just in theatre, but in any form. That is, an Aboriginal family who have money, who are not oppressed but who are culturally quite strong.

*(Wild 2019)*

In her Introduction to the play's published edition, Lui goes on to say that she "wanted to write something that didn't come from a place of sorrow, or from death…where I'd have to rehash that intergenerational trauma. This was actually about something that had hope and happiness in it" (Lui xii).

Bringing us back to farce, Lui "thinks laughter is the heart opening the door, and the more we can laugh, the more open and bigger our hearts get" (Lui xiii). As of this writing, *Black is the New White* has not been seen outside of its native Australia. Although the play speaks directly to a contemporary Australian audience, the universal (and complicated) truths about love and family which Lui's characters learn to recognise over the course of the play speak to all of us, and how neither can be defined simply by status, privilege, politics, and the colour of one's skin.

### *Larissa FastHorse:* The Thanksgiving Play *(2018)*

In spring of 2023, Larissa FastHorse became the first female Native American playwright to have a play premiere on Broadway. Taking on cultural appropriation and liberal 'wokeness', *The Thanksgiving Play* (2018) focuses on a group of three teaching artists (Logan, Jaxton, and Caden) and an ethnically ambiguous 'professional' actress (Alicia) who have been awarded multiple grants to devise a piece of theatre celebrating Thanksgiving and Native American Heritage Month. In their attempt to produce a carefully 'politically correct' pageant for elementary school students within a compressed time frame, their efforts are seen to be increasingly self-involved, and wildly inappropriate. As the quartet rehearses the show, attempts to be respectful and instructive begin to falter. In one horrifically hilarious set piece, an eager effort is made to underscore the Pilgrims' role in the brutal killings of Native American families. As per FastHorse's stage directions, one of the 'Pilgrims' pulls from a bag "two crafted heads that have long, dark hair [and] are oozing a red, blood-like liquid. He drops them on the ground. Blood sprays" (FastHorse 46). Soon, the heads are being kicked, tossed, and 'bowled' 'in sport', covering the high school classroom in blood. This leads to the following conversation:

> *Logan:* How is killing off hundreds of Indigenous people and then kicking their heads a proper celebration of Native American Heritage Month?
> *Caden:* It's true, and gets a Native American presence into our play.

> *Jaxton:* It's like those programs in high school where they make you visit a prison to stay out of prisons and see a crashed car to stay out of drunk driver cars and visit a morgue to…stay out of morgues.
>
> *(FastHorse 47)*

In his review of the Broadway production, *New York Times* critic Jesse Green observes that

> …farce is not an end in itself. Rather, it is the hilarious envelope in which [FastHorse] delivers a brutal satire about mythmaking, and thus, in a way, about theater itself. The stories we create can do almost as much harm as the false histories they purport to commemorate, she shows. And well-meaning people can, too.
>
> *(Green 2023)*

FastHorse purposely threads a fine line between what it means to be an 'accomplice' and assuaging white guilt. She "sends up the idea that anyone could claim that authority – a reflexive acknowledgement of her own position – instead turning her attention to those who have co-opted the history and representation of indigenous people in their absence. Adult diehards for high school drama are inherently funny, sure. But educators and entertainers are also the primary storytellers passing down America's legacy" (Kumar 2023).

At the end of the play, the foursome comes to what is both absurdly funny and also telling when it comes to 'white inaction.' After surmising that doing 'nothing' is the solution, the best way not to offend anyone, and in their woke minds combat "the cycle of lies, stereotypes and inequality" (FastHorse 62), we see FastHorse highlighting through satire and farce what happens when people talk themselves out of doing the difficult work when it comes to social activism. In the closing lines of the play, Jaxton and Logan seem to have a spiritual epiphany about 'nothing':

> *Logan:* How can the play be more than nothing?
> *Jaxton:* Not the play. We need to be less. Do less. That's the lesson. By doing nothing, we become part of the solution. But it has to start here, with us.
> *Logan:* Yes.
> *(They appreciate the nothing a moment more…)*
>
> *(FastHorse 63)*

## A Few More Contemporary Social Farces

Marius Von Mayenburg's *Perplex* (2010) is an absurdist farce with echoes of Pirandello, Stoppard, and Ionesco (like his *The Ugly One*). Two married couples lose their identities, gain new ones, swap partners, and engage in existential discussions about reality. Appearances from Nietzche, a Nazi, and an Elk coincide with some fourth-wall breaking that "highlights the unreliability of everything around us, be it the physical world or our social, ethical, and political structures" (Lenny 2018).

In queer icon Charles Busch's *The Tribute Artist* (2014), Jimmy, an ageing and unemployed female impersonator, assumes the role of his recently deceased landlady, Adrianna, in order to convince Adrianna's niece to forgo her legal claim to the Greenwich Village Townhouse. A classic deception farce, *The Tribute Artist* is notable for featuring a young trans character whose gender identity is not only a given but also integrated as an emotional character foil for Jimmy. This is unique for a genre which has historically appropriated trans culture as a plot development device.

Lynn Nottage's 15-minute play *Poof!* (2005) uses elements of farce to explore domestic violence in an African American household and the power of speaking out against those trying to silence or control you. After Loureen tells her abusive husband to 'go to hell', he spontaneously combusts. With the help of her friend Florence, Loureen must come to terms with what his 'leaving' means, and literally (with a dustpan) clean up the mess her husband has made of her life.

Egyptian American playwright Yussef El-Guindi's *Threesome* (2015) lures the audience in with a first act that plays out with bedroom farce hilarity. A Middle Eastern couple trying to repair their relationship invite a white photographer into their bedroom. This gives way to a tonally different second act that explores "a story of sexual trauma inflicted by dictatorships, American adventurism in the Middle East, and the shameless nature of a publishing industry that prizes salacious content over truth" (Najjar xxvii).

As our global community continues to wrestle with intricate issues pertaining to gender politics and identity, LGBTQ+ rights, class disparity, racism, and inequity, the theatre community is going through its own reckoning as well. Institutional racism and harassment are being called out, casting practices are evolving, and more diverse stories are being welcomed not only to regional stages but also to commercial theatres on Broadway and in the West End. Contemporary playwrights are grabbing hold of this moment in an optimal way, addressing these pressing social concerns that continue to dominate our headlines and impact us personally.

The plays discussed in this chapter use farce as a means to push the social envelope when it comes to confronting these 'hot-button' topics. Many of these playwrights write from a place of pain, from personal experience. Comedy, and more specifically satire and farce, become potent avenues to enter into dialogue with audiences. Additionally, we are seeing playwrights confidently switching stylistic gears; oscillating between genres, even shifting towards a more serious, dramatic tone.

The laughter generated by these social farces is not only disarming, but often shocking and uncomfortable. Farce has the ability to engage its audiences in controversial discourse without being preachy. Instead of hitting us over the head with messages, the thematic ideas are embedded in the comical set-ups and situations.

Beneath these social farces lie anger, confusion, and a need to be accepted. The characters in these farces obsess over their status; not only their financial status but also their status in society. They worry how they are perceived by others, and passionately seek to be 'seen.' Post-Covid, the world may be open for business again, but it is no longer 'stage' business as usual. Farce is an ideal and compelling theatrical form to interrogate such sensitive and challenging subject matter.

**Works Cited**

Barnett, Jeremy. Personal Interview. 6 Jun. 2020.
Bartlett, Mike. *Scandaltown*. Nick Hern Books, 2022.
Benjamin, Nell. "Nell Benjamin on Laughing at Bullies and the Sentimental Inspiration Behind Her Play the Explorers Club." *Broadway.com*, 17 Apr. 2017, www.broadway.com/buzz/170035/nell-benjamin-on-laughing-at-bullies-the-sentimental-inspiration-behind-her-play-the-explorers-club
Benjamin, Nell. *The Explorer's Club*. Dramatists Play Service, 2014.
Berman, Sabina, and Bixler, Jacqueline (Introduction). *The Theatre of Sabina Berman: The Agony of Ecstasy and Other Plays* (Translator Adam Versényi). Southern Illinois University Press, 2002.
Boenisch, Peter M. "Dissecting European Lives under Global Capitalism." *Contemporary European Playwrights* (Edited by Maria M. Delgado, Bryce Lease and Dan Rebellato). Routledge, pp. 129–149.
Boles, William C. *Understanding David Henry Hwang*. University of South Carolina Press, 2013.
Bradshaw, Thomas. *Intimacy and Other Plays*. Theater Communications Group, 2015.
Brantley, Ben. "The Ritz - Review - Theater." *The New York Times*, 11 Oct. 2007, www.nytimes.com/2007/10/12/theater/reviews/12ritz.html
Brantley, Ben. "Thomas Bradshaw's 'Intimacy' Makes Sex Neighborly." *The New York Times*, 30 Jan. 2014, www.nytimes.com/2014/01/30/theater/thomas-bradshaws-intimacy-makes-sex-neighborly.html?auth=login-facebook
The British Library. "Loot." www.bl.uk/works/loot
Burke, Gregory. *Gagarin Way*. Faber and Faber, 2001.
Busch, Charles. *The Tribute Artist*. Samuel French, 2014.
Buzwell, Greg. "Homosexuality, Censorship and British Drama during the 1950s and 1960s." *The British Library*, www.bl.uk/20th-century-literature/articles/homosexuality-censorship-and-british-drama-during-the-1950s-and-1960s
Charney, Maurice. *Joe Orton*. Macmillan Press, 1984.
Callow, Simon. *Acting in Restoration Comedy*. Applause, 1990.
Coppa, Francesca. "A Perfectly Developed Playwright: Joe Orton and Homosexual Reform." *The Queer Sixties* (Edited by Patricia Juliana Smith). Routledge, 1999, 87–104.

Demastes, William W. *Understanding John Guare*. The University of South Carolina Press, 2017.
Durkin, Kai. Dundee Review of the Arts. *A Short Interview With Cora Bisset, Director of Dundee Rep's Gagarin Way*. 26 Oct. 2018, dura-dundee.org.uk/2018/10/26/a-short-interview-with-cora-bisset-director-of-dundee-reps-gagarin-way
Dürrenmatt, Friedrich (2006). *The Physicists* (Translated by Joel Agee). Grove Press, 2006.
FastHorse, Larissa. *The Thanksgiving Play*. Samuel French, 2019.
Fisher, Mark. "Gagarin Way – Review." *The Guardian*, 26 Mar. 2020, www.theguardian.com/stage/2011/feb/23/gagarin-way-review
Green, Jesse. "Review: In 'The Thanksgiving Play,' Who Gets to Tell the Story?" *The New York Times*, 21 Apr. 2023, www.nytimes.com/2023/04/20/theater/thanksgiving-play-review-larissa-fasthorse.html
Guare, John. *A Free Man of Color*. Dramatists Play Service, 2014.
Guare, John. *Six Degrees of Separation*. Vintage Books, 1994.
Guindi, Yussef El, and Najjar, Michael Malek (Introduction). *The Selected Works of Yussef El Guindi*. Methuen Drama, 2019.
Hwang, David Henry, and Rich, Frank (Introduction). *Yellow Face*. Theatre Communications Group, 2009.
Isherwood, Charles. "'The Ugly One,' a Satire about Beauty, at Soho Rep." *The New York Times*, 20 Feb. 2013, www.nytimes.com/2012/02/08/theater/reviews/the-ugly-one-a-satire-about-beauty-at-soho-rep.html
Jefferson, Margo. "*BOMB* Magazine | Thomas Bradshaw." *BOMB Magazine*, 23 Oct. 2017, bombmagazine.org/articles/thomas-bradshaw
Kumar, Naveen. "'The Thanksgiving Play' Review: Larissa FastHorse's Broadway Satire of Wokeness Is Outpaced by History." *Variety*, 20 Apr. 2023, variety.com/2023/legit/reviews/the-thanksgiving-play-review-broadway-darcy-carden-scott-foley-1235589845
Lahr, John. *Prick Up Your Ears*. University of California Press, 2000.
Lawson, Mark. "Farce Is Everywhere on Stage – But Why?" *The Guardian*, 26 Mar. 2020, www.theguardian.com/stage/2012/jun/10/farce-is-everywhere-why
Lee, Esther Kim. *The Theatre of David Henry Hwang*. Methuen Drama, 2015.
Lenny, Barry. "Review: A NEW BRAIN at Star Theatres, Theatre One." *BroadwayWorld.com*, 14 Oct. 2023, www.broadwayworld.com/adelaide/article/BWW-Review-PERPLEX-at-Bakehouse-Theatre-20180819
Lui, Nakkiah. *Black Is the New White*. Griffin Press, 2019.
Maas, Danielle. Email Interview. 29 June 2020.
Marsh, Walter. *Review: Black Is the New White – the Adelaide Review*. 15 Nov. 2019, www.adelaidereview.com.au/arts/performing-arts/2019/11/15/review-black-is-the-new-white
Mayenburg, Marius Von. *Three Plays*. Oberon Books, 2015.
Mayenburg, Marius Von. *The Ugly One* (Translated by Maja Zade). Methuen Drama, 2007.
McNally, Terrence. *15 Short Plays*. Smith and Kraus, 1994.
Melendez, Priscilla. *The Politics of Farce in Contemporary Spanish American Theatre*. University of North Carolina Press, 2006.
Murphy, Tim. "Q. and A. | Playwright Thomas Bradshaw on Race, Porn and Suburbia." *T Magazine*, 30 Jan. 2014, archive.nytimes.com/tmagazine.blogs.nytimes.com/2014/01/29/q-and-a-playwright-thomas-bradshaw-on-race-porn-and-suburbia/?action=click&module=RelatedCoverage&pgtype=Article&tion=Footer

Neilson, Anthony. *Plays: 2*. Methuen Drama, 2008.
Nottage, Lynn. *Poof!* Playscripts, 1993.
Orton, Joe, and Lahr, John (Introduction). *Complete Plays*. Methuen, 1976.
Orton, Joe, and Mayne, Andrew (Commentary). *Loot*. Methuen Drama, 2013.
Orton, Joe. *The Orton Diaries* (Edited by John Lahr). Da Capo Press, 1996.
Orton, Joe. *What the Butler Saw*. Methuen Drama, 2017.
"Ortonesque – English Definition, Grammar, Pronunciation, Synonyms and Examples | Glosbe." *Glosbe*, glosbe.com/en/en/Ortonesque
Outtraveler Staff. "Terrence McNally Recalls the Making of 'the Ritz'" *Advocate.com*, 17 Nov. 2015, www.advocate.com/arts-entertainment/entertainment-news/2007/10/12/terrence-mcnally-recalls-making-the-ritz
Parker, Emma. "A Close Reading of Loot." *British Library*, Sept. 2017, www.bl.uk/20th-century-literature/articles/a-close-reading-of-loot
Parker, Emma. "What the Butler Saw: Joe Orton's Savage Satire on Rape Is as Relevant Now as It Was in 1969." *The Conversation*, theconversation.com/what-the-butler-saw-joe-ortons-savage-satire-on-rape-is-as-relevant-now-as-it-was-in-1969-112239
Pfefferman, Naomi. "Director Relishes the Humor in 'What the Butler Saw' at Taper." *Jewish Journal*, Nov. 2014, jewishjournal.com/current_edition/143366
Plunka, Gene A. *The Black Comedy of John Guare*. University of Delaware Press, 2002.
Raymond, Gerard. "Under Your Skin: An Interview with Burning Playwright Thomas Bradshaw." *Slant Magazine*, Sept. 2022, www.slantmagazine.com/features/under-your-skin-an-interview-with-burning-playwright-thomas-bradshaw
Reid, Trish. *The Theatre of Anthony Neilson*. Methuen Drama, 2018.
Rothstein, Mervyn. "For Neil Simon, the Prescription Was Farce." *The New York Times*, 13 Nov. 1988, www.nytimes.com/1988/11/13/theater/for-neil-simon-the-prescription-was-farce.html
Rothstein, Mervyn. "THEATER; It's Great to Be a Playwright, but Oh, the Pain." *The New York Times*, 15 Oct. 2000, www.nytimes.com/2000/10/15/theater/theater-it-s-great-to-be-a-playwright-but-oh-the-pain.html
Shewey, Don. "SEX IN THE THEATER: Thomas Bradshaw's INTIMACY." *Food for the Joybody*, 5 Mar. 2014, joy-body.com/2014/03/05/sex-in-the-theater-thomas-bradshaws-intimacy
Simon, Neil. *Neil Simon's Memoirs*. Simon and Schuster, 2017.
Simon, Neil. *The Dinner Party*. Samuel French, 2002.
Simon, Neil. *Rumors*. Samuel French, 1990.
Smith, Leslie. *Modern British Farce*. Barnes and Noble Books, 1989.
Soloski, Alexis. "David Henry Hwang's 'M. Butterfly' Followup: 'M. Turkey'." *New York Times*, 4 Nov. 2020, www.nytimes.com/2020/11/01/theater/face-value-david-henry-hwang-broadway.html
Stirling, Rachael. "When Covid Shut the Theatres, I Became My Mother's Carer. Returning Feels Defiant." *The Guardian*, 21 Mar. 2022, www.theguardian.com/culture/2022/mar/20/rachael-stirling-scandaltown-interview-theatre-covid-diana-rigg
Stott, Andrew. *Comedy*. Routledge, 2005, p. 156.
Taylor, Amy. *Cora Bissett on Her Gagarin Way Revival – The Skinny*. www.theskinny.co.uk/theatre/interviews/gagarin-way-cora-bissett-dundee-rep
Tongue, Cassie. "Black Is the New White Review – Nakkiah Lui Brings Politics to Christmas in Hilarious Family Farce." *The Guardian*, 26 Mar. 2020, www.theguardian.com/stage/2017/may/12/black-is-the-new-white-review-nakkiah-lui-brings-politics-to-christmas-in-hilarious-family-farce

Wicker, Tom. "La Cage Aux Fliles Review: Non-musical Adaptation Finds the Bitter Heart of the Classic Gay Comedy." *Time Out London*, 20 Feb. 2020, www.timeout.com/london/theatre/la-cage-aux-folles-review

Wild, Stephi. "Review: A NEW BRAIN at Star Theatres, Theatre One." *Broadway World.com*, 14 Oct. 2023, www.broadwayworld.com/adelaide/article/BLACK-IS-THE-NEW-WHITE-Comes-to-State-Theatre-Company-South-Australia-20191023

Wolfe, Peter. *The Theatre of Terrence McNally*. McFarland, 2013.

Wood, Claire. "Gagarin Way." *The Wee Review*. theweereview.com/review/gagarin-way

Weitz, Eric. *The Cambridge Introduction to Comedy*. Cambridge University Press, p. 184

Young, Harvey. *Theatre & Race*. Red Globe Press, 2013.

Young, Harvey. "Interview with Thomas Bradshaw (Playwright), Jan. 2014." *Northwestern*, May 2014, www.academia.edu/6026257/Interview_with_Thomas_Bradshaw_Playwright_Jan_2014?email_work_card=thumbnail

# 3
# POLITICAL FARCE

Politics has always been a ripe target for comedy. Every generation is beset by ineffective or corrupt leaders, government overreach and hypocrisy, dire global issues, and those whose political views are in direct conflict with the majority, resulting in extremist behaviour. Unsurprisingly, farce is often the 'go-to' genre for playwrights wishing to expose the machinations of those in power, or to highlight the absurdities when ego and agenda come before the best interests of the people.

The contemporary political farces found behind Door Number Three are direct descendants of Aristophanes (*Lysistrata*), Nikolai Gogol (*The Government Inspector*), Arthur Wing Pinero (*The Magistrate*), Alfred Jarry (*Ubu Roi*), Odon Von Horvath (*The Belle Vue*), Nikolai Erdman (*The Suicide*), and Eugène Ionesco (*Rhinoceros*).

Political farce revolves around the upholding or rejection of institutional and/or governmental policies and practices. Such farce may take on war, immigration, healthcare, economics, the environment, or the justice system. These plays reflect the contemporary politics of the playwright's time, and have been written as direct responses to the arguments and issues of the day. As with social farce, satire is an ingredient often found in political farce. However, where social satires/farces often leave audiences squirming uncomfortably, political satires/farces keep us at arm's length, allowing us to remain detached observers of the action. We are given an outlet (and permission) to laugh at those in high places, who may take advantage of their positions for personal benefit (be it political, economical, even sexual). Similarly, these contemporary satires/farces can help us understand complicated points of view and help us make sense of a landscape in turmoil. It is no surprise that during election campaigns, many turn to late night comedy programmes and talk shows for

DOI: 10.4324/9780429268809-5

their 'news'. These expert satirists and farceurs cut through the double talk, political dodges, and vagueness to decode the issues for voters.

The plays surveyed in this chapter feature a wide range of characters, many of whom either abuse their positions for gain, or, by circumstance, must fend off the threat of their power being usurped or stripped away. Whether it's a common citizen, a civil servant, an elected official, or even a political extremist, in one form or another, these characters are willing to sacrifice everything, comically, even their lives. We bear witness to those instigating or victimised within said political systems.

Before encountering a selection of 21st-century political farces, we must consider one of the foremost farceurs of the 20th century: a political 'guillare' or 'jester', who saw farce as a great political weapon – the Nobel Prize-winning, Italian playwright, Dario Fo.

### Dario Fo: Farsa Politica

If Joe Orton was a farceur of misrule, Italian playwright, actor, and political activist Dario Fo was the equivalent of the King's 'wise fool' who populated Mediaeval and Elizabethan stages.

As one of the great political jesters of the 20th century, Fo was inspired by the *commedia dell'arte*, and also the work of his fellow countrymen Carlo Goldoni and Carlo Gozzi. He also drews on Moliere, Feydeau, and Brecht, using farce to highlight corruption within government and law enforcement, bringing attention to economic hardship, class inequality, and censorship.

Although predominantly known for his political theatre, during Fo's 'bourgeois period', towards the beginning of his career, he was primarily concerned with "ridicul[ing] his bourgeois characters because of the way they behave, because of the beliefs they hold and because of the discrepancies between the two" (Farrell 1995). Beneath these tidily crafted boulevard comedies, Fo was not afraid to push the grotesqueness and absurdity of social situations in order to call out class hypocrisy. In contrast to Feydeau, Fo's farces cut deeper, going so far as to break the fourth wall. Joseph Farrell writes that "Fo is the distorted mirror image of Feydeau; where Feydeau asserts that all is well, Fo replies that all could be made well" (Farrell 1995). In these two playwrights we see a 'familial lineage' linking them to the Roman poets (and satirists) Horace and Juvenal. Their respective brands of social and political satire can be seen in the work of these two modern French and Italian farceurs. Like Feydeau, Horatian satire was "concerned with maintaining moral standards and wishing to improve the ethics of his contemporaries by suggesting a point of equilibrium between extremes" (Stott 157). This lines up with Feydeau's domestic farces, all of which are tinged with social commentary that decidedly calls out, with clockwork precision, bourgeois hypocrisy. On the other hand, Juvenal's satire was known for its "savage indignation, the bitter condemnation of venal and stupid humanity" (158). We see this indignation in the work of Fo, brought to bear with similar fiery passion for change. One could argue that Fo had the innate ability to fuse the urbane social critic, Horatio, with the rage of Juvenal to create work that made audiences laugh while skewering political oppressors.

Fo was known as the people's playwright and it is no surprise that theatre artists keep coming back to his plays. Although his work originates in a specific time (the 1960s, 1970s and 1980s) and is located in a specific place (Italy), what continues to resonate is the topicality of the subject matter. *Accidental Death of an Anarchist*, for example, speaks to fascist or oppressive regimes attempting to silence political or social outrage. *Can't Pay? Won't Pay!* imagines a world where civil disobedience, through the looting of grocery stores, is the only way women can combat an economic crisis in order to put food on their family's tables. *Trumpets and Raspberries* (or *About Face*) is a response to terrorism. The wealthy and the privileged are given farcical treatment in *The Virtuous Burglar*, a one-act Feydeau-inspired comedy, and *Kidnapping Francesca*, a full-length piece about a banker in bankruptcy who stages her own abduction (adapted as *Abducting Diana* in the UK). And in *Female Parts*, written with his wife, Franca Rame, a series of women's monologues ferociously and humorously address female oppression. Fo's work continues to be produced because it remains in dialogue with changing times, with productions often referencing local or global events. His gift for improvisation and clowning, coupled with his deep understanding and attention to farcical structure, ensure a spirit of anarchy is maintained through his work. For contemporary theatre artists with a deep sense of social justice, political acuity, and desire to enact change, Fo's plays continue to feel both dangerous and attractive. What better way to challenge complacent audiences than through the weaponization of comedy?

Together with Rame, Fo's theatrical body of work includes full-length plays, one-acts, radio and television plays, adaptations, and writings about the art and craft of theatre. *Accidental Death of an Anarchist*, and *Can't Pay? Won't Pay!*, in particular, continue to find resonance as countries struggle with government corruption and neglect of the citizenry. Their fearlessness and outspoken left-wing rhetoric led to phones being tapped, multiple arrests, denied entry to the USA, and Franca being kidnapped and raped by right-wing political extremists.

Fo's work is unafraid and imbued with rebelliousness, driven to take on a full spectrum of political issues, proving that through comedy we can make change, or at least strive for it.

### *Morte accidentale di un anarchico* (Accidental Death of an Anarchist, 1970)

In 1969, Italy was a country in political turmoil. The newly elected "Christian Democrat government, having deposed the centre-left coalition, tried to crack down on the Left and dissipate its forces" (Mitchell 101). A deeply divided Italy saw a rise in terrorist groups on both the left and the right. At the time,

> there had been 173 bomb attacks in Italy, 102 of which had been proved to have been organised by fascists. More than half the remaining 71 appeared to have been organised by the Right with the intention of bringing suspicion and blame on the Left.
>
> *(101–102)*

Meanwhile, the working class and students were protesting the new government over low wages, long hours, and poor working conditions, all to no avail. In the absence of progress, instead of looking for ways to reform the country, the left began mobilising, emphasising revolution rather than reformation.

On December 12th, 1969, a bomb was detonated in the Banca dell'Agricoltura, at the Piazza Fontana, killing sixteen people and injuring ninety. Although the responsible parties were never brought to justice, at the time, widespread rumour-mongering by the police, politicians, the military, and journalists immediately shifted the blame onto Far Left extremists. Within days of the bombing, the police began rounding up known anarchists, arresting ballet dancer Pietro Valpeda and railwayman Giuseppe (Pino) Pinelli, and charging them not only with the bombing of a train station but also the Piazza Fontana incident.

After being held in custody and interrogated for a period of 72 hours, at approximately 12 a.m. on December 16th, Pino Pinelli plunged to his death from the fourth floor of Milan's police headquarters. Although ruled an 'accident', his death was immediately viewed as suspicious. The inconsistencies and contradictions that came to light following a 'private inquiry' into Pinelli's death had all the makings of a conspiracy or, at the very least, a cover-up. This would provide the impetus for Fo's play.

We provide this political backstory to set the scene for Fo's *Accidental Death of an Anarchist*, a play that finds new audiences in times of fascist behaviour, government overreach, police brutality, and the oppression of dissenting voices. On the surface, it may appear that Fo was exploiting the death of Pinelli, especially so soon after the bombing and the questionable circumstances surrounding his death. In Fo's own words, however, there was little information available about the events. The press was either not writing about it or when they did (even in the left-wing papers), they were deliberately not taking sides. Fo found those

> who were coming to see our shows – workers, students and progressives – were asking us to write a full-length piece on the Milan bombings and the murder of Pinelli, a piece which would discuss the political motives and consequences of these events.
>
> *(Fo 207)*

Political Farce 105

Before publishing any potential incendiary conclusions, the press seemed to be biding their time, waiting for concrete facts to be revealed. For Fo and company, striking while the events were fresh in people's minds

> was precisely the time to make a fuss, with every means available: so that people who are always thinking about other things…could be told how the State is capable of organising a massacre and at the same time organise the mourning, the public outrage…
>
> *(Fo 207)*

The time is 1970. The place is Milan. In the wake of a series of bombings, and an anarchist's 'accidental' fall from a fourth-storey window of a police station, we discover at the rise of the curtain that a 'Maniac' has been arrested (again) for impersonation and is being interrogated in the office by one Inspector Bertozzo. Having previously been arrested by Bertozzo for impersonating a surgeon, a bishop, and an army captain (among others), he is currently being held for impersonating a psychiatrist and charging patients an astronomical amount of money for their services. After cleverly talking his way out of being charged for fraud, the Maniac is released from custody only to sneak back into Bertozzo's office, where he begins to throw arrest sheets of those he believes are undeserving victims, out the window. In the process he discovers a folder that contains information connected to the case of the 'Anarchist.' The farce that plays out sees the Maniac adopting multiple disguises – including that of a judge, bishop, and forensics expert – and "interrogating the police officers who were present at the time of the 'leap'", at one point "convinc[ing] them the only solution is to follow the anarchist's example and leap out the window" (Mitchell 362). The Maniac talks circles around the officers, first poking holes in the credibility of their stories and then encouraging them to concoct a new version of what happened in order to appear sympathetic in the eyes of the public. Things become even more complicated when a reporter from a magazine shows up, seeking to interview the police about the incident. Masquerading as a forensics expert, the Maniac assures the police he will help them out. Instead, he uses the reporter's presence as an opportunity to both indict the police and illuminate terrible working-class conditions.

Drawing on various facts, reports, and interviews which emerged from the inquest into both the bombing and the death of Pinelli, Fo challenges his characters with the same questions and inconsistencies. He highlights for audiences not only the absurdities in how the original story has been framed, but also in how it has been manipulated, with scapegoats cast to protect the truth.

Although different adaptations have taken liberties with the end of the play, the constant factor is the revelation that the Maniac has recorded the proceedings at the police station. What happens next has varied. Fo himself had created two endings. In one version, the Maniac "appears to blow himself up offstage, in an ironic replay of the police version of the anarchist's death, only to reappear as the 'real' examining magistrate, reverting to the play's opening situation" (Mitchell 263). The second version (and Fo's intended ending) sees the Maniac threatening to detonate the bomb that Bertozzo has brought into the interrogating office, thereby allowing him to escape with the recordings, with plans to share it with media outlets, political groups, and other authority figures. This is an important delineation because the adaptations that see the bomb go off, blowing up the police station (with either the police and/or the journalist still handcuffed to the wall), fly in the face of Fo's original intentions. For Fo, the blowing up of the police station is an act of terrorism and does not allow for justice to be adequately served in the public eye. Instead,

> the central argument of [the play] was that the police should be exposed publicly for their responsibility for the death of Pinelli...The play also exposed their collusion with the fascist group responsible for the Piazza Fontana bombing, and called for them to be brought to justice.
>
> *(ibid. 263)*

Like Brecht, Fo was interested in activating his audience, stirring up their sense of indignation with the goal of igniting them into action. Catharsis is not the endgame. In describing his ideal response to *Anarchist*, Fo wanted "to liberate the indignation of the people who come along. We want them to keep their anger inside them, and not be freed of it, so they can take action on events, and get involved in the struggle" (113). The difference between the two playwrights lies in their form and execution. Where Brecht's work, through his *verfremdungseffekt*, or alienation technique, is designed to keep the audience's emotional involvement at a distance, so they could focus on the issues, Fo wanted his audience to laugh, to be lured into the satirically grotesque proceedings. Drawing on clowning conventions which oscillate between comedic innocence and experience, and elements of bouffon, a form of physical performance connected to the art of social mockery, Fo's playmaking returns to its jester roots. As master teacher Jacques Lecoq notes, employing these comedic forms brings us "back to the tradition of the king's fool, who, far from being a real madman, was licensed to express truths in all its forms" (Lecoq 118).

Returning to catharsis, Fo has stated,

> if we had created a dramatic play instead of a comic, grotesque and satirical play, we would have another liberating catharsis. But this play doesn't allow you this outlet, because when you laugh, the sediment of anger stays inside you, and can't get out. It's no wonder dictatorial governments always forbid laughter and satire first, rather than drama.
>
> *(Mitchell 363)*

For Fo, laughter becomes a powerful way to activate communities. The 'Fo Clown' becomes a conduit for change, with the ability to directly confront targets and engage audiences without retribution, addressing many of the same issues preoccupying the work of Boal's Theatre of the Oppressed: "economic inequality, racism, and other social, health and human rights injustices" (Theatre of the Oppressed NYC 2019).

There have been numerous translations and adaptations of *Accidental Death of an Anarchist* since its premiere in 1970. Finding the balance between Fo's original play and political agenda, and unearthing the resonant connective tissue for contemporary audiences has always been a challenge in the script. Adaptations of the play have largely kept it in its native Milan, but have also relocated the action to Rome (Richard Nelson), England (Alan Cumming and Tim Supple, 1991; Simon Nye, 2003), India (Chanakya Bhardwaj, 2015), and Toronto (Paula Wing, 2015). In 2015 and 2018, two productions of the play, produced on opposite sides of the globe, showcased unique and very specific points of view from both a social and political perspective.

The first of these, Soulpepper Theatre Company's Toronto production, adapted by Paula Wing and directed by Ravi Jain, reset the play in the city of Toronto. The play was consciously cast with actors of the global majority, including the Afghan-Canadian actor Kawa Ada in the role of the 'Madman.' This was with the specific intention of representing the cultural mosaic of the city, and unique in that an actor of colour played a role that was not about race. For Jain, "the content was relevant because of…Black Lives Matter and where we were with our own relationship with the Toronto police as well" (Jain 2020). Discussing some of the challenges that come with relocating the setting, Jain goes on to say

> the two biggest areas we engaged in were 1) how to integrate the physical comedy into the writing…and then 2) how to modernise and update [the play] to a Toronto context without reducing it to something too 'inside baseball'…how to be judicious and efficient and precise with the references so that it feels relevant.
>
> *(ibid.)*

For the production's adapter and dramaturg, Paula Wing:

> [Fo's] plays are demanding. Demanding not only in their…political content, but it is [also] a…rigorous use of farce. And if you do not have…well tuned farce skills, you can't carry the political – it's necessary that it's sidesplitting funny in order for its political message to truly land, I think. And that's very difficult to achieve, both from the point of view of the actors, but also the

direction of it. You need somebody with a very, very well developed sense of farce, physical farce, wordplay…And then you have to make the audience question things. That's the goal, is to say to them, "what the fuck? Seriously".

*(Wing 2020)*

Wing's comment is a reminder that the imagination demanded in staging farce emerges from the blueprint of the text. The physical manifestation of action requires not only a reading between the lines, but also a strong commitment to the moment. And in the case of Fo, the political moment that is being scrutinised. Oftentimes, actors will read a farce script and wonder how it's funny? Laughter might be evoked from clever wordplay, but stage directions that describe physical business are merely guides; actors in conjunction with the director and designer must discover the physical 'alchemy' together.

In 2020, with racial protests and civil unrest occurring globally in the wake of George Floyd's death at the hands of Minneapolis police officers, more cases of police misconduct were being reported. One particular case from Toronto drew attention not only because of its current resonance, but because of its echoes of Fo's play.

On Wednesday May 20th, 2020, Regis Korchinski-Paquet fell from the 24th floor of her apartment building after her mother had called 911 to report her daughter's state of "distress." "I asked the police if they could take my daughter to CAMH [Toronto's Centre for Addiction and Mental Health], and my daughter ended up dead," stated Claudette Korchinski-Beals (Nasser 2020). From there, "Korchinski-Paquet, her brother and mother met police in the hallway of their 24th-floor apartment." Words were exchanged

between her and police. Not long afterward, she said she had to use the bathroom. [Six] Police went into the unit with her but did not allow her mother or brother to enter…Within a minute or two…the family heard commotion. Then, they heard Korchinski-Paquet cry out, 'Mom help. Mom help. Mom help'…Moments later, there was silence.

*(ibid.)*

Although the family has alleged that police pushed Korchinski-Paquet from the balcony, and some inconsistencies surfaced based on videocam footage, a Special Unit Investigation concluded that Korchinski-Paquet scaled the balcony on her own and that the law enforcement officers did nothing wrong. Given these tenuous times, where there is an inherent distrust of law enforcement, due to numerous acts of police brutality, one can't help but be reminded of the Pinelli case.

In 2018, the Australian director Sarah Giles and her co-adaptor Francis Greenslade fashioned a new version of *Anarchist* for the Sydney Theatre Company, with Giles adding a unique directorial twist. Employing an all-female cast, Giles had five of them play the male roles in drag, with the journalist remaining a female identifying character. Discussing this choice, Giles has said,

> the incompetence and the cruelty of those policemen…it just felt so right for women to inhabit those powerful bodies and kind of destroy them from within…And there was something about how the Maniac inveigles his/her way through this space that just felt so resonant to me in terms of how women have to navigate male space.
>
> *(Giles 2020)*

There is something fascinating about Giles' decision to use Fo's farce as a means to address not only the political issues embedded in the original play, but also the oppressiveness of gender politics. By pushing the grotesquerie of the farce (which Fo might certainly have applauded), the production takes on a Brechtian call to arms, with the 'performative-ness' of gender inviting the audience to laugh *with* the company at the various levels of authoritative oppression. Keeping the play in both its original time and setting means the audience remains at arm's length, allowing us to not become emotionally invested, and instead see our world with more insight. Giles discovered "the distance we've travelled politically [since the play's premiere]…is not so far, that I found it actually…brought out the horrors of what's happening today in a more pertinent way" (Giles 2020).

Giles, who also directed a new adaptation of *No Pay? No Way!* for the Sydney Theatre Company in 2020, believes Fo's work is important because "the things that he is picking apart and poking at are the fundamental flaws of society, the fundamental problems of democracy, and how capitalism now is highlighting them further and further. They're all about how the individual suffers at the hands of power" and that farce as a form is "the best way to interrogate the power structures that we're all suffering from, to interrogate the systems that are governing us…because if you can get everyone together laughing, then maybe you can get them listening in a way they wouldn't" (Giles 2020).

Most recently, British playwright Tom Basden (*The Crocodile*) had his new adaptation of *Anarchist* premiere at Sheffield Theatre's Playhouse in Fall of 2022. Set squarely in contemporary London, the play is "laced with topical references to police malpractice, from dodgy WhatsApp groups to officers taking selfies with murder victims…" (Fisher 2022). Amidst the expected shenanigans, Basden and the production ensure Fo's action-evocation is upheld. A bold design choice sees 'red tally marks' scribbled innocuously on the walls of the set. Projected on the set, their meaning

> is revealed with a short statement: 'Since 1970, there have been over 3,000 deaths in police custody in England and Wales. Each tally represents one of

these deaths.' We see a QR code linking to the website of Inquest, a charity campaigning for justice for those who have died in state-related incidents.

*(Ruck 2022)*

In 1982, speaking to the importance of making political theatre, Fo said:

> There's now a huge blackout on loads of things: terrorism, the Mafia, everyday crimes. There's no resentment or indignation any more, just passive acceptance…My job is to defeat indifference. The most dangerous thing that could happen today is for people to abandon political and social commitment. Theatre is movement, it's never theory. What I've always been looking for is the right screw to fix people into their seats.
>
> *(Behan 133)*

With this quote in mind, one can see farce being that 'right screw'. It is a form of theatre using a universal language to speak directly to the people, challenging their political values. In the program note for Washington Arena Stage's 1984 production of *Anarchist*, Fo clarifies the difference between comedy and farce, imploring us:

> Don't call my play a comedy. There is a misunderstanding of the word. I call it farce. In current language, farce is understood as vulgar, trivial, facile, very simple. In truth, this is a cliche of official culture. What they call comedy today has lost the rebellious strain of ancient times. What is provocative and rebellious is farce. The establishment goes for comedy, the people for farce.
>
> *(Mitchell 47)*

Dario Fo died in 2016, but his legacy as one of the pre-eminent political farceurs endures. The fact that 50 years on, his plays continue to speak to audiences proves both prescient and unfortunate, begging the question: How far have we really come politically and socially?

---

### Farce and the Government

Over the years, playwrights have enjoyed 'taking the piss' out of their government officials. The government has long been a ripe area for ridicule, satire, and farce, given that scandals have (and continue to) pervade these offices in one form or another. Much like the 'status' comedies discussed in the previous chapter, there is considerable pleasure in watching those in positions of power forced to reckon with dire situations, leaving them and those they represent professionally and personally vulnerable. Political farce demands characters to manipulate, scheme and 'spin' situations with a degree of 'savvy' to extract or protect themselves or those they work for, from embarrassing situations that put office and country at risk. In some political farces, reputation and risk are also tied to inappropriate behaviour, colliding with political responsibility. Political farce takes this behaviour to extremes, landing characters in career-ending positions where time is of the essence, the stakes are immense, and critical decisions must be made.

The popularity of political farce can be attributed to our repeated exposure to questionable behaviour by elected or bureaucratic officials. Whether it's the image of a 'stuffy' member of the British Parliament, or a loud-mouthed member of American Congress, there is voyeuristic delight in watching these elected officials' loss of control take centre stage. With their defences down, the glad-handing public face disappears and the private face is on public display. We depend on our leaders to put up a strong and stable front, to behave with decorum and represent their office with integrity and professionalism. The fun in political farce comes when those chosen to lead are forced to use their well-honed political skills to manoeuvre their way out of trouble. Sometimes they get away with their indiscretions and sometimes they don't.

The farces discussed in the following two sections look specifically at British and American elected officials who, through a series of questionable decisions or bad luck, end up landing themselves in hot water. We also witness the unsung heroes who work tirelessly to protect their boss's reputation, their party's image, and their own jobs.

**Farce and the British Government**

With the British domestic farce dominating modern stages, but waning in the 21st century, political satires and farces about the British parliament and levels of government have always found popular homes on both the radio and television, with shows like *Yes Minister* and *Yes, Prime Minister*, *Spitting Image*, *The Thick of It*, *The New Statesman*, and *Absolute Power*. And, although British politics has been given a voice onstage in more serious fare by the likes of Howard Barker, Caryl Churchill, David Hare, and, more recently, James Graham, political farce and satire have not been staples. Perhaps one of the challenges is how to construct surprising farces when reality is stranger (and sometimes funnier) than fiction.

Television programming notwithstanding, with contemporary domestic farces on a downswing, we have seen more political farces and satires open on UK stages in the 21st century. Works by Alistair Beaton (*Feelgood*) and James Graham (*The Culture*) take on governmental politics at the federal and municipal levels, respectively. Lucy Kirkwood's *Tinderbox* portrays a dystopian fallout from a Brexit-like decision.

Setting the stage for these contemporary works is a rare 20th-century government-focused farce.

### Tom Stoppard: *Dirty Linen* (1976)

Having already had critical success with plays like *Rosencrantz and Guildenstern are Dead*, *The Real Inspector Hound*, and *Travesties*, Stoppard tried his hand at an old-fashioned 'knickers farce.' Written in 1976, *Dirty Linen* "is a non-political play populated by politicians" (Nadel 260). These seven members (six men and one woman) comprise the 'Select Committee on Promiscuity in High Places', and have been tasked to investigate lurid charges surrounding an unknown individual responsible for seducing more than a hundred British MPs. This individual soon becomes known to the audience as the committee's new secretary, Maddie Gotobed. Furthermore, over the course of this cheeky, yet sly one-act farce, we come to learn that five of the six committee members (including MP Mrs. Ebury) have slept with Maddie. All of the individuals are trying to hide their affairs and none of them have an interest in getting to the bottom of the issue at hand.

With names like McTeazle, Withenshaw, Cocklebury-Smythe, Ebury, and Chamberlain, platitudes of self-importance rival the need to uphold the dignity of the Prime Minister's office. A recurring visual gag involving multiple pairs of Maddie's 'French knickers' randomly appearing from jacket pockets, handbags and briefcases, becomes a clever indicator as to who else has been 'with' her. Characters covertly try to coach Maddie into hiding their indiscretions. Stoppard plays with language, as "confusions pile upon one another with quips, jokes, double entendres in Latin and French, tongue twisters and inverted logic flying about…" (Nadel 262). As the committee members tie themselves up in knots, it becomes obvious that the real compass of common sense is Maddie. Stoppard sets her up and then subverts our expectations from the very beginning, by having a "sexy dumb blonde [walk] on and [who] is utterly patronised, and the play ends with the entire committee adopting the resolution which she said they ought to adopt on page four…" (Page 53).

We do not get the sense that Maddie's sexual proclivities have any agenda behind them. Her dream job may be to one day become Permanent Under Secretary, but there is no indication in the script that she is sleeping her way to a position. Maddie is a cheerful woman with political ambitions, who also happens to be sexually liberated…and proud of it.

What angers Maddie is the committee's cowardice. Instead of defending their right to privacy, the committee seeks to craft a bureaucratic report denying any wrong-doing by the numbered members of the House of Commons. When it becomes clear none of them will acknowledge their trysts, she rhymes off with Stoppardian dexterity, all of the places where their liaisons took place, making sure to link each member and location.

Before anything can be resolved, though, the committee is called away to vote on another matter, leaving Maddie fuming. She yells after them "…I wouldn't have bothered if I'd known it was supposed to be a secret – who needs it?" (Stoppard 116). For Maddie, the lack of acknowledgement makes her feel devalued.

Remaining behind is Mr French, the lone proponent of upholding the committee's civic duty of exposing the seducer (and also the only MP that hasn't slept with Maddie). Before he heads off to vote, Maddie asks him where the ladies' bathroom is, and, predictably, he is more than happy to show her. Following a brief interlude, the committee returns, as do Maddie and eventually French, who has done an about-face, crafting a report stating:

*French:* Paragraph I. In performing the duty entrusted to them your Committee took as their guiding principle that it is the just and proper expectation of every Member of Parliament, no less than for every citizen of this country, that what they choose to do in their own time, and with whom, is…

*Maddie:* …between them and their conscience.

*French (simultaneously with Maddie):* …conscience, provided they do not transgress the rights of others or the law of the land; and that this principle is not to be sacrificed to that Fleet Street stalking-horse masquerading as sacred cow labelled 'The People's Right to Know'. Your Committee found no evidence or even suggestion of laws broken or harm done, and thereby concludes that its business is hereby completed.

*(Stoppard 136)*

Earlier, Maddie had chastised the Committee and their rambling report for "playing into [the Press'] hands…All you need is one paragraph saying that M.P.s have got just as much right to enjoy themselves in their own way as anyone else, and Fleet Street can take a running jump" (Stoppard 105). As a former journalist himself, Stoppard appears to be calling out the press and "the behaviour of journalists who write such gossip not for their readers but for other journalists" (Nadel 262).

The play points out hypocrisy among government representatives; officials who claim to uphold moral standards, but who themselves engage in inappropriate acts without owning up to them. Although the play was not written as a direct response to it, British audiences would be hard-pressed not to connect Stoppard's play to the Profumo Scandal that had rocked the British parliament a decade prior.

In the end, French's diplomatic crafting of words gives everyone an out, and takes the power away from the tabloids. Inadvertently, Maddie's free love for her fellow citizens may bring opposing sides of the government together in more ways than one. As Withenshaw observes, "As you know sexual immorality unites all parties" (Stoppard 93).

Two of the three contemporary political farces that follow consider the federal and municipal echelons or factions, respectively, of the British government. Alistair Beaton's *Feelgood* calls attention to the culture of 'spin' that had engulfed the Labour Party in the late 1990s and early 2000s. James Graham's *The Culture* examines the inner workings of a government-funded cultural festival, and what happens when elected officials, civil servants, and ordinary citizens, all with the best of intentions, collide in a municipal office. The third play in this section, Lucy Kirkwood's *Tinderbox*, imagines a dystopian UK; a result of government failure.

### *Alistair Beaton:* Feelgood *(2001)*

Alistair Beaton's 2001 satirical farce, *Feelgood*, takes place at a British seaside hotel during an unnamed party's annual conference (though all clues point to the Labour Party). The Prime Minister is set to give a speech in 24 hours. At rise, Eddie, the PM's driven and manipulative Press Secretary, is working tirelessly with Paul, the PM's speechwriter, to craft a career-saving speech for the Prime Minister, whose popularity has been waning.

As the two men struggle to write the speech, Eddie's problems are compounded when he finds out that George, one of the Cabinet Ministers, has been growing genetically modified 'hops' on his estate, in order to make beer. Aside from the fact that George stood up in the House of Lords and lied to Parliament that no secret crop trials were taking place on his land, an unfortunate mix-up has taken place, resulting in a bad batch of harvested hops, which had been earmarked for destruction, being delivered to a local brewery where they were used to make a dozen barrels of beer which ended up on tap at local pubs. The result: a number of men who drank the beer have grown breasts. To compound matters, George had unknowingly licensed the bad batch of beer and it's been on sale for three months…at 14,000 pubs. Throw in a comedy writer hired by the PM to punch up the speech, environmental protesters, anti-capitalist rioters, and Eddie's ex-wife Liz, an investigative journalist, threatening to break the 'hop-breast' story, and Eddie must use every skill in his 'spin' arsenal to take care of the situation and avoid a scandal that could bring down both Prime Minister and Party. Whether it's bribing his ex-wife to kill the story, threatening to have the comedian's sitcom cancelled if he opens his mouth, blackmailing George to resign, selling information to the press, or even arranging a fatal 'accident', Eddie will stop at nothing to preserve the office of the PM.

*Feelgood* is set in 2001, at a time when damage control happened via landlines, pagers, and floppy disks. Twenty years on, Beaton's play remains relevant as politicians around the world continue to make questionable, and sometimes abhorrent, choices or decisions, requiring effective spin. There are simply more ways to reach people, resulting in truth and fact frequently being called into question. Politics has become more combative, contentious, and seldom takes the 'people' into consideration. We have reached a place where politicking is more about putting on a show, and rarely for the benefit of society.

> Liz: You want to take the politics out of politics.
> Eddie: No, we want to get beyond the politics of left and right.
> Liz: Oh, come on, you know where all that consensual bollocks takes you. You end up trying to govern without choosing. Which can't really be done. So all you end up with is presentation. Government by headline. Making people feel good. It's the feelgood factor. It's all you care about.
> Eddie: You can't achieve anything if you don't get people onside.
> Liz: You can't have everyone onside! If that's your aim, you'll just keep on tinkering around the edges.
>
> *(Beaton 74)*

With James Brown's high-energy 1965 song "I Got You (I Feel Good)" opening and closing the play, Eddie has done his job. The Prime Minister has weathered a storm and the impact is that the people are going to be taken care of and everything is "nice, like sugar and spice." But the audience is left wondering: is this really what the country needs?

Speaking about why the government is a prime target for theatrical comedy, Beaton says:

> Politics, being about how we are governed, is a deadly serious business, which is why it lends itself so well to comedy. Whether we call it satire or not doesn't really matter. What matters is that theatre can thereby combine the playful and the serious. Entertaining the audience is an honourable endeavour; provoking and informing the audience is equally honourable.
>
> *(Beaton 2016)*

---

### *James Graham:* **The Culture *(2017)***

In recent years, James Graham has established himself as one of the most astute chroniclers and satirists of British politics (*This House*), society (*Ink*) and culture (*Quiz*). When the city of Hull was named UK City of Culture 2017, Graham (who had gone to university in the city) was commissioned to write a play for Hull Truck Theatre's Year of Exceptional Drama. Granted 'behind-the-scenes' access to the inner workings of the Festival, he was afforded the opportunity to see what goes into creating the year-long 'City of Culture Festival', observe the culture of the city itself, and examine the culture that drives the *creation* of this kind of festival. The result was a farce set within the Marketing and Communications offices (or 'Marcomms') of the 'Culture Company', an entity that was set up specifically "to deliver a 365-day programme of transformative culture" and which oversaw "more than 2,000 events at more than 250 venues and public spaces across the city…" (Graham vii).

Graham's play, *The Culture*, takes place in January 2018, post-Festival. The Monitoring and Evaluation team is set to make a presentation to Clive, the Leader of Coventry City Council, hosts of the next UK City of Culture, and Imelda, the Permanent Secretary from the Department of Digital Culture, Media and Sport (DCMS). Lizzie, the coordinator of M&E, is feeling the pressure to ensure her presentation goes well, and that the statistics and analyses that have been compiled justify the important role 'culture' plays in the well-being of a city.

As Lizzie and her team prepare to meet these officials, Dennis, a Hull citizen, wanders into the 'Marcomms' offices with a complaint. Apparently, his old furniture isn't being picked up by the sanitation department because local students have turned them into art installations. While waiting to speak with someone, Dennis is mistaken inadvertently for both the Permanent Secretary *and* the Leader of Coventry City Council. Lizzie, worried that this will be perceived poorly, and thereby feeding the narrative that Hull is incompetent and "'…can't do this, Hull's not up to it, it'll be a total and utter – *farce.*' And here we are, at the final hurdle, finally proving them fucking right…" (Graham 52). Instead of owning the mistake and being perceived poorly by those in higher places, Lizzie recruits Dennis to continue the charade. Four doors, two cakes, a bunch of emojis on sticks, a box full of sex toys, and one Dutch photographer all contribute to Lizzie's heightened panic as she attempts to set things right for her presentation. With four of the six actors portraying two or more roles, Graham peppers the proceedings with characters from various corners of Hull society, inviting well-choreographed confusion. One minute an actor will be playing a government official, the next, a civilian volunteer for the Festival.

The play is a love letter to the City of Hull and a celebration of what makes it culturally unique. As could be expected, the play is very Hull-centric. In one sequence, a local 'Hull celebrity' is recruited to record a voiceover for visual artist Dixon's 'Touch' Exhibition (which is a suitcase filled with objects from Hull). Mistakenly, Dennis brings in the box of sex toys, leaving the guest narrating a voiceover about Hull objects and Imelda (blindfolded) demonstrating how the 'objects' work. Graham also cheekily references Richard Bean's historical political farce *The Hypocrite*, which had been premiered by Hull Truck Theatre earlier in their 2017 season.

In his review of the play, James Willstrop asks: "What does culture really do for a place like Hull? How do we quantify it?" (Willstrop 2018). Graham has written a play that uses the microcosm of Hull to remind us that culture in any city (or country) cannot be quantifiable, regulated, or controlled. At the beginning of the play, Lizzie describes what she does as "[m]easuring the impact of [the Festival] on the city, the people, by collecting data, tracking indicators, monitoring trends" (Graham 8). By the end of the play, with the humanity of the city shining through, Lizzie realises that "you can also 'feel' [culture]. In a way that can't be measured…you have to be out there. In the city. Talking to people. Seeing them lift their heads that little bit higher than before…" (Graham 93). Under ridiculous pressure, we witness the citizens of Hull rise from the ashes and proudly demonstrate what it means to be from Hull.

Arts organisations and cultural institutions are constantly asked to submit numbers, analytics, and statistics for government funding. This is, of course, necessary to justify how and where government money is being spent. Graham's play reminds us, however, that 'culture' is a product of the people, and not of politicians or government officials.

### *Lucy Kirkwood:* Tinderbox *(2008)*

Mixing farce with the Grand Guignol (a popular genre of 19th-/early 20th-century French theatre that combined horror and comedy), Lucy Kirkwood's *Tinderbox* imagines a fractured United Kingdom where England and Scotland are not only 'on the outs' but now separated by a 38-mile-wide Hadrian's Channel. Kirkwood, who refers to the play as a 'dystopian farce', may not have set the piece within the walls of a government office, yet one feels the government's Orwellian presence, while offering a glimpse into a society that has been failed by those elected to serve them.

Set in Bradford, Yorkshire, in an undisclosed year that we assume is the not-too-distant-future, the play takes place in a butcher's shop, run by sixty-year-old Saul Everard and his wife Vanessa, who was once an aspiring actress, and who was well known for starring in a series of "short party-political pornographic films intended to broaden the appeal of the Conservative Party to the masses" (Kirkwood 23). Peter Perchik, a Scottish artist, on the run after painting a not-so-flattering erotic portrait of the Prime Minister, decides to hide out in Saul's shop. With the Scottish and English each perceived as a threat and not welcome in their respective countries, Perchik finds his life in danger. We soon learn Saul and Vanessa had two children who "were slaughtered…by people like [Perchik]. Immigrants with backpacks and accents. During the 2012 attacks on Stratford" (Kirkwood 22).

Luckily for Perchik, Saul offers him a job as his assistant. Unluckily for Perchik, however, it was less an offer and more blackmail, with Saul threatening to 'out' Perchik to the police if he didn't accept. What Perchik doesn't know is that Saul's previous assistants haven't lasted very long in the position.

Most businesses, including the butcher's shop, have fallen on hard times. There is constant rioting in the streets. Global warming weighs on people's minds as a blazing February heat wave engulfs Bradford. This is a world where "eating bananas is frowned upon because of the 'Brazilian wandering spiders' infiltrating the country, where tobacco is a Class-A drug and where the morning's post is treated as a potential weapon of biological warfare" (Loveridge 2008). Meat is a rare commodity. And after Vanessa ladles a pair of spectacles out of a bowl of soup, we soon discover that Saul has taken a page out of the Sweeney Todd handbook and has been feeding his assistants into the cement mixer. When one can't find meat, one improvises.

When the play opened in 2008, Britain, in common with most of the Western world, was in the midst of the Great Recession. Banks collapsed, businesses failed, and productivity plummeted, resulting in high unemployment and a housing crisis.

The title of the play offers multiple meanings. The fragility of the nation is reflected in Saul's discussion of the butcher's shop being akin to "a veritable tinderbox. The walls are little more than parchment, and what you must remember is: who holds the matches..." (Kirkwood 15). Although Saul refers to himself as the one holding the matches, when a love triangle ignites, it serves as a metaphor for a UK at the point of combustion.

In an interview with Kirkwood, Guardian writer Tim Adams refers to "the dystopian extremes of *Tinderbox*, which, at the height of the financial crash, picture[s] a Britain of the near future unhinged by riots and cannibalism, and managed to find some bleak comedy in the fallout" (Adams 2012).

Kirkwood, who is more readily known for her sprawling 2013 political drama *Chimerica* and her apocalyptic *The Children* (2016), allows *Tinderbox* to bubble with a humour that "owes a considerable debt to Joe Orton's black comedies" (Billington 2009). Kirkwood also reveals an appetite for Gothic humour. This heightens both the farcical elements and the violence embedded in the play.

Kirkwood was determined though not to "...have a first play – you know, living room, domestic situation, problem... Loads of people have done that. I was excited by the fact that it was weird and metaphorical" (Jones 2009).

This is not your conventional middle- or upper-class 'farce room' waiting to fall apart. This is a grungy butcher's shop infested with maggots and bad meat. Desperation bleeds from the walls. Yet Kirkwood still manages to find an abundance of humour within its dereliction. In addition to the shop featuring a front and back entrance, characters leap behind counters, stash themselves in a walk-in ice box, and hide themselves in sacks. We even get a domestic wrench thrown into the proceedings when Perchik and Vanessa fall for one another and must hide their 'affair' from the murderous Saul, so they may escape to a better life. However, once Saul is out of the picture, Perchik finds himself mistakenly tapped as the 'new' Mr. Everard, and is presented with a financial situation of which he had been previously unaware. Vanessa, who is determined to leave and start anew, confronts Perchik, who takes on the same abusive attributes that defined Saul, dismissing her as 'stupid'. Initially, this seems to be a full circle moment, with Vanessa remaining trapped in a life she has never wanted; however, she proves herself to be a formidable opponent (like Stoppard's Maddie Gotobed) and leaves Perchik and the butcher's shop in a 'blaze' of glory. For Kirkwood, this theatrical statement lines up with her "[interest] in how you fight from a position of implicit inferiority" (Jones 2009).

Kirkwood began writing *Tinderbox* after graduating from university:

In 2006 it seemed to me like everything that had felt new and young and revolutionary for a while had revealed itself to be as old and reactionary as what came before it. So it was about change seeming impossible. A series of white men running the show. But it was also about how difficult change is for those at the sharp end of it. A country is a delicate organism and some parts are more exposed than others to the arrival of foreign bodies. I wanted to be honest but generous about this. Saul is a racist, but he is also a man who has been culturally and economically displaced by forces beyond his control. Modernity. Multiculturalism. Weather. He's a crook and a murderer and – worse – very sentimental. But he is grieving, and while his grief is sometimes presented comically, I don't find it entirely sentimental…

*(Kirkwood vi)*

Given the current state of affairs in the UK, reading the play through a 2023 lens feels oddly prescient. Its take on political affairs, economics, and how people may cannibalise one another in order to survive feels more urgent, and may resonate more now than it did in 2008. Similarly, the play's allusion to a rather dire climate change situation, mirrors much of what we are laden with today.

In her *Curtain Up* review, Charlotte Loveridge wrote that *Tinderbox* was

full of black wit…a darkly playful attitude to a society in flux and is unafraid to plumb to grisly, cannibalistic depths…where social fads are exposed and overturned but mankind is shown to be still the same flawed species in thrall to ideas of empire, to possession and to love.

*(Loveridge 2008)*

With the UK having officially 'Brexited' from the European Union amid concerns such as trade and immigration, and hearing rumblings of Scotland's desire to separate from England and re-join the EU, the play's imagined future is reflected in real life today. The world of *Tinderbox* is no longer a dystopian 'notion', but plausible. Kirkwood herself has said: "writing this introduction in the months after the Brexit vote it feels like its prevailing concerns are alive and kicking violently" (Kirkwood vi).

### Farce and the American Government

In contrast to the British, who have made an art form out of skewering their government, Americans are not as quick to take on political office in their theatrical works. Apart from the 1931 Pulitzer Prize-winning musical *Of Thee I Sing* – which is more satire than farce – political farces about the government are rare. Given the number of political scandals in the USA – with politicians lying about their credentials, embroiled in child trafficking rings, appropriating campaign funds, or meddling in elections, one would think American politics offers much to the genre. Yet those are not the stories being told. Donald Trump's four years in the White House produced, on a daily basis, response after response that bordered on farce. When the government itself is a farce, why do we need to see one? In addition, when you have well-written television programmes like *The West Wing*, *Madame Secretary*, and *House of Cards*, speaking to the present moment with alarm and alacrity, while also providing intrigue, thrills, and inspiration, crafting a farce may not be the genre American writers wish to enter.

Having said that, this section considers two plays offering unique perspectives on different levels of government. The extremes of farce vary, but they both examine the intersection of leadership, governance, and public appearance. In Tracy Lett's 2018 play *The Minutes*, a municipal meeting goes from innocuous and absurdly funny to sinister and downright scary. By contrast, Selina Fillinger's *POTUS: Or, Behind Every Great Dumbass Are Seven Women Trying to Keep Him Alive*, involves an all-female cast of characters demonstrating where the real intelligence lies behind the Commander-In-Chief.

### Tracy Letts: The Minutes (2017)

Tracy Letts, well known for his award-winning *August: Osage County*, and 'pulp' crime plays *Bug* and *Killer Joe*, explores the state of the nation through the lens of a municipal city council. Premiering in November 2018 at Chicago's Steppenwolf Theatre and then on Broadway in 2022, Letts describes his impetus for writing *The Minutes* not as "a condemnation of President Trump, or any particular politician. Rather, it's an examination of how we make myths about ourselves as a society and how that informs how we treat one another" (McKinley 2020). Speaking to *Newsweek*, Letts said that the play did "[grow] out of his observations of the 2016 presidential election: 'I wrote this play in the summer of 2016. During the Hillary Clinton–Donald Trump presidential campaign, I was just thinking about the way we conduct our politics in this country and the moment we were politically'" (Westerfield 2022).

*The Minutes* takes place in the small Midwestern town of Big Cherry in the present day. Set during a weekly city council meeting, and playing out in real time (minus one flashback), the 11 elected members who comprise the council are a group of devoted officials who, on the surface, want what's best for their town. The play begins with the council members discussing "the quotidian minutiae of small town life: stolen bicycles, parking spaces, a proposed redesign of a fountain in the town center" (Caggiano 2022). There is something sinister that pervades the proceedings. Soon, "[p]etty rivalries surface and simmer. We get repeated hints of some intrigue concerning an absent council member and the missing minutes from the previous meeting" (Caggiano 2022). Newcomer (and paediatric dentist) Mr. Peel had to miss the previous week's meeting because of the death of his mother. As he attempts to find his place within the group, his natural curiosity invites him to ask about the whereabouts of Mr. Carp (he of the empty chair) and the missing 'minutes' from the previous week. Initially, both queries are dismissed handily, but as he pressures them for an answer, it is clear that something ominous has happened. No one wants to chat about either.

Like Tom Stoppard's *Dirty Linen*, Letts has assigned his characters Dickensian names such as 'Assalone', 'Oldfield', 'Peel', 'Carp', and Mayor 'Superba' (whom Letts apparently named after the KitchenAid refrigerator), indicating personality traits that may or may not be readily apparent (at least to the characters themselves). This lends an air of fiction to the proceedings, as if we have stumbled upon a make-believe town. One marvels at how these people Letts has 'lovingly', yet broadly drawn, reel the audience in with their obsessions about the town. He "strings us along with a group of sanctimonious people who might as easily be delivering farce" (Cohen 2022).

Letts has given us a dark political farce wrapped up in an *Our Town*-type setting. In the words of actress Blair Brown, who played the self-involved 'Ms. Innes' on Broadway, the play is "an investigation of what ordinary people will do to maintain the status quo" (Broadway World 2022). This speaks to the pride and passion that drives the members of the council, and the lengths they will go to in order to protect their town and maintain a self-mythologising narrative concerning its history.

With council members seated for long stretches at a time, voting sporadically on minor issues, one might be hard-pressed to term *The Minutes* as a farce. But we can argue that the farce lies in the inertia of the government. The petty preoccupations that consume these characters typify, even at the municipal level, why nothing ever really gets done in government. The inability to listen coupled with an innate desire to be right is embedded in politics at any level. The play "…examines the secrets at the heart of regional and national identity…" (Fahy 7).

Predominantly a verbal farce of the mundane, *The Minutes* often leaves us shaking our heads. Like the "nonsensical proposal of Mr. Blake…the council's sole African-American, for the town to create a 'Lincoln Smackdown' in which a mixed-martial artist dressed as Honest Abe would take on all comers in a steel cage match" or when

> in the middle of the meeting, the members, except for the newcomer Mr. Peel, spontaneously perform an elaborate reenactment of the 1872 'Battle at Mackie Creek,' the victory over bloodthirsty Indians that has defined the town ever since. But, as we eventually learn, that local history, as well as the town's name, is built on a web of lies.
>
> *(Scheck 2022)*

Within the confines of this council room, "the town's complicity in lying about its origins reflects the country's ongoing desire to erase historical truths about white occupation and exploitation. It reflects a failure on the part of America to take responsibility for the past" (Fahy 8).

The play may not be traditional knockabout farce, but the mechanics of how 'political business' is conducted invites us to view the proceedings as farce. Looming dread is shrouded in comedy. Amidst ridiculous conversations, serious consequences await these characters. In one particular exchange, Mr. Peel questions why the council is voting to approve the minutes from two weeks ago, and why the minutes from the previous week are missing. Letts captures mundanity in an almost vaudeville-esque tone, with a slight underscoring of menace:

*Peel:* Right, I just thought we got the minutes from the last meeting at the next meeting. Meaning I would have thought the minutes from the October 18th meeting would have been distributed at the October 25th meeting and that the minutes for the October 25th meeting would be distributed tonight.
*Superba:* I understand your question, Mr. Peel. It would appear that the minutes for the meeting in question have not been prepared for distribution and so we'll have to wait until the next meeting to review those minutes.
*Peel:* I understand…But before we continue. I'm curious, the minutes missing in this way, is that uncommon?
*Superba:* The minutes are not missing, Mr. Peel, they are simply delayed.
*Peel:* Right. And is that uncommon?
*Superba:* I couldn't speak to how common that is.

*(Letts 26–27)*

While laughing, one feels the play building towards something distinctly unfunny, and in the end the audience is hit with a gut punch – a chilling cult-like blood ritual. One leaves the theatre feeling complicit in the cover-up and indoctrinated by what we have witnessed.

We recognise parallels to our own world. Letts does not need to identify political parties, or reference what goes on in Washington DC. Instead, Big Cherry becomes a farcical and horrific microcosm of the country.

*The Minutes* is "both a political comedy and a wicked, methodically plotted horror show, not unlike American democracy and its original sins. The play's razor-sharp edge is all the more cutting for being polished with easy wit, like tickling a captive before releasing the guillotine" (Kumar 2022).

### *Selina Fillinger:* POTUS *(2022)*

In April of 2022, playwright Selina Fillinger's farce, *POTUS: Or, Behind Every Great Dumbass Are Seven Women Trying to Keep Him Alive* opened on Broadway. As previously noted, it is rare these days to have a 'self-proclaimed' farce open on the Great White Way, let alone one that did not have an out-of-town tryout or open off-Broadway prior to its premiere.

Even rarer, and unique to Fillinger's play, it is composed of an all-female cast of characters.

Set in the White House in the present day, the play follows seven women as they navigate the fallout after the President offhandedly uses a certain 'c-word' expletive during a press conference in reference to his wife. The word, which is also the play's first line of dialogue, is repeated six times in the first three pages, indicating that we are in for a 'no-holds-barred' evening, and that Fillinger will not allow her characters to stand politely on ceremony. The seven women who populate *POTUS* are confident, ballsy, and crude. They are all connected to the White House through either their jobs or their personal relationship to the President. Spearheading the 'spin' effort is Harriet, the President's Chief of Staff (a position no woman has held in real-world American politics), who is assisted to varying degrees by Jean (his press secretary), Margaret (the FLOTUS), and Stephanie (his secretary). Complicating matters is Bernadette (his ex-con, lesbian sister) looking for a pardon, Chris (a journalist) looking for a story, and Dusty (a fling) flown in by the President to discuss her pregnancy. To top matters off, the President is scheduled to speak at an event on women's rights. This is assuming he is not dead after accidentally being hit in the head by a hurled vase. To protect the unnamed and never seen Commander-in-Chief, these seven women must come together to prevent a national scandal.

Fillinger wisely keeps the focus off the President. Although an unseen presence, he remains a cipher; a compendium of past Presidents. Although Donald Trump's name is never invoked, like Tracy Letts, Fillinger's inspiration for the play is rooted in the 2016 election cycle. Fillinger was

> really fascinated by all the women around [Trump's] campaigns…They were in this loop of headlines about powerful men abusing their power. And I was really fascinated by the women in their orbit, who keep these guys going day after day.
>
> *(Tauer 2022)*

The play could easily have been centred on a buffoon-like but dangerous President, as David Mamet does in his 2008 political farce, *November*. Instead, Fillinger uses this timely moment in political history to craft 'a farce about women's relationship to male power — how they access it, what they are allowed to do with it, and who else they subjugate along the way'. 'I love farces, but they typically rely on sexist and racist tropes,' Fillinger said. So she wrote a comedy about women struggling to adhere to the rules of the patriarchy, which "literally causes a farce on a day-to-day basis" (Hess 2022).

On Friday June 24th 2022, two months after *POTUS* opened, the US Supreme Court overturned *Roe* vs. *Wade*, ending federal abortion rights in the United States. At the performance that night, a singular moment saw the real world clash with the farce world. Pregnant Dusty (played by actress Julianne Hough) proudly announces she is a "volunteer at a clinic back in Iowa. Affordable, safe reproductive health care is a basic human right" (Fillinger 43). This line transformed from an unexpected character reveal to a heartbreaking and defiant rallying cry, lifting audience members to their feet in mid-show. We highlight this to recognize the irony in a bawdy, profane farce featuring empowered and unapologetic women navigating the patriarchy, being juxtaposed with the stripping of a woman's right to autonomy over their body.

In the end, the women successfully keep the President out of personal and political trouble. At what cost though? Harriet finds out from Dusty she is being fired because "people were saying that [she's] the real brains in the White House" (Fillinger 82). Dusty discovers the President has been sleeping with an analyst, long before she was in the picture. Clearly, FLOTUS, as well as the remaining women on staff, will continue to be disrespected. The play is an indictment of entitled and privileged men in positions of power. However, Fillinger is not about to let her ending become defeatist. Underpinning this are Fillinger's,

> …own politics and ideas around what is hopeful and what is not. When I see ungrounded hope that doesn't uplift me, that's a person who is out of touch. But if I see people who are fully aware of the work ahead, of the collective power that has yet to be harnessed…you don't need hope because you have resilience. You don't need hope because you have endurance. And there is something so energising about that to me.
>
> *(Fillinger 2021)*

This is alluded to at the end of the play, with Chris imploring Harriet to go on the record and liberate the proverbial skeletons from the White House closet. While the President smiles through clenched teeth before the Female Model Leadership Council, his sister Bernadette observes:

*Bernadette:* He's white knuckling that podium but the fucker's still smiling.
*Harriet:* 'Course he is. He doesn't know.
*Chris:* Know what?
*Harriet:* …There's a cunty dawn coming.

*(Fillinger 87)*

The last lines of the play are a hark back and a warning. In this final moment, farce has the power to unite members of an audience through collective laughter. Citing the absurdity of power structures' inability to change, Fillinger believes this laughter becomes:

…a shared understanding that we are in a room of people who also think that this is absurd, and that's incredibly threatening to the powers that be; that want us to accept our reality as normal and natural. And so, when we're laughing at something together, you are essentially [building a] little army. I hear this person laugh. [And] I hear this person laugh. I'm laughing, and I'm realizing that we have aligned values. And we were strangers standing apart. But right now, I know that we could stand together and we could be a political mass and a political movement.

*(Fillinger 2021)*

### Farce and the Radical

One does not automatically associate 'radical' with farce, yet the seeds can be found in the 'leftist activism' in the work of Dario Fo. In *Accidental Death of an Anarchist*, Fo's use of satire and farce is clearly intended to call out law enforcement for its abuse of power.

Contemporary playwrights have employed the genre to engage audiences in discourse about extremist behaviour. The 21st century is fraught with acts of extreme violence in the name of political ideology. From the horrors of 9/11 to domestic terrorism, cities globally have fallen victim to radicalised political groups, or individuals. Similarly, these acts impact how we view and treat our fellow citizens. Distrust, even paranoia, often colour our interactions.

More recently, the insurrection of January 6th, 2021 in Washington DC, saw Trump supporters storm the halls of the Capitol Building in an effort to stop Congress from certifying the 2020 presidential election. It re-introduced the word 'coup' to the American lexicon, a word not applied to the USA for almost 90 years.

The next section introduces two late 20th-century political farces, George Tabori's *Mein Kampf: A Farce* and Mustapha Matura's *The Coup*, which lay the groundwork for a focus on Martin McDonagh's contemporary political farce *The Lieutenant of Inishmore* (2006).

### *George Tabori:* Mein Kampf: Farce *(1987)*

Hungarian-born, Berlin-raised, Jewish playwright George Tabori took the name of one of the most infamous books written by a would-be politician and used it to explore the relationship between victim and victimizer. Written in 1987, *Mein Kampf: Farce* is one of the playwright's most popular and most produced plays. Originally based on a short story built on a piece of historical fact, Tabori slyly sets two opposing forces against one another: the young German, Adolf Hitler, and the slightly older Jew, Shlomo Herzl.

The play takes place in a dilapidated rooming house where Herzl makes a living selling copies of the Bible and the 18th-century erotic novel, *Fanny Hill*. Hitler has come to Vienna to try and enter art college, which he is ultimately denied. Herzl is trying to survive, doing what is necessary to make a living. Drawing on a recurring theme in his work, Tabori asks us to see what happens when "victim and victimizer become inseparable partners in an unholy symbiosis, making them engender and need each other" (Carl Weber 40)

Herzl takes the unapologetically antisemitic Hitler under his wing, helps him sell his paintings, and encourages him to pursue a career in politics, yet never stoops to Hitler's schoolboy level of hate with his own. In an oddly hilarious and chilling sequence, we watch Herzl prepare Hitler for his college interview, grooming a 'hippie' Hitler into the image we know of him today. Tabori turns the transformation into a clever piece of comic business, where Herzl:

> *[Stage Directions]:* ...combs up Hitler's moustache, it drops, he clips one end, then the other, they won't stay even, lopsiding the face, until Herzl gets the bush down to a respectable toothbrush nestling in the nose. Then he brushes Hitler's hair, it won't stay up, a lock keeps falling onto his forehead. Herzl rubs a bit of schmaltz into it, finds the parting.
> 
> *(Tabori 55)*

We learn that Herzl is trying to write a memoir, but that he has not got past the first sentence. More concerned about the title, Herzl was originally going to call it "My Life", but it's dismissed by his other roommate Lobkowitz (who also believes he is 'God'). After going through a series of other titles including: 'My Memoirs', 'Shlomo in Wonderland', 'Waiting for Shlomo', and 'The Merry Shlomos of Windsor', he offers up "Mein Kampf", or "My Struggle". The title is ultimately purloined by Hitler, as Tabori is essentially saying the future Fuhrer had no original ideas.

Tabori's characters engage in slapstick, physical comedy, and vaudeville-like banter, with "wit and wordplay foreshadow[ing] the actual Hitler and the Holocaust without directly addressing it" (Meirich 57). Laughter is employed to augment the dramatic irony of the situation, and "the humor in the play is created by either the absurdities of the situation, or by the macabre allusions to history" (ibid.). Despite knowing who and what Hitler will become, all we are allowed to witness is a brat; a self-indulgent, ignorant man-child who can barely take care of himself.

Herzl inadvertently opens the door to the rise of Nazism. In the play, Tabori has the figure of Death appear. She has arrived to take "Herr Hotler, or Hutler – no Hitler" (Tabori 73) as his name appears on her list. Seeking to protect his 'friend' who has now given him purpose in life, Herzl insists Frau Death must have the wrong Hitler and asks if she can come back later. Frau Death responds: "I'm not interested in your friend as a corpse. As a corpse, as a victim, he is absolutely mediocre. But as a criminal, as a mass murderer, as an exterminating angel, a natural talent" (Tabori 77).

Additionally, the comedy is not afraid to go to low-brow lengths with cartoonish violence, a Keystone Cop-like chase, and even Schlomo's chicken, Mitzi, taking a 'big shit' in Hitler's hand. A short Act Five sees Schlomo's chicken (portrayed by an actor) cooked in a pot, a clear allusion to Jews dying in concentration camps.

Herzl's subconscious tells him that he has unleashed a monster by not giving him up to Death. In his efforts to survive, Herzl has enabled Hitler and this will lead to travesty. Lobkowitz appears to Herzl at the end of the play and says "Grief ain't enough, Boobele. In the heart of each joke hides a little holocaust" (Tabori 83). In the dream, Frau Death has not come to take Hitler to the afterlife. Instead, she says this is "the beginning of a wonderful friendship." Hitler responds: "I will not disappoint you" (Tabori 82).

Tabori pursues a line of writing asking us to consider how our personal beliefs – political, religious, sociological – bind us. There is, of course, tension in the title *Mein Kampf: Farce* itself. He makes sure to include 'Farce' in the title as a means of taking back power and to demonstrate the fine line between comedy and tragedy. This is tragic farce. Even though no characters are killed, we know where this story is heading and we can't stop it. The farce of watching this ridiculous man, whom we know as one of the most ruthless figures in history, is shocking, especially as Tabori portrays him – both inept and scary. For Tabori, "Associating the genesis of Hitler's infamous autobiography and political manifesto with a Jewish figure and implying that a Jew was partly responsible for Hitler's career are examples of the outrageous premises with which Tabori seeks to shock" (Crowe 68). Prior to Tabori, only a few had used comedy to take on Hitler and the Third Reich, including Charlie Chaplin (*The Great Dictator*, 1940) and Mel Brooks (*The Producers*, 1968). More recently, Taika Waititi attempted the same in *Jojo Rabbit* (2019). However, aside from Brecht's *The Resistible Rise of Arturo Ui* (1941), "German-language theatrical representations of this period had hitherto been dominated by [a] kind of solemnity..." (ibid.). For this reason, "*Mein Kampf* cemented Tabori's reputation in the German speaking world as a taboo-breaker" (ibid.).

For many, the Holocaust remains 'off-limits' in terms of comedic subject matter. Tabori, whose own family perished in Nazi concentration camps, consciously uses this taboo subject to get our attention through laughter, not to glorify Hitler or provide any kind of psychological understanding of the man. Tabori wants us "to recognise that the Holocaust and events surrounding it 'are taboos that must be broken or they will continue to choke us'" (My 2013).

By weaving this story as a farce, Tabori sounds a warning. The warning here is not to underestimate or dismiss. We have seen it in the United States with the rise of Donald Trump. Like Hitler, he was underestimated, even laughed off, and he ended up leading the country.

### *Mustapha Matura:* The Coup – A Play of Revolutionary Dreams (1991)

Premiering in 1991 at the Royal National Theatre, Mustapha Matura's play *The Coup* is about the power of foreign influence over government, and what happens when misguided uprising leads to ineffectual revolt. Matura, a Trinidadian playwright living in Britain, was known to combine humour and drama to interrogate and criticise "social and political changes that followed independence" (Peacock 189) in Trinidad.

*The Coup – A Play of Revolutionary Dreams*, was commissioned by the National Theatre a year after the unsuccessful Jamaat al Muslimeen coup against the Trinidad and Tobago government. This coup attempt, which played out for six days in July of 1990, saw insurgents take the Prime Minister of Trinidad and members of his cabinet hostage, bomb the Police Headquarters and storm television and radio studios.

Matura, at the time "Britain's leading black playwright" (Peacock 195), began writing about a fictional coup that descends quickly into farce. A group of Trinidadian rebel soldiers have overthrown the government and imprisoned their President, having taken it upon themselves to: "...liberate the people from [the President's] corrupt and oppressive regime", they 'charge' him with "being a traitor to the people of Trinidad an Tobago...of running a corrupt, decadent and oppressive government on behalf of [his own] family...opened several Swiss bank accounts where the proceeds of [his] corruption now exceed

15.2 million dollars, and on foreign trips [has] paid visits to brothels, had the use of call girls…" (Matura 13).

Unfortunately, the rebels are in over their heads, and no match for President Edward 'Eddie' Jones. From his cell, Jones ably manipulates various lieutenants and sentries who come and go. Their lack of leadership experience, along with their ineptitude and infighting, leads to soldiers accidentally shooting themselves, and, towards the end, sees two of the rebel leaders unintentionally blowing themselves up "by lighting cigars as a sign of rapprochement in front of a leaking petrol tank…killed by the substance that would provide the petrol-dollars necessary to establish a new regime!" (Peacock 196).

Interviewed for the National Theatre's world premiere production, Matura cites the power of "giving 'fatigue'…a Trinidadian weapon. To ridicule the politicians and the customs and manners of the so-called ruling class…poking them in the ribs a bit" (Matura 1991). Matura is 'giving fatigue' not only to those in power but also to those 'incompetents' with revolutionary dreams. This is a comical look at civil war; an examination of what happens when those in charge betray the people, and what the people do when they lose faith in their leaders.

It is readily apparent that Eddie is a 'pro-capitalist', a President who knows how to play the political and economic game in order to live in the lap of luxury. The rebels charge him with taking money from Americans to fuel a lifestyle of BMWs and Miami prostitutes in exchange for illegal goods.

The final irony of the play sees Eddie accidentally killed after going to extreme lengths to free himself from imprisonment. Standing by the President's coffin, a church 'Workman' speaking with his friend describes how:

*Workman:* A hear some reactionary elements, aided and abetted by South African mercenaries tried to rescue him from de people's custody an a Uzi machine pistol fall out if a sleeping sentry hand an start firing by itself an one of de bullets hit a nail on a bean over he head and on de nail was a old iron anchor an dat fall on he head.

*(Matura 67)*

Laughing at this farcical explanation might not seem appropriate, yet Matura uses the farce of the moment to point out how it's the small things that can have the biggest impact. Political blindness and ambition may lead not only to chaos, but loss of life. This is a theme to be explored further in Martin McDonagh's play *The Lieutenant of Inishmore*.

Mustapha, who passed away in 2019, "once said that his constant aim was 'to examine the effects of colonialism, political and psychological, on the colonisers and the colonised'. The Coup…has suddenly acquired a new and chilling relevance" (Billington 2020).

### Martin McDonagh: The Lieutenant of Inishmore *(2001)*

Emerging in the mid-1990s, alongside Joe Penhall, Anthony Neilson, Sarah Kane, and Mark Ravenhill, Irish-British playwright Martin McDonagh embodied the British 'In-Yer-Face' Theatre movement. With its liberal use of profanity, shocking violence, macabre humour, and taboo-breaking subject matter, McDonagh's work has regularly aimed to jolt us out of complacency. Outrageous laughter is juxtaposed with extreme visceral responses. Pedestrian conversations give way to brutal acts. McDonagh seeks "to bring sensation back into the theatre: 'I think people should leave a theatre with the same feeling you get after a really good rock concert. A play should be a thrill'" (Sierz 224).

A McDonagh play is something of a thrill ride. He "display[s] the masterly mechanics of Georges Feydeau, the richly idiosyncratic dialogue of Synge, and the gallows humor of Joe Orton" (O'Toole 2006). In addition to these theatrical influences, McDonagh's plays regularly embrace the storytelling techniques of contemporary cinema. It is no surprise that the theatre of Martin McDonagh has been compared to the films of Quentin Tarantino, specifically in terms of the way in which their respective fictional universes find a precarious balance between comedy and violence. Mundane conversations about sick cats and foot massages are tangential to acts of torture and contracted murder. It's in these mundane moments that Tarantino and McDonagh's characters are given surprising dimensions.

Terrorism. Dismemberment. Exploding cats.

In *The Lieutenant of Inishmore*, McDonagh's Orton-esque use of farce allows him to attack terrorism, and comment on our oversaturated exposure and increasing numbness to violence. Set against the backdrop of the 'Troubles' in Northern Ireland, *The Lieutenant of Inishmore* is "McDonagh's thoroughly ethical appeal against terrorism…is unequivocal: base means can never serve noble ends" (Middeke 222).

The year is 1993. The setting is the Aran Island of Inishmore, County Galway.

Davey, a local teenager on the island of Inishmore, finds a dead cat, Wee Thomas, on the side of the road. He brings it back to Donny Osbourne, which sets off a chain reaction of events leading to an end rivalling any number of Jacobean revenge tragedies. Donny accuses Davey of killing the cat by running him over with his bicycle. Davey denies the accusation. Donny, who was charged with protecting Wee Thomas while his son Padraic was away, does not want to be held responsible for the cat's death and elicits a false confession from Davey. Together, they concoct a plan whereby they gradually inform Padraic of Wee Thomas' declining health, before eventually breaking the bad news that he has passed away. Unfortunately for both, things do not go according to plan.

Padraic Osbourne, an INLA terrorist, and the play's 'Lieutenant of Inishmore', is in the middle of torturing a drug dealer when Donny calls, informing him about Wee Thomas. Devastated, Padraic informs his Dad that he will be leaving immediately for Inishmore. Donny recognizes that this does not bode well for either himself or Davey. Padraic, who was turned down for membership of the IRA because of his extreme emotional instability, and who plans on splintering off from the INLA (itself a splinter group) and starting his own 'splinter splinter' organisation, will be merciless in avenging the irresponsibility that has led to the death of his best friend, Wee Thomas.

What none of them know is that Wee Thomas was actually killed by three members of the INLA who seek to draw Padraic out into the open, and assassinate him. Padraic's decision to form his own splinter organisation presents potential conflicts for the INLA, and his obsessive torturing of drug dealers is causing the terrorist group to lose money.

Meanwhile, in anticipation of Padraic's arrival, Donny and Davey find another cat, paint it with black shoe polish and hope to pass it off as Wee Thomas. Soon after, McDonagh's black farce shifts into high gear with Padraic, Donny, Davey, the three INLA members, Davey's younger sister Mairead (an expert sharpshooter, and Padraic's brief love interest), all converging on the Osbourne cottage. What plays out next is an amalgamation of genres – with homage to crime drama, westerns, and horror. All of this is wrapped in farce: obsession, lies, misunderstandings, and a complete lack of self-awareness. By the end, we are left with a body count of four men, two cats, and a gasp-inducing reversal that is both dark joke and shattering change in audience perspective.

Speaking to Guardian writer Sean O'Hagan in 2001 about his impetus to write the play, McDonagh describes

> having grown up Catholic and, to a certain degree, Republican, I thought I should tackle the problems on my own side, so to speak. I chose the INLA because they seemed so extreme and, to be honest, because I thought I'd be less at risk. I'm not being heroic or anything – it was just something I felt I had to write about. The play came from a position of what you might call pacifist rage. I mean, it's a violent play that is wholeheartedly anti-violence. The bottom line, I suppose, is that I believe that if a piece of work is well written, you can tackle anything.
>
> *(O'Hagan 2001)*

Famously, the play had a storied journey to production. Even though McDonagh's previous plays had garnered critical and commercial acclaim, this black farce did not immediately find traction with major theatres of the day. Whether it had to do with the play's politics or its graphic violence, theatres were not prepared to programme it. In McDonagh's words, Trevor Nunn (Artistic Director of the Royal National Theatre at the time) "thought the play was so inflammatory that its production might threaten the Northern Irish Peace process..." (ibid.). McDonagh was asked by O'Hagan about his decision to court controversy and write a farce about the IRA, and...

> Did it ever cross his mind that there were certain places that you just cannot go with comedy? [McDonagh pauses] "No, never. I probably should, but it's those very places that intrigue me. I kind of felt that this stuff had to be dealt with in the blackly sick way in which we sometimes react to it. I think a lot of the stuff that has happened in the past 25 years has been a sick joke. I'm not trying to solve anything, the same way as I am not trying to damage anything; just looking at it in a different way. I mean, how else can you react to all that has happened through writing, or art or whatever you want to call it, if not through absurdity?"
>
> *(ibid.)*

McDonagh, who had originally written the play back in 1994 "before the peace process gained momentum in Northern Ireland[,]...presents a savage critique of Irish-nationalist terrorism [that] was intended to provoke" (O'Toole 2006). O'Toole goes on to observe that because of the play's "graphic depiction of torture, murder, and dismemberment, even within the framework of a madcap farce, [it] was deemed both offensive and politically insensitive" (ibid.). One can argue, however, that it is *because* of the farce framework we are able to connect with the story.

Like Tabori's *Mein Kampf*, farce allows McDonagh to interrogate taboo material without becoming didactic. Eamonn Jordan writes that McDonagh's "commitment is to take the subversive potential of farce to the politics of violence so that certain contradictions and anomalies are exposed, without regard to the pieties of Republican thinking, an approach that some find to be disrespectful" (Jordan 374). It is in these contradictions that McDonagh's work finds a kinship with Joe Orton. McDonagh himself acknowledges that his play is "much more in the Joe Orton tradition than in any tradition of Irish drama" (369). Highlighting aspects of the play that border on the same kind of artificiality one sees in Orton's work, Jordan goes on to note that *The Lieutenant of Inishmore* displays elements of "...a metatheatrical farce...pushing violence in one specific direction, but also calling attention to its theatricality, blatancy, and constructedness...it is a world that goes into free fall, when a cat is thought dead" (Jordan 383–384). And like the incestuous family reunion in Orton's *What the Butler Saw*, *The Lieutenant of Inishmore*'s 'happy ending' can only be left in quotes. On the one hand, the terrorists have been neutralised and a certain furry companion unexpectedly reappears. On the other hand, a heart has been broken, a father has lost his son, and four bodies are dismembered onstage. McDonagh, like Orton and Enda Walsh, offers the audience a superficial conclusion; in reality, "…there is no return to order, what is left is chaos" (Jordan 383).

When the play premiered in 2001 at the Royal Shakespeare Company, it was coming on the heels of the 1998 'Good Friday Agreement' or 'Belfast Agreement', that had all but ended 'The Troubles.' Still, some felt it was too early to be 'laughing' at the violence associated with political conflict in Northern Ireland.

Ironically, the play's transfer to the West End in early 2002 provided audiences an outlet for processing the events of 9/11. "The play's treatment of terrorism seemed to resonate with people who were struggling to come to terms with Britain's role in the emerging 'War against Terrorism'" (Lonergan lii). Suddenly, this black farce, which only a few months prior was an Irish-centric story, exploded with global popularity, being translated into almost 30 languages by 2003. Theatre artists saw the play not only as an explicit commentary on the 'War on Terrorism', but also as an exploration of questions of morality, political responsibility, and society's relationship to violence. By the time the production had reached Broadway in 2006, "McDonagh's play about terrorism was seen as a sign that New York was at last starting to come to terms with the trauma its citizens had experienced just over four years previously" (Lonergan lvi).

In 2018, British director Michael Grandage mounted the first major West End revival of *The Lieutenant of Inishmore*, featuring an all-Irish cast. McDonagh's play now has some distance between both the conflict in Northern Ireland and 9/11. Yet, the play remains resonant because acts of terrorism – both international and domestic – remain present in the news.

In his 2006 review of the play, Ben Brantley called the play "brazenly and unapologetically a farce. But it is also a severely moral play, translating into dizzy absurdism the self-perpetuating spirals of political violence that now occur throughout the world. I kept thinking of Macbeth's forlorn recognition that 'blood will have blood'" (Brantley 2006). Reviewing the 2018 revival, *Time Out*'s Andrzej Lukowski

> …Not that *The Lieutenant of Inishmore* lacks purpose – it also functions as an absolutely brutal satire on the absurdity of sectarian conflict. The reasons why the characters clash are unutterably stupid. When Chris Walley's brilliantly hapless Davey asks at the end whether it was all pointless or not, it is very apparent that it definitely was – and there is a sort of bleak poetry in the total futility of the play's events. Whether you want to call the cat a metaphor for religion, the peace process, or just a cat, McDonagh's subversive intent is pretty undeniable – it's his gift to show relatively normal people tottering blithely into the abyss.
>
> *(Lukowski 2018)*

It is testimony to McDonagh's skill that his play continues to entertain as well as speak to contemporary audiences. Michael Grandage observes that "many great writers can make you laugh and cry in a single sentence but McDonagh's ability to make you laugh and gasp in a single sentence is particularly brilliant" (Grandage 2020).

Grandage, who also directed McDonagh's *The Cripple of Inishmaan*, is drawn to McDonagh's

> …subversiveness. It's wonderful to watch how he makes an audience laugh at things they would normally regard as off limits - and in doing so, he catches them out. Also, his characters are more empathetic than people think and I love the way he lets his audience discover that.
>
> *(ibid.)*

For this reason, one has to temper the tonal balances in the staging of McDonagh's work, so that the characters' humanity may emerge alongside the technical demands of the farce. At a certain point in the process, the technical and the instinctual must merge. Grandage observes that:

> …farce is very difficult to rehearse because it's mainly a technical genre. Instinct comes later when you have all the beats in place and an audience may want to steer you in another direction. But to get it perfect, it has to be mapped out beat by beat and in McDonagh's case, he has already gone through every beat (and every variation of a beat) in his head. So the road map that is the script in the case of something like Inishmore is open to little interpretation in the more extreme farcical sections. In other words, there is usually only one way to get it right. If you shoot the cat on a different beat to the one in the script, it won't work. He is a precise writer with a total understanding of the structure of farce. All departments have to respond to that precision – you can't design an interior that doesn't reflect the detailed things that have to happen in that space. It could feel constraining for some interpretive artists but the rewards are so great when it works that there is usually a consensus that it is worth the effort…His work isn't easy to stage. He breaks all the laws of playwriting with haircuts, live animals, bleeding body parts, extreme violence in full view, etc, etc, but it all comes from an uncensored imagination and so it's worth finding ways to solve any technical challenges. McDonagh's laughter is universal. Unlike his contemporaries, or even those Irish writers who came before him, McDonagh's portraits of Ireland are uniquely his, filtered through a funhouse of mirrors.
>
> *(Grandage 2020)*

Because of this, he:

...provides audiences globally with a play that sets out to challenge them – to force them to reconsider their responses to violence, that demands that they examine how terrorism has entered their lives, and that asks them to consider why they find themselves laughing so hard at events that are so utterly horrific and tragic...[the play is] a powerful corrective to the beautification of violence in contemporary culture, and a hilarious farce.

*(Lonergan lvii)*

—

### Two Modern and a Few More Contemporary Political Farces

Australia's David Williamson and Britain's Alan Ayckbourn each take on smaller levels of political bureaucracy with their respective modern political farces *The Department* (1975) and *Ten Times Table* (1977).

Set during a college departmental faculty meeting, the "all-important central character of *The Department* is the meeting itself. All the subsidiary characters, with two exceptions, are trapped, controlled and defeated by the meeting just as they are trapped, controlled and defeated by their professional lives" (Williamson viii). Like Letts' *The Minutes*, the farce of *The Department* does not overtly manifest comically in the actions of the physical body. Instead, the farce at hand is witnessing the characters' futile attempt to rally against the administrative and bureaucratic hurdles that threaten their engineering department, preventing them from doing what they love to do: teach.

In contrast, over the course of seven months, *Ten Times Table* follows an assembled committee of local Pendon citizens who have come together to plan and execute a town pageant based on the little-known historical events surrounding the community's 'Massacre of the Pendon 12'. As political ideologies clash over what the event should represent, the committee devolves into chaos with everything coming to a farcical head at the historical recreation of the 'massacre' on Festival Day. "The play then works on two levels. As a study in political polarisation. Think [Brexit] Remain versus Leave" (O'Brien 2020). Based on his own observations and fascination with meeting procedures and protocols, Ayckbourn's play dissects the personality of the 'committee member' and the minutiae that keeps committees from getting anything done.

British playwright Steve Thompson's contemporary satirical farce *Whipping It Up* (2006) could be viewed as a companion piece to Alistair Beaton's *Feelgood*. With a recently elected Conservative Party holding a very slim majority in Parliament, Thompson offers audiences a peek behind the closed doors of the office of the Conservative 'Whips.' With a bill on the line that will see Gypsies and Boy Scouts taxed, the Chief, Deputy, and Junior Whips wheel, deal, bully and bribe a small group of holdouts in order to ensure the bill goes through. Set the week before Christmas, the Conservative whips face off against their equally formidable Labour counterparts, while manoeuvring around a manipulative research journalist keen on exposing the political scandals emanating from the Whips' office. Rioting Boy Scouts, a possible coup, a bit of blackmail, tests of loyalty, and a safe full of secrets, are all part of a day's work for the whips of Westminster.

Richard Bean's 2008 play *In the Club*, subtitled 'A Political Sex Farce', moves away from the hypocritical halls of Westminster, landing the audience in a posh hotel in Strasbourg, France. Philip Wardrobe, a Minister of the European Parliament, is trying, unsuccessfully, to balance his personal and professional lives. He awaits the imminent arrival of his ovulating partner, Nicole, for an afternoon 'romp', while simultaneously attempting to secure his position as the next President of the European Parliament. Wardrobe must also ward off the amorous advances of Beatrice Renard, the French Chair of the Women's Committee, mollify an angry Turkish Ambassador, accommodate his stern German Socialist Whip, and placate a gruff Yorkshire pig farmer. A possible spy hiding in the closet notwithstanding, all of the aforementioned keep upending his political and romantic aspirations.

Like James Graham's *The Culture*, Richard Bean's historical political farce *The Hypocrite* (2017) was commissioned and co-presented by Hull Truck Theatre and the Royal Shakespeare Company, during Hull's 2017 UK City of Culture Festival. Drawing on Hull history, Bean presents us with Sir John Hotham, the 17$^{th}$-century Governor of Hull, who finds himself caught between his duty to Parliament, and his loyalty to King Charles I. Tasked by Parliament to protect their massive arsenal and deny Charles and his 'Royalists' entry into Hull, Sir John must decide where his allegiances lie, make a decision that could lead to Civil War, or most assuredly cost him his head. Hotham's own domestic situation is also in upheaval, further complicating matters, and resulting in the worst day of Hotham's life.

Christopher Durang's *Why Torture is Wrong, and the People Who Love Them* (2009), is a 9/11 play, although not one directly about 9/11. With a title ripped from an episode of tabloid television, it "reads like a warped combination between a morality pamphlet and a self-help guide" (Chirico 169). Durang's dark, at times absurdist, farce paints a picture of a neurotic, paranoid, and discombobulated America in the wake of the terrorist attacks.

As the play opens, Durang presents the audience with a moment right out of a psychological thriller. Felicity wakes up in a strange motel room, wearing a slip, with a strange man (Zamir) in her bed. As she probes him for answers, Zamir – who appears to be Middle Eastern and possessed of a violent temper – explains how they had met at a Hooters restaurant, got drunk, and been married (while she was unconscious) by a minister (Reverend Mike), who also happens to direct porno movies. Pressured by Zamir, Felicity introduces him to her parents, Luella and Leonard, her right-wing father who secretly belongs to a homegrown militia. Leonard calls upon his network of spies ('Hildegarde' and 'Looney Tunes') to 'investigate' Zamir. While spying on Zamir at a local restaurant, Hildegarde overhears Reverend Mike pitching him the 'orgy scenario' for his next porno film and mistakes it for a terrorist plot:

> *Reverend Mike:* Look, next Tuesday, we're doin' it – The Big Bang, that's what we're callin' it. And they're goin' be doing it all over, man – in New York, in D.C., in San Francisco. And you can be part of it. Shoot it out, man. I mean, explosions, man, all over the place. It's gonna be awesome. Dirty, dirty. The Big Bang.
> *Zamir:* Can I wear a mask?
>
> *(Durang 38)*

Hildegarde's 'intel' results in Zamir being captured and held hostage by Leonard, who proceeds to interrogate him about 'The Big Bang.' Zamir's multiple attempts to explain away the misunderstanding further enrage Leonard who tortures him, resulting in Zamir's loss of three fingers and an ear.

With his trademark comic subversiveness, Durang uses

> madcap farce to illustrate the insecurity and fear caused by the perpetual threat of domestic terrorism…The play exposes fallacious rhetoric, false assumptions, and other misrepresentations, such as the irony behind the Department of Homeland Security making us feel *less* secure.
>
> *(Chirico 175)*

Farce allows Durang to underline how 'abnormal' things felt in America post-9/11.

Chicago-bred playwright and actor Matthew-Lee Erlbach's 2017 play *The Doppelganger (an international farce)* combines elements of Plautus and Feydeau, with clever allusions to the movies *Dave* and *Weekend at Bernie's*. The play is set in Bangui, the capital city of the Central African Republic, at the colonial mansion of British businessman Thomas Irdley and his wife, Theresa. Thomas is preparing for the arrival of a group of international 'investors', each hoping to negotiate a deal with Thomas for his valuable copper mine. Parallel events occur: Thomas' doppelganger, Jimmy Peterson (a kindergarten teacher and volunteer for Habitat for Humanity whom he met in America), arrives unexpectedly. Also, Thomas has accidentally taken a zebra tranquiliser instead of his blood pressure medication, leaving him (possibly) dead.

Caught in the middle of it all is Rosie, the Irdleys' put-upon maid, the one person who keeps the household on track. Rosie, who has her own humanitarian agenda, sees this as an opportunity to "secure decent wages and conditions for the vast, long-exploited labor force of her country – the copper miners and others who remain impoverished as others reap huge profits" (Weiss 2018). With an American General, a British envoy, an Asian-American technocrat, a bisexual Saudi prince, and the ousted dictator of the CAR (among others), descending on the Irdley mansion, Rosie convinces Jimmy to assume Thomas' identity, enlisting him as an ally to help forward her agenda with the international entourage.

As the action plays out, Rosie must do everything in her power to ensure no one discovers the truth about Thomas (which requires a lot of hiding, haranguing, and body hauling). Jimmy attempts to negotiate with Thomas's guests on Rosie's behalf and ends up doing more harm than good, resulting in a comically bloody end, not far removed from the work of McDonagh.

Expertly weaving classic farce tropes, including misunderstandings and miscommunication, lies and cover-ups, tightly choreographed physical comedy, and eleven doors, the play also seethes with an activist's desire for change.

For Erlbach, farce is a way to engage audiences in this subject matter:

> [If] you're giving me two hours of your time, more or less, I want to have a conversation with you. And I can't have you leave the theatre without taking you through [the issues] because what we're talking about is so dire. And, I had to do it through this vehicle because that was the best way I was going to get your attention. So I want to make it really clear that the vehicle of farce was in order to exploit the natural absurdity and eccentricities of this topic and also engage the audience in a conversation about it afterwards.
> 
> *(Erlbach 2022)*

Finally, in an act of storytelling expertise that would make Alan Ayckbourn proud, Canadian playwright Kat Sandler created two, intertwining political farces, *The Party* and *The Candidate*, which were originally designed to be performed simultaneously in adjacent theatre spaces by the same cast. On the surface, Sandler's work shares technical similarities with Ayckbourn's domestic farce *House & Garden*. What differentiates the two is the additional challenge she sets out for the actors (and production team). The two plays are set nine months apart, requiring the actors to traverse not only performance spaces, but also time. One could take in either *The Party* or *The Candidate* and enjoy a solidly constructed, incisive evening of political farce. Taking in both, and remembering they are being presented simultaneously, highlights a different type of performance virtuosity. Beyond the need to keep two storylines straight and maintain the changing nature of character relationships from moment to moment, there is the added pressure of simply making entrances and exits on time, so that the story can move forward in each space.

*The Party* takes place at a birthday party for media baron Butch Buchanan, brother of Woodruff Buchanan, the country's current 'Chief Leader.' The party also doubles as a political fundraiser which sees two prospective 'Left Party' candidates schmoozing with audience members and vying for Butch's endorsement. These two candidates, Heather Straughan (a Hilary Clinton-like character, complete with pant suit and adulterous husband) and Bill Biszy (the politically 'innocent', black, gay, action star of the popular *Sharkman* film franchise), must navigate both professional and personal obstacles over the course of the evening in order to secure Butch's support.

*The Candidate* takes place nine months later, on the eve of the election for Chief Leader. With a more traditional eye towards the door-slamming farces of modern playwrights, Sandler injects the work with a hard-edged, contemporary take on political and social issues. The events and fallout from *The Party* have landed all of the characters in new (and unexpected) situations. Vague political policies, same-sex marriage, non-traditional families, political correctness, and the media are all fair game. As political and personal allegiances shift, new romantic relationships form, old ones collapse, babies are born, and scandals threaten to break. When the election dust clears and the next 'Chief Leader' is revealed, one question remains: what lies ahead for the country?

Witty, profane, silly, and corrosive, and complemented by a host of bawdy visual gags that Orton would applaud, Sandler allows her characters to live prominently in the mess they've made of their lives. Speaking to this, Sandler sees contemporary farce as:

> …an unfixable mess that somehow gets fixed a little bit, but not permanently. And I think, just because of how the world is, we're actually better at imagining horrible, hilarious, ludicrous situations for people to be in. Heaping the most awful fucked up shit onto our characters and watching them struggle against it and laughing at them….[there is] something about watching people try to unfuck a fucked up situation that just keeps getting more fucked up.
>
> *(Sandler 2022)*

Intriguingly, the 'fictional mess' of the play is echoed in the structural complexity of executing these two plays. The very act of producing them is, in and of itself, an exercise which could *potentially* result in a theatrical mess. An audience knowing both plays are running simultaneously, invites the question: "Will they pull it off?" Needless to say, this project is a perfect example of the collaborative spirit required from all involved – to ensure the event flourishes. The above question surfaces time and again with many of the cultural farces discussed in the next chapter.

*The Party* and *The Candidate*, commissioned by the Citadel Theatre in Edmonton, Alberta, provided Sandler the opportunity to address, through farce, the fractious political landscape in North America, saying "what was happening in Canada, but primarily the States…It's Rome. It's Rome falling in real time. And I don't think enough people are making fun of it in a smart way" (Sandler 2022).

In both plays, Sandler finds the comic and frustrating intersection between politics and celebrity. Politics is a fickle business where flash can overshadow substance; where it's not what you say, but how you say it. It is no wonder the 2016 US election has inspired, to varying degrees, more works of political satire and farce in recent years. It's important to note, however, that Sandler's characters are not cartoonish. They are equally ambitious and fragile. We see the toll public life takes on these characters' private affairs. One never gets the sense everything has wrapped up nicely. Sandler sums it up:

> …You know, there's going to be another problem. There's just a slightly more cynical, modern edge to an ending now where we acknowledge that. The most ludicrous thing about a farce is that it would end happily, completely happily. It's just more interesting to create stories and characters who are more deeply flawed than that.
>
> *(Sandler 2022)*

Although the playwrights discussed in this chapter have plunged their characters into highly exaggerated, ridiculous and even improbable situations, the events they depict are often a reflection of the fears we have when those people or institutions we trust to do right by us, abuse that trust, and bring us 'that close' to catastrophe.

Similarly, we see the extreme responses to those institutions. Characters preferring to live on the fringe rather than abide by what they see as oppressive regimes (real or imagined), resulting in them taking matters into their own hands, with bloody consequences to follow.

The difference we see in the political farces today is a sense of looming or pending violence, a tinderbox if you will that is ready to be lit up. Political figures have always been easy targets to ridicule. Contemporary political farces lure us in with innocuous scenarios or dim-witted characters only to pull the rug out from under us, exposing harsh truths about government, and our present-day political systems. There is an anger, even rage that pulses under these farces, borne out of disregard and betrayal, where political agendas take precedence over human decency.

It may be too soon, but the odds are that someone will use the COVID pandemic, or the conflicts in Ukraine or the Middle East, or a global natural disaster as fodder for farce. As we come to terms with a world increasingly plagued by crisis, and with politics appearing to be in free fall, we can at least take comfort in knowing there is much humour to be mined.

**Works Cited**

Adams, Tim. "Lucy Kirkwood: 'Boys Are Force-Fed This Very Plastic Sexuality on a Mass Scale'." *The Guardian*, 8 Sept. 2021, www.theguardian.com/stage/2012/oct/21/lucy-kirkwood-nsfw-pornography-play-interview

Ayckbourn, Alan. *Joking Apart and Other Plays*. Penguin Books, 1979.

Bean, Richard. *In the Club*. Oberon Books, 2007.

Bean, Richard. *The Hypocrite*. Oberon Books, 2017.

Beaton, Alistair. *Alistair Beaton: "If You're Bored, It'll Be My Fault"*. 8 Apr. 2017, theartsdesk.com/theatre/alistair-beaton-if-you%E2%80%99re-bored-it%E2%80%99ll-be-my-fault

Beaton, Alistair. *Feelgood*. Methuen Drama, 2001.

Behan, Tom. *Dario Fo: Revolutionary Theatre*. Pluto Press, 2000.

Billington, Michael. "Forgotten Plays: No 3 – the Coup (1991) by Mustapha Matura." *The Guardian*, 15 Jun. 2020a, www.theguardian.com/stage/2020/jun/15/forgotten-plays-no-3-the-coup-mustapha-matura

Billington, Michael. "Tinderbox." *The Guardian*, 26 Mar. 2020b, www.theguardian.com/stage/2008/apr/29/theatre4

Brantley, Ben. "Terrorism Meets Absurdism in a Rural Village in Ireland." *The New York Times*, 28 Feb. 2006, www.nytimes.com/2006/02/28/theater/reviews/terrorism-meets-absurdism-in-a-rural-village-in-ireland.html

Broadway World. TV - Press Previews. "THE MINUTES Enters Its Final Two Weeks of Broadway Performances." *BroadwayWorld.com*, 12 Jul. 2022, www.broadwayworld.com/article/BWW-TV-Hangin-with-the-Cast-of-THE-MINUTES-on-Broadway-20200220

Caggiano, Christopher. "Theater Review: 'the Minutes' on Broadway Beguiles and Befuddles - the Arts Fuse." *The Arts Fuse*, 12 Oct. 2023, artsfuse.org/255454/theater-review-the-minutes-on-broadway-beguiles-and-befuddles

Chirico, Miriam M. *The Theatre of Christopher Durang*. Methuen Drama. 2021.

Cohen, Alix. "The Minutes– Revisionist History – Woman around Town." *Woman Around Town*, 19 May 2022, www.womanaroundtown.com/sections/playing-around/the-minutes-revisionist-history

Cox, Gordon. "'The Minutes' Review: New Broadway Comedy Is a Cunning, Sensational Indictment of American Democracy." *Variety*, 17 Apr. 2022.

Crowe, Sinead. *Religion in Contemporary German Drama*. Camden House, 2013.

Durang, Christopher. *Why Torture Is Wrong, and the People Who Love Them*. Dramatists Play Service, 2011.

Erlbach, Matthew-Lee. *The Doppelgänger*. Unpublished manuscript, 2018.

Farrell, Joseph. "Fo and Feydeau: Is Farce a Laughing Matter?" *Italica*, vol. 72, no. 3, American Association of Teachers of Italian, Jan. 1995, p. 307, https://doi.org/10.2307/479721

Fahy, Thomas. *Understanding Tracy Letts*. University of South Carolina Press, 2020.

Fillinger, Selina. Personal Interview. 9 Sept. 2022a.

Fillinger, Selina. *POTUS*. Samuel French, 2022b.

Fisher, Mark. "Accidental Death of an Anarchist Review – A Riotous Satirical Farce Brought Bang up to Date." *The Guardian*, 2 Oct. 2022, www.theguardian.com/stage/2022/oct/02/accidental-death-of-an-anarchist-review-sheffield-crucible-tom-basden-daniel-rigby

Fo, Dario. *Plays: 1*. Methuen Drama, 1992.
Fo, Dario. *Plays: 2*. Methuen Drama, 1994.
Fo, Dario, and Nye, Simon (Translator). *Accidental Death of an Anarchist*. Methuen Drama, 2003.
Fo, Dario, and Joe Farrell (Translator). *The Tricks of the Trade*. Routledge Publishing, 1991.
Giles, Sarah. Personal Interview. 1 Aug. 2020.
Graham, James. *The Culture*. Bloomsbury Methuen Drama, 2018.
Grandage, Michael. Email Interview. 10 Jun. 2020.
Greene, Alexis. *Durang in an Hour*. In an Hour Books, 2011.
Gussow, Mel. *Conversations with Stoppard*. Grove Press, 1995.
Hess, Amanda. "The 'POTUS' Playwright Is Making a Farce of the Patriarchy." *The New York Times*, 22 Apr. 2022, www.nytimes.com/2022/04/22/theater/potus-selina-fillinger-broadway.html
Jain, Ravi. Personal Interview. 12 Jul. 2020.
Jones, Alice. "Lucy Kirkwood: Britain's Brightest Young Stage Writer | the Independent." *The Independent*, 27 Oct. 2009, www.independent.co.uk/arts-entertainment/theatre-dance/features/lucy-kirkwood-britain-s-brightest-young-stage-writer-1809848.html. variety.com/2022/legit/reviews/the-minutes-review-broadway-play-tracy-letts-1235234223/amp
Jordan, Eamonn. "Martin McDonagh's 'the Lieutenant of Inishmore': Commemoration and Dismemberment through Farce." *JSTOR*, vol. 15, no. 2, 2006, pp. 369–386, www.jstor.org/stable/41274485
Kumar, Naveen. "Variety." *Variety*, 17 Apr. 2022, variety.com/2022/legit/reviews/the-minutes-review-broadway-play-tracy-letts-1235234223
Kirkwood, Lucy. *Plays: One*. Nick Hern Books, 2016.
Lecoq, Jacques. *The Moving Body*. Routledge, 2001, p. 118.
Letts, Tracy. *The Minutes*. Samuel French, 2023.
Lonergan, Patrick. *The Theatre and Films of Martin McDonagh*. Methuen Drama, 2012.
Loveridge, Charlotte. CurtainUp. *Tinderbox, a CurtainUp London Review*, www.curtainup.com/tinderboxlond.html
Lukowski, Andrzej. "'The Lieutenant of Inishmore' Review." *Time Out London*, 5 Jul. 2018, www.timeout.com/london/theatre/the-lieutenant-of-inishmore-review
Matura, Mustapha. *The Coup: A Play of Revolutionary Dreams*. Methuen Drama, 1991.
McDonagh, Martin. *The Lieutenant of Inishmore*. Methuen Drama, 2009.
McKinley, Jesse. "Tracy Letts Can't Fight with His Playwright." *The New York Times*, 26 Feb. 2020, www.nytimes.com/2020/02/26/theater/tracy-letts-the-minutes.html
Meirich, Hanni. "'A Laughing Matter: The Role of Humor in Holocaust Narrative'" *Core.ac.uk*, 2013, core.ac.uk/download/pdf/79566609.pdf
Middeke, Martin. *Martin McDonagh. The Methuen Drama Guide to Contemporary Irish Playwrights* (Edited by Martin Middeke and Peter Paul Schnierer). Methuen Drama, 2010.
Mitchell, Tony. *Dario Fo: People's Court Jester*. Methuen Drama, 2006, pp. 101–102.
Mitchell, Tony (Compiled by). *File on Fo*. Methuen Drama, 1989.
My, Myron. "REVIEW: George Tabori's MEIN KAMPF." *Theatre Press*, 17 Aug. 2013, theatre-press.com/2013/08/16/review-george-taboris-mein-kampf
Nadel, Ira. *Tom Stoppard: A Life*. Palgrave Macmillan, 2002.

Nasser, Shanifa. "Toronto Police Chief Warns of 'Opportunists,' 'Misinformation' after Woman's Fall from Highrise." *CBC*, 1 Jun. 2020, www.cbc.ca/news/canada/toronto/regis-korchinski-paquet-toronto-police-1.5590296

National Theatre Black Plays Archive. *Mustapha Matura Biography | BPA*, www.blackplaysarchive.org.uk/featured-content/interviews/mustapha-matura-biography

O'Brien, John. "Alan Ayckbourn's Ten Times Table at Richmond Theatre | Review." *LondonTheatre1*, Jan. 2020, www.londontheatre1.com/reviews/play/alan-ayckbourns-ten-times-table-at-richmond-theatre-review/#:~:text=Ten%20Times%20Table%20(1977)%20is,spending%20many%20hours%20in%20meetings

O'Hagan, Sean. "The Wild West." *The Guardian*, 1 Dec. 2017, www.theguardian.com/lifeandstyle/2001/mar/24/weekend.seanohagan

O'Toole, Fintan. "A Mind in Connemara." *The New Yorker*, 27 Feb. 2006, www.newyorker.com/magazine/2006/03/06/a-mind-in-connemara

Page, Malcolm (Compiled by). *File on Stoppard*. Methuen Drama, 1986.

Peacock, D. Keith. "Home Thoughts from Abroad: Mustapha Matura". *A Companion to Modern British and Irish Drama, 1880-2005* (Edited by Mary Luckhurst). Wiley-Blackwell, 2010, pp. 188–197.

Poggioli, Sylvia. "Valle Giulia Has Taken on Mythological Stature." *NPR*, 23 June 2008, www.npr.org/templates/story/story.php?storyId=91819083

Ruck, Victoria. "Accidental Death of an Anarchist's Hard-Hitting Messages Remain Relevant 50 Years On." *Now Then Sheffield*, 19 Oct. 2022, nowthenmagazine.com/live-reviews/2022/accidental-death-of-an-anarchists-hard-hitting-messages-remain-relevant-50-years-on-tom-basden-daniel-rigby

Sandler, Kat. *The Party/The Candidate*. Playwrights Canada Press, 2024.

Sandler, Kat. Personal Interview. 29 Sept. 2022.

Shewey, Don. *Tom Stoppard's "Dirty Linen and New-Found-Land" and "Dogg's Hamlet, Cahoot's Macbeth"*, n.d. Reviewed in 1979 by Don Shewey. www.donshewey.com/theater_reviews/dirty_linen.html

Sierz, Aleks. *In-Yer-Face Theatre: British Drama Today*. Faber and Faber, 2001, p. 224.

Stoppard, Tom. *Plays: One*. Faber and Faber, 1996.

Stott, Andrew. *Comedy*. Routledge, 2005, pp.157–158.

Tabori, George. *Mein Kampf (A Farce)*. Drama Contemporary: Germany (Edited by Carl Weber). Johns Hopkins University Press, 1996.

Tauer, Kristen. "WWD." *WWD*, 3 Jun. 2022, wwd.com/eye/people/meet-selina-fillinger-the-young-playwright-behind-three-of-this-years-tony-nominations-1235187751

"Theatre of the Oppressed NYC." *Theatre of the Oppressed NYC*, www.tonyc.nyc

Thompson, Steve. *Whipping It Up*. Nick Hern Books, 2006.

Weiss, Hedy. "In 'The Doppelgänger,' Insiders and Outsiders Greedily Savage an African Nation." *WTTW News*, 23 May 2018, news.wttw.com/2018/04/19/doppelg-nger-insiders-and-outsiders-greedily-savage-african-nation

Westerfield, Joe. "Tracy Letts Talks about 'The Minutes,' His New Comedy of Menace on Broadway." *Newsweek*, 29 Mar. 2022, www.newsweek.com/tracy-letts-talks-about-minutes-comedy-menace-broadway-1692118

Williamson, David. *The Department*. Currency Press, 1975.

Willstrop, James. "Review: The Culture (Hull Truck Theatre)." *WhatsOnStage.com*, 21 June 2023, www.whatsonstage.com/news/review-the-culture-hull-truck-theatre_45664

Wing, Paula. Personal Interview. 23 Jul. 2020.

# 4
# CULTURAL FARCE (OR 'FARCE REMIXED')

Our fourth door leads us into a room where culture has provided the foundation for many of the most popular farces that have graced our stages in the last 20 years. These farces derive their inspiration from source material drawn from literature, film, theatre, television, and popular culture. The recognition factor of this material often plays a role in generating laughs based on how the playwright celebrates or subverts the work they are adapting or creating.

Moving beyond satire, cultural farces often use parody to lampoon cultural touchstones. There may be a self-aware, even metatheatrical quality to the work. Characters break the fourth wall to engage the audience, inviting complicity. Reducing epic works to their theatrical essence, small casts of actors are asked to perform athletic feats of storytelling, whisking the audience to settings far and wide, suggesting a location with a simple set piece or prop. Actors take on multiple roles, playing different ages, nationalities, genders, even races, with split-second changes. These farces not only beg the question, 'Will they pull it off?', but ask 'How will they pull it off?' Half the fun is watching the impossible become possible.

Within the genre, cultural farce has emerged as the most popular form in the 21st century. With audiences sticking to what they know, name and/or content recognition can play an important role in determining whether a patron will pay $100 for a theatre ticket. Whether it's a play based on their favourite novel or movie, or a new slant on a classic work, audiences are more apt to take in a farce based on a work they admire or with which they have a previous history.

Because of this, contemporary playwrights are under more pressure to find a way to interrogate and transcend the source material, so it resonates with a contemporary audience. It's not enough to do a straightforward retelling of

*The Three Musketeers*, or a Sherlock Holmes novel. The contemporary playwright must not only reimagine the source material for the *stage*, but also recognise that the play may be performed in various spatial configurations, deal with touring demands, and allow for either a pre-determined or flexible ensemble of actors.

Cultural farces, when successful, are models of adaptation. These farces must figure out a way to illuminate their source material to create a whole new theatrical entity. Not only must they figure out a way to re-think a 300-page novel, a five-act classical text, or a three-hour movie, but they must also consider how the genre will reveal something new about the material or offer audiences a unique viewing experience. In certain cases, the playwrights or creators must consider the expectations or 'baggage' that accompanies a popular or well-known work of art.

Adapting a classic play or popular movie does not beget success. When a playwright considers adapting a previous work for the stage, there are important questions to consider: What does the source material offer a contemporary audience that gives it resonance? What is it about the source material that speaks to the playwright and inspires them to adapt it for the stage? What form does the adaptation need to take? It may pay homage to the original, be it in the dialogue or the style of the play. It may use the original as a jumping-off point to explore the piece in a different medium. It may flip the original on its head and breathe theatrical life into the storytelling in unique and innovative ways.

The playwright might also ask: how much of the original source material are audiences anticipating? Are there quotable lines, especially if it is building on an entity's cult status? If the play is based on an historical character or event, how faithful must the story remain, or can the playwright take liberties?

What is laudable about said playwrights is that they all took significant risks in their approach to adapting these pieces for the stage. As we've come to see, farce is already a tricky prospect to execute well. These adaptations are actor-driven, use simple but clever stagecraft techniques, and put their trust in the audience to fill in any remaining gaps.

The art of adaptation is not easy, and crafting a farce for the stage based on other material is doubly difficult, especially when it was written for another medium. It takes ingenuity to translate for the stage. Yet we have seen several successful 'remixes' in the 21st century. The term 'remix' is offered, because that is what a good adaptation is: Taking a previously produced piece of media and altering it, changing it, bending it and in the process producing a new artistic entity that still contains the DNA of the source material.

When source material meets an active imagination, the result can be theatrical bliss. For this reason, we offer up a subtitle to this chapter, *Farce Remixed*.

Canadian adaptor and playwright Paula Wing offers the following to describe the process of adaptation:

> A long time ago, I gave a talk about adaptation and the metaphor that I used was [the] headstand…to learn a headstand, which according to Yoga teaching is exactly like standing on your feet, you're just reversing it. But because you have had way more practice on your feet, you need to use a wall at first. And the script, the old thing, is like a wall and you gradually learn how to come off the wall and then eventually you're in the room alone. No wall. And you can stand there and you understand where everything is. But it takes a long time in learning a headstand, to know where your feet are, where your hips are, where your chest is. You know, when you watch a kid learn to walk, that's what they're figuring out…They're figuring out that, "Oh, my God. No, this is not working".
>
> *(Wing 2020)*

This chapter will break the work into four sections: Farce and the Novel, Farce and the Silver Screen, Farce and the Theatrical Adaptation, and Farce and the Cultural Icon.

---

### Farce and the Novel

Have you ever read a novel and wondered how this could translate into a movie or play, without losing the author's voice or story elements that make the novel unique? Those in the theatre (and in film) do this on a regular basis, finding inventive ways to translate those sweeping, epic novels to the stage or screen.

At first glance, farce is not a genre that one associates with 'great literature.' These classic works of fiction enthrall readers with their language and scope. Adaptations are drawn from the Industrial Age, the Romantic and Victorian eras, and also Gothic, mystery, and espionage novels. Yet farce becomes an ideal vehicle for the theatricalisation of a novel because it requires virtuosic imagination from the actors, the director, the designers, and the audience to compress 300–1000 pages of words, locations, and characters into a two-hour act of storytelling. Speed and economy must be employed to execute these types of cultural farces.

Whether from Dickens, Doyle, or Dumas, brilliance in ingenuity is demanded when being translated for the stage.

Over the last 20 years, we have seen a rise in one particular brand of hilarity: the literary farce. Playwrights have found fascinating ways to condense these books into successful theatrical events. With hundreds of characters, ever-changing locales, and period fashion that would wipe out a play's costume budget, the adaptation of novels has forced playwrights to innovate. One solution: crafting plays where a small ensemble of actors change roles in the blink of an eye by simply adding a hat or changing their physicality. Umbrellas become car wheels. A table may represent a desk or a boat.

There seem to be three things at play here: these reimagined takes on classical works capture the energy and thrill of reading a great story. They provide a company of artists with an artistic challenge; how to tell a particular story using traditional stagecraft and the actors' transformative ability, while harnessing the audience's imagination. The approach to the work is serious and must remain grounded in truth. And although some of these pieces have crossover with the 'Backstage Farces' to be surveyed in the next chapter, these literary farces have a wonderful sense of 'play' about them, both celebrating and poking fun at the original material.

### Peepolykus & Le Navet Bete

British companies Peepolykus and Le Navet Bete are characterised by their commitment to physical comedy, mask and clown work. Ensemble-driven, they share a history of creating devised work as well as putting their own unique spin on literary classics.

Led by Co-Artistic Directors John Nicholson, Javier Marzan and David Sant, Peepolykus has been touring original shows built around their brand of physical comedy and clowning for over twenty-five years. In 2007, the company premiered their first literary adaptation, a three-person re-telling of Sir Arthur Conan Doyle's *The Hound of the Baskervilles*. In 2016, the company premiered their four-person *The Massive Tragedy of Madame Bovary* (*Gustave Flaubert's Complex Novel Lovingly Derailed By Peepolykus*). In both plays, a small cast of actors is asked to assume anywhere between two and eight roles, including versions of themselves. In both cases, the fourth wall is broken almost immediately, and a rapport is established between performer and audience member. Playwrights Steve Canny and John Nicholson state in their Authors' Note to *The Hound of the Baskervilles* that "their inspiration [was] drawn from the many memorable solo, double- and triple-act performers whose physical-comedy routines were honed in front of a live audience" (Canny and Nicholson 5). In describing the key to performing the piece, they note that "the physical pace and dexterity of the performers is as important as the pace in which the text is played" (ibid.). In the case of *Bovary*, writers Nicholson and Marzan reduced Flaubert's 300+-page novel to a 100-page script. It should also be noted that, amidst the 'anarchic' comedy, the authors once again share insight into approaching the play. They describe how, in their research, "we explored the pendulum swing between comedy and tragedy and how, when juxtaposed, comedy can expose tragedy and tragedy can expose comedy" (Nicholson and Marzan 3).

Le Navet Bete (which roughly translates as 'The Daft Turnip') was co-founded in 2007 by Nick Bunt, Al Dunn and Matt Freeman, who had met as undergraduates at the University of Plymouth in 2003. Drawing on their love of bouffon clowning, Le Navet Bete, like Peepolykus, began creating devised works of physical comedy with non-narrative structures, before finding their niche touring theatrical adaptations of classic stories. These include *Treasure Island* (2019), *The Three Musketeers* (2019), and *Dracula: The Bloody Truth* (2017), which were devised and written in collaboration with Peepolykus' John Nicholson. These works feature a healthy combination of slapstick and physical comedy, with a quartet of actors portraying up to 40 roles, each play finding unique ways to embrace recognizable traits defining the original novel.

For *Treasure Island*, "the action is suspenseful and gripping…But in places it's also irreverent, anarchic and screwball". A coming-of-age story told from the perspective of fourteen-year-old Jim Hawkins,

> [Robert Louis] Stevenson's timeless novel gets pretty graphic in places – murder on the high seas and all that. We were keen not to sanitise these more lurid aspects of the book…We also wanted to create characters who were as funny and playful as they were ruthless, as deliciously Machiavellian as they were ridiculous.
>
> *(Nicholson 5)*

On the other hand, *Dracula: The Bloody Truth* utilises a framing device where the vampire hunter Abraham Van Helsing (who hates the theatre) has hired a trio of amateur actors to help him "broadcast the true events that happened to him and his friends; the true events that Stoker shamelessly fictionalised" (Nicholson v). Playing scores of characters, including exaggerated versions of themselves, this rag-tag quartet perform

> a serious (albeit wooden) script, within which terrible directorial decisions have been made and which is primed to derail at every turn…sometimes the actors share characters, sometimes an actor is keeping three characters alive in one scene…But despite it all, the company somehow pull it off.
>
> *(Nicholson v)*

And pulling it off is crucial for Van Helsing. The audience must know, "that Bram Stoker's *Dracula*, is in fact…fact" (Le Navet Bete & Nicholson 5). To spread the truth, Van Helsing and his actors tour Europe, educating their audiences. Similarly, with a commitment to make their work accessible for all audiences, Le Navet Bete devises their work to tour. Based in Exeter, the company has "quickly become one of the UK's most ridiculously outrageous, much loved outdoor acts" (Le Navet Bete 2) performing their shows at home and abroad.

For both companies, the fourth wall does not exist. Audiences are addressed directly by the actors and even pulled into the chicanery, becoming enmeshed in the storytelling. This relationship with the audience becomes a recurring element in a number of cultural and backstage farces, where we are unwittingly cast in the role of 'audience', while watching the play proper, a lovely little coup de théâtre.

### The Goodale Brothers: Jeeves and Wooster in Perfect Nonsense (2013)

Hyper-awareness of the audience is also present in the Goodale Brothers' 2013 play *Jeeves and Wooster in Perfect Nonsense*. Based on the comic works of P.G. Wodehouse, including *The Code of the Woosters*, the eponymous Bertie Wooster is egged on by his drinking pals to rent out a West End theatre and to present one of his recent 'fixes' as a one-man show. With his ever-faithful butler Jeeves at the ready as a would-be stage manager (and playing four other roles), they are joined by Seppings, the butler of Bertie's Aunt Dahlia, who dutifully takes on the remaining five characters in the story. Together, these three recreate a country house weekend debacle which sees Bertie playing matchmaker to classic Wodehouse characters Gussie Fink-Nottle and Madeline Bassett, a situation that almost results in him marrying the undesirable Madeline himself. Of course, as is his wont in the books, Wooster's loyal butler Jeeves helps Bertie out of his predicaments within the story, but also helps him rectify the theatrical mess he is making onstage.

### Tom Basden: The Crocodile (2015)

In Tom Basden's 2015 play *The Crocodile*, Basden updates Fydor Dostoevsky's short story of the same name, to create a farce exploiting the cult of celebrity. Taking place in 1865, at a zoo in St. Petersburg, Russia, Basden's adaptation follows Ivan, a deluded actor who lacks any self-awareness. His one-man shows leave much to be desired, blaming an uneducated audience. Even Ivan's close friend Zack believes he needs to redirect his creative energies elsewhere:

> Zack: …if it's not changing anything, if you're not getting anywhere, if the audience for the last one was made up of me, [your ex-girlfriend] Anya, and that man with the dog, then why…don't keep doing it! Don't keep getting cross with the public because they'd rather watch a bear balancing on a ball than a grown man pretending to be a potato–
> 
> Ivan: I wasn't pretending to be a potato! Thank you. I was portraying the famine in Northern India from the point of view of the crops – it was highly theatrical.
> 
> *(Basden 15)*

On a sojourn to the Zoo with Zack, Ivan is swallowed by a crocodile. Surviving the ordeal, but now 'lodged' inside the large reptile, Ivan suddenly finds himself attaining the notoriety he has so desperately craved. Audiences are suddenly captivated by him, willing to pay good money to see 'The Croc Monsieur' performing Ivan's similar 'dreck', railing against a system he knows little about. Ivan's new-found fame even captures Anya's attention, and in the end she gives herself over to Ivan/Crocodile, literally becoming one with him. A fourth actor takes on a multitude of roles – playing everything from an entrepreneurial crocodile owner to the Tsar of Russia, all with the simple change of a hat. With echoes of Ionesco and Theatre of the Absurd, Basden takes on artistic integrity, capitalism, and political propaganda.

### Ken Ludwig's The Game's Afoot *(2011)* and Baskerville *(2015)*

In addition to his array of domestic and backstage farces, Ken Ludwig has also adapted a number of classic literary novels, including his own versions of *The Adventures of Tom Sawyer* (2001), *The Three Musketeers* (2006), *Treasure Island* (2009), and *Sherwood: The Adventures of Robin Hood* (2017). Filled with Ludwig's trademark wit, these adaptations put a greater emphasis on the element of adventure, capturing the swashbuckle, sword play and those clearly defined cultural heroes and villains that have captured our imaginations in books and on the silver screen.

Another genre that Ludwig has also returned to on numerous occasions is mystery. In particular, his strong affection for Sherlock Holmes has led him to revisit the character of Holmes in one form or another on four different occasions.

Modelled on an earlier play entitled *Postmortem* (1983), Ludwig's *The Game's Afoot or Holmes for the Holidays* is set on Christmas Eve 1936, at the Connecticut castle of actor William Gillette. Famed for his onstage portrayal of Sherlock Holmes, Gillette has invited castmates to his home for a weekend of holiday festivities, while he recuperates after an attempt on his life. The soiree takes a turn after one of the guests is stabbed to death. Embracing the detective persona that has defined his career, Gillette and company try to solve the murder before another person meets their untimely end. *The Game's Afoot* is a linear mystery in the tradition of Agatha Christie, with elements of farce peppered throughout; aspects include slapstick comedy, irreverence in the face of death, the persistent hiding of a body, and a set that surprises with games, gadgets and mirrors. Ludwig pays homage to both the Sherlock Holmes character and Gillette, while affectionately poking fun at theatre people.

*Baskerville: A Sherlock Holmes Mystery* (2015), Ludwig's adaptation of *The Hound of the Baskervilles*, features a cast of five, who take on approximately 40 roles. Filled with lightning-fast costume and scene changes, taking us from the city setting of London into the country moors, the audience is propelled through Conan Doyle's classic mystery story with fluid verve and hilarity. Where

Peepolykus' version of the play consciously acknowledges the audience's presence in a metatheatrical way, Ludwig employs Watson as a narrator figure (as he is in the original novels) who addresses the audience directly. But there is no 'play-within-a-play' in operation here. Ludwig is interested in the performative doubling and tripling of characters harking back to classical theatre, noting "it is often a source of theatrical joy" (Ludwig 8). This joy is echoed by costume designer Whitney Locher:

> …I mean it is a kind of virtuosity right? Because as a costume designer you have to become more and more clever every time you do a change or a reveal. Is this a tearaway moment? Is this a melt-away moment? What's your plan for getting people into things that are bigger, faster, funnier? Right. It's like how do you do that without slowing down the momentum of the show? The momentum is what makes it funny.
> 
> *(Locher 2020)*

Ludwig goes on to reference a quote from playwright J.B. Priestley about the dual nature of performance. Ludwig is reminded

> that when we go to the theater we feel two things at the same time. First, we see characters who tell us a story. Second, we're conscious that professional actors are playing those characters and telling the story on a small wooden stage…I believe that this knowledge can enrich the experience of seeing a play, and reminds us that play-going is not merely life, but life enhanced.
>
> *(Ludwig 8)*

Ludwig's new Sherlock Holmes play, *Moriarty*, opened at the Cleveland Playhouse in 2023. Like *Baskerville*, it features a cast of five playing over 40 roles. Drawing on Conan Doyle's short story "A Scandal in Bohemia", the play features not only Holmes and Watson, but also the American actress Irene Adler (who appeared in the original story) and Holmes' arch-nemesis, Professor Moriarty.

Though not immediately obvious, mysteries and farces share a range of common attributes. In both, the plots are almost always linear, with little time to develop a subplot. Similarly, an emphasis is put on the mathematical plotting of the story rather than the psychological development of the characters. There is a sense of performance in a mystery, with characters hiding behind their secrets or disguises, attempting to get away with a crime. In farce, however, the audience is privy to the lies. Mysteries keep us in the dark for as long as possible. Finally, in speaking about the endings of mysteries, Ludwig says: "…society rights itself after a period of discord. In a sense, that's the very definition of a mystery. Order from chaos" (Ludwig 8). As we have discussed, farces aim to do the same thing, just with laughs.

**152** Cultural Farce (or 'Farce Remixed')

*Patrick Barlow:* **The 39 Steps** *(2006)*

As we have seen in this first section, the phenomenon of the epic story/small cast has been a favoured mode of storytelling. Arguably, the most popular example is *The 39 Steps*, adapted by Patrick Barlow. Based on an original concept by Simon Corble and Nobby Dimon, *The 39 Steps* started life at the West Yorkshire Playhouse in 2005 before transferring to the West End in 2006 under the directorial eye of Maria Aitken. It then moved to Broadway in 2008.

The play is based on both the book by Scottish novelist John Buchan and the 1935 Alfred Hitchcock movie. Barlow's rollicking adaptation is at turns theatrically imaginative, a masterclass in performance, and a thrill ride all wrapped up in one. A spy story that ricochets around the United Kingdom is simultaneously a cultural farce taking its cue from literary and cinematic references (especially ones from the Hitchcock oeuvre).

Richard Hannay, who is living a relatively boring life in London, decides to go to the theatre one night. His world is upended when he meets Annabella, a beautiful foreigner who informs him she's a spy, on the run. She insists he take her back to his place. Less than a few hours later, Annabella is dead, having been stabbed in the back. Hannay, who 15 minutes ago was complaining about being bored, now finds himself caught up in international espionage. The play is an homage, a spoof and, most of all, a fast-paced farce that is dependent on the main character clearing his name, winning the girl, and saving humanity from 'The 39 Steps', a secret sect with plans for world domination.

*The 39 Steps* is a giddy concoction, mixing farce, and elements of English pantomime, musical hall convention, and Monty Python. Barlow has taken key ingredients from both Buchan's book and Hitchcock's movie and reimagined them for the stage. One can look at the constantly changing characters the two Clowns play in the show and simply see it as a gimmick; yet when we return to the book, we learn that Richard Hannay was a master of disguise, constantly changing his personality, dialects and personas to fit a situation. Barlow's decision to use this as a conceit is thus not only clever, but also in keeping with the source material. At the same time, we witness four actors pulling off a performance feat. Actor Mark Price, who has played a Clown in multiple productions, discusses the approach to performance he adopts in *The 39 Steps*:

> The thing that I think makes these directors of comedy, particularly farce, so intelligent and so spot on is their heart underneath it. These comedies do not work if there is not a heart at the core of all of this chaos. What [director]Mark Shanahan…said [on Price's production is] that this play is not about a bunch of people entertaining an audience or entertaining each other. It is about this troupe of people understanding that they can do the impossible. And being able to get to that, to that heart underneath all of

those changes, the Mr. Memory, the milkman, all of that, the two train guards, it's still in service of saying, "hey, look, we can do the impossible", [and] that's really what the play is about. So, it's not necessarily about this love story…it is about this core of four actors suggesting that if you want to, you can do the impossible. And there's also the hope or there's also the danger that they may not be able to do it. And if you go back and look at that play through that lens, you can see in each one of the scenes that there is that slight sort of dip to where the character may not be convinced that they can actually do that thing. The writing supports it. And I just was blown away by that insight.

*(Price 2020)*

The play captures the breathless pace of the book and the movie. To keep the audience engaged, the production must ensure that a) the audience doesn't get ahead of the actors, and b) the storytelling is clear and the journey is fun.

Along the way there is word play, visual gags, some metatheatrical commentary, and a love story. The play finds its joy in the storytelling. The play demands the audience remain invested in the lives of Hannay and the character of Pamela, his love interest. The threat of danger, however, must always lurk in their shadows. As soon as we don't believe that anything could happen to them, we don't care. If at any point, the audience senses that the production starts to wink or 'nudge', the stakes plummet. The inventiveness of the piece is a love letter to the stage and reminds us of the 'sense of play' and imagination required to put on a show. In his book, *Good Nights Out*, Aleks Sierz highlights some examples of the theatrical ingenuity:

> The Fourth Bridge from which Hannay dangles is created by means of a ladder suspended between two step-ladders; the train roof is built from three upturned trunks; a length of cloth creates a stream. The Highland chase sequence is told using shadow puppets…Gorse is created by bent fingers. Fogs billow. Mime rules.
>
> *(Sierz 142–143)*

Barlow invites productions to embrace the economy, pace and reversals in the storytelling, encouraging each production to find what works for their company. Karen Sheridan, who directed the play for Peninsula Players Theatre, concurs, saying:

> I think the trap of any show is thinking you have to do things by the book – whatever that means. *The 39 Steps* is built on surprise and invention. It is theatrical, narrated by the main character. The first death is about 10 minutes in. And then that body becomes one of the first big gags. We have to have fun, but not make the play an excuse to show how clever or funny we

are. It's about an unfolding story compounded by people who get involved and seem to multiply. It's about a bored man who goes to the theatre one day and his entire life changes. If you see photos from different productions of *The 39 Steps*, they may all resemble each other. But anyone watching in the room will be enveloped in the storytelling of that particular company.

*(Sheridan 2021)*

In 2014, Sean Fitzpatrick of *The Civilized Reader* wrote the following about Buchan's book: "There is a very real need to believe in the impossible these days – to believe in miracles, especially political miracles, where one man can overcome all odds and make a difference in the fate of a nation. *The Thirty-Nine Steps* engages and enacts this dream, and thereby serves to keep the hope alive that the impossible may, in fact, be possible. Such fantasies are important in these days when, as John Buchan wrote, 'the wildest fictions are so much less improbable than the facts'" (Fitzpatrick 2014).

Although Fitzpatrick was writing about the novel, he could easily have been speaking to the very thing actor Mark Price references – the thrill of watching those commit fully to their passion (or obsession), and achieve the impossible. The 'impossible' does not come readily, yet requires everyone involved to make it look effortless. Actor Jill Paice shares her own experience, coming in as a replacement to the Broadway production:

Stepping into *The 39 Steps* was intimidating and I kept thinking I would be asked to leave. I felt way out of my league, but the company was so welcoming. Arnie Burton, Jeffrey Kuhn, and Sean Mahon, the stage management team, the crew – everyone was there in support of the show. At my final run-through before officially taking over the role, I had a small cry after rehearsing the scene where we are all running around in the dark with puppets and flashlights. It went so horribly and I felt like such an utter failure. Jeffrey came right over to me, hugged me, and told me this was when he cried at his put in too. I prepared for the show by watching it over and over for many weeks. At night, at home, I would run the blocking in my sleep. In the morning, I would say all of my lines in the various dialects and I would visualize my tougher costume changes. My time with Maria [Aitken] was limited though she would drop in and give notes. It was a tough experience because I never felt comfortable in the roles. Some nights, Pamela would slot right in, but Annabella would be all over the place. On the nights I was able to really commit to Annabella, Margaret would take two steps back. It was tough! I think I was much harder on myself than was necessary and I do wish I would have been able to relax and enjoy it a bit more. For heaven's sake, I was running around with a flashlight. How many notes could I possibly give myself? The answer is hundreds.

*(Paice 2020)*

What seems to characterise all of the farces in this section is a childlike return to storytelling and a shared experience between performer and audience. Because the audience is a component in most of these plays, the notion of being scrutinised becomes even greater.

With *The 39 Steps* taking its partial inspiration from the silver screen, we now pay further attention to farces that have been adapted or inspired by the world of film.

**Farce and the Silver Screen**

A stage adaptation of a movie gives the playwright the chance to expand on scenes, often adding dialogue, backstory and even emotional depth that may have only been hinted at or communicated with a look or subtext. Likewise, a playwright must also contend with the very real problem of translating a movie's various locations to the stage; where trying to recreate the reality of multiple settings can result in long and unnecessary scene changes. Playwrights looking to adapt a movie for the stage must ask themselves: How can the theatrical form help to illuminate or reveal something new about the source material? What form or structure will help with this? What is the theatrical experience I am looking to offer my audience? When it comes to farce, how can the screen to stage adaptation capture the energy of the movie, while not diffusing the comedy or slowing it down? Finally, a decision has to be made about how faithful the play must be to the source material.

Cinematic cult classics are ripe for adaptation. Although they may have found fandom in certain circles, they have often divided audiences and critics. These are attractive commodities to draw on for adaptation because they are generally not weighed down by awards, box office, and 'prestige'. There is room to fill them out and find new ways through the medium to tell their story.

The three plays discussed in this section are based on two cult classics, and an Oscar-winning movie that became a Tony Award-winning musical.

***Graham Linehan:* The Ladykillers *(2011)***

*The Ladykillers*, written by Irish writer Graham Linehan ("Father Ted"), is based on the 1955 Ealing Studio movie of the same name by screenwriter William Rose, and featuring Alec Guiness and Peter Sellers.

The year is 1956. Over the course of five days in November, a gang of low-rent thieves come together to pull off a security van robbery at King's Cross Station, London. Led by their devious leader Professor Marcus, the five men masquerade as a string quartet while plotting their heist. To place them in proximity to their target, Marcus rents multiple rooms in the boarding house of elderly (and unrelentingly nosy) Mrs. Wilberforce, who unwittingly becomes an accessory in their criminal activity. Following the report of the robbery and the inadvertent reveal of the money the men stole, Mrs. Wilberforce connects them to the recently reported crime and politely tells them she must call the police. Before she can do this, a gaggle of Mrs. Wilberforce's friends arrive to hear the men play. With no choice, and unable to hide behind the gramophone recording they have been using to perpetrate their 'brilliant musicianship', the men proceed to give a concert of ear-piercing awfulness. Outed as incompetent musicians, the men plead their case, making up sad stories for why they need the money, and even scaring Mrs. Wilberforce with the threat of jail, given her part in the robbery. She stands firm and insists they turn themselves in. The five men recognise they have no choice but to 'bump off' Mrs. Wilberforce. Unfortunately, things don't go according to plan and soon each one of them meets their untimely end in turn, either by accident, by murder, or through sheer bad luck.

The idea to adapt the original Ealing comedy into a stage play was not Linehan's. In the case of cult classics such as *The Ladykillers*, fans can be very protective. Linehan was:

> ...approached by the producers – and they said something like, 'You like *Ladykillers* don't you?' And I said, 'Yeah, it's good.' And they said, 'Could be funnier though, couldn't it?' And I thought, 'Yeah, it really could be!' Because *Ladykillers* is a very dry, mordant comedy. I thought if you got it on stage you could amplify the farce. In the film the farce stuff is just lots of pratfalls and chasing parrots, so I thought there's a kind of gap where the farce should be.
>
> *(Chortle 2011)*

Discussing his approach to adapting the original film for the stage, Linehan says: "In adapting – often but not always – you must first plant dynamite around the ground floor of the original. After the detonation, you keep what's still standing and bid farewell to the rest..." (Linehan 2011). Perhaps the biggest change is in the tone. Where the original had a much darker hue (not just in the filming), Linehan's version ups the farcical aspects, with more visual gags (the house becomes a character in itself), running jokes (including comic foreshadowing involving a scarf), and the ultimate drive to escape with the money. Linehan goes on to say that there were elements guiding him in his writing: "There were some other rules, of course: Mrs Wilberforce's final line had to be as satisfying as the original film's...The bodies had to disappear without a trace; and all the events had to happen within the house. Furthermore, my adaptation could never contradict what [screenwriter] Rose saw as the film's moral: 'In the worst of men, there is a little bit of good that can destroy them'" (Linehan 2011).

The play was an immediate hit upon its premiere at the Liverpool Theatre, and it was greeted with even more success when it opened in the West End at the Gielgud Theatre.

In 2017, the Lyric in Belfast cast five women in the roles of the robbers, "heightening the artifice and pretence" (Meany 2017). This also gave an added layer of meaning to the play's title, *The Ladykillers*.

### Sandy Rustin: Clue *(2020)*

In 1985, the classic Parker Brothers murder/mystery board game Clue was adapted and directed by British filmmaker Jonathan Lynn. Featuring a cast of brilliant comic actors, the movie version of CLUE was set to become a hit. Offering audiences the gimmick of seeing one of three different 'whodunnit' endings (each presented at different theatres), the movie was a moderate box office hit, but it was met with derision from the critics. Over the years, however, it has achieved cult status. With screwball dialogue bordering on the absurd, deft physical comedy, memorable quotes ("…To make a long story short –" "Too late!") and manic farce energy, many have come to see the movie CLUE as an all-time favourite.

In 2018, Hunter Foster, Eric Price, and Sandy Rustin (*The Cottage*) adapted the movie's screenplay for its world premiere at Bucks County Playhouse. Featuring the same cast of characters, the playwrights were charged with translating the fun and energy of the movie onto the stage. Since then, Rustin has revised the script and is now given sole credit for the adaptation (though Foster and Price are still listed as having contributed additional material).

Set in New England in 1954, the plot of the play sees an eclectic group of dinner guests, with pseudonyms matching parts of their wardrobe, invited to the home of a 'Mr. Boddy.' Upon arriving, they are greeted by Mr. Boddy's butler Wadsworth. He reveals that each one is being blackmailed by Mr. Boddy, for various 'un-American' acts, and tells them the police have been called. Wadsworth offers that this is their opportunity to expose 'Mr. Boddy.' Mr. Boddy arrives, hands each guest a box holding a weapon, and presents them with two scenarios: If they 'out' him as a blackmailer, they will be forced to confess their crimes and secrets to the public, facing both personal and professional disgrace. Alternatively, they can kill Wadsworth, leave quietly, with no one being the wiser, although Boddy will continue to blackmail them. Boddy then turns off the lights, and a shot rings out; when the lights come back on, Boddy lies dead. As the six guests and Wadsworth attempt to unmask the murderer, random visitors arrive, and soon more bodies begin to pile up.

One can see how *Clue* lends itself to stage adaptation. The play has one setting (the house), a relatively small cast of characters (eight, with two ensemble members playing all the other roles), a classic whodunnit storyline with many twists and reversals, and an escalating situation epitomising the classic farce structure: passion, persistence, panic, preservation. In Rustin's revised adaptation, the threats of communism and McCarthyism appear more present. The jokes around Mr. Green's homosexuality have been tamped down. The house again becomes a character. A clever scenic design approximates all the different rooms in which the murders take place (by whom and with which weapon). Discussing the challenges of adapting *Clue*, Rustin says:

> Crafting *Clue* for the stage has been both the greatest joy and greatest challenge of my career! My task was to take the iconic and beloved script from the movie CLUE and adapt it to an entirely different medium – without losing the spark that made it great in the first place! In the film, they were able to zoom in on expressions and private moments, they were able to cut away to fresh locations, they had the benefit of…a CAMERA! Ha! On stage, of course, everything must happen without zooming in, without cutting away…so the first step for me, was to determine how the set could function so that the pace of the "room to room" storytelling could still exist. I imagined how that might work (though later, director Casey Hushion and set designer, Lee Savage imagined it far better than I ever could and created a MASTERPIECE of a set!), and once I had that first piece of the puzzle clear in my mind, the rest began to fall into place. I came into the project after the previous writers had departed, so rather than being active collaborators, I had the benefit of learning from their early efforts and using my fresh eyes to craft something new. My collaboration was with my dear friend, and director, Casey Hushion, who came into this project with a clarity of vision that was electric and inspiring. Together, we set out to create a stage version of *Clue* that clings to the truth of the stakes of a murder mystery, while celebrating the unique tone of this comedy. We thought if we can REALLY make audiences wonder "whodunnit," while laughing at every turn, we will have done Jonathan Lynn's brilliant film justice.
>
> (Rustin 2020)

Rustin captures the spirit of the original, but has also economised as necessary. Certain story elements have been elaborated on or altered, lines have been changed or cut – in both cases, because they feel dated or simply do not work for the stage. Even for those not familiar with the original movie, the play can be enjoyed as a frantic murder/mystery farce. In the case of those who know the original intimately, one may bask in Rustin's clear affection for the movie. The popularity of her stage adaptation has generated numerous productions at the professional, college, and community level.

### Mel Brooks & Thomas Meehan: The Producers *(2001)*

Few farces or musicals with strong farce elements have achieved prominence within the musical theatre canon. Rare successes have included *A Funny Thing Happened on the Way to the Forum* (1963), *Promises, Promises* (1968), *On the Twentieth Century* (1978), *Lucky Stiff* (1988), *Spamalot* (2005) and *A Gentleman's Guide to Love and Murder* (2014).

In 2001, a tsunami of musical comedy took America by storm, winning a record 12 Tony Awards and cementing a reputation for itself in the lore of musical theatre. *The Producers* offered the theatre world a memorable theatrical experience, rooted in farce.

Returning to the scene of his Oscar-winning movie of the same name, the legendary filmmaker and comedian Mel Brooks fulfilled a lifelong dream with *The Producers*, by writing an original score for Broadway. Brooks' previous Broadway credits were as a librettist for the musical revue *New Faces of 1952*, and co-writer of the musicals *Shinbone Alley* (with Joe Darion, who would go on to write *Man of La Mancha*) and *All-American* (with music and lyrics by Lee Adams and Charles Strouse of *Bye Bye Birdie* fame). Ironically, he was not the first choice to write the score for *The Producers*. The movie mogul David Geffen had initially contacted *Hello Dolly* and *La Cage aux Folles* composer/lyricist Jerry Herman to write the score. Brooks writes about meeting Herman who tells him that he said 'no' to Geffen "because the first time he called I instantly thought of another songwriter who would be absolutely perfect for the job…I know and admire all of your songs. You happen to be a very good songwriter" (Brooks and Meehan 19–20).

Brooks invited Tony Award winners Thomas Meehan (co-writer) and Susan Stroman (director/choreographer) to collaborate with him on the musical. Together, they set out to adapt a cult classic movie for the musical stage. Upon agreeing to partner with Brooks, Meehan said

> What we've got to do…is to take the screenplay of *The Producers* entirely apart, as though we are disassembling the works of a finely crafted Swiss watch, and then put it back together again, adding new pieces where necessary, taking out old pieces that no longer fit the new construction, and end up with it still ticking.

Citing another metaphor, Meehan says "…turning the screenplay of *The Producers* into the musical book of *The Producers* will be not unlike trying to translate it from English into Serbo-Croatian." Brooks' response: "In other words…it's going to be a very hard job" (Brooks and Meehan 22).

Meehan's metaphors aptly describe the process of adaptation. Adapting a book, movie, or a play for the musical stage can be uniquely challenging because ultimately the new work has to literally and metaphorically sing. When writers adapt a property for film, the screenwriting mantra is "show it, don't say it." Film is a visual medium, which allows viewers to move fluidly from location to location. A close-up or silent reaction shot can speak volumes. In musicals, the mantra is: when characters can no longer speak their feelings, they sing them. And when singing isn't enough to express their emotions, they dance. The most successful musicals need to find both a theatrical language that situates them on stage, and a musical vocabulary – the marriage of words and music – that helps define the world of the play. One cannot simply transfer a screenplay to the stage, scene for scene. The source material needs to be reimagined for the stage and the question posed: what does a musical version of *The Producers*, a 1968 comedy, have to say to a 21st-century audience? And how does one tell that particular story through song, while allowing the laughs to translate?

The story in question is set in New York City in 1959. Once regarded as "The King of Broadway", producer Max Bialystock hasn't had a hit in years. Down on his luck, and relegated to sleeping with little old ladies in order to finance his productions, his most recent production *Funny Boy* – a musical version of Hamlet – has received the worst reviews of his career. One day Leo Bloom, an accountant from the firm of Whitehall and Marks, shows up at his office to look at Max's books – which, of course, are a mess and indicate fraudulent activity. Leo whimsically surmises that "it's absolutely amazing, but under the right circumstances, a producer could make more money with a flop than he could with a hit" (Brooks and Meehan, p. 90). A lightbulb goes off for Max (complete with musical 'sting'). He sees an opportunity to make a lot of money by producing just such a show. Preying on Bloom's innocent pipe dream of wanting to be a producer, Max convinces Leo to join him as co-producer. Together, they set out on a mission to produce the worst show on Broadway, one that will open and close the same night (if not by intermission).

After scouring piles of scripts, they believe they have hit the jackpot with a new musical entitled *Springtime for Hitler*. Written by Nazi fanatic Franz Liebkind, the show is a valentine to Adolf Hitler. Reluctantly taking the 'Siegfried Oath' and proving to Liebkind that they are serious about producing his show, Max, Leo, and Franz agree to move ahead with the production. Max and Leo hire the worst director, designers, and actors in New York. They also hire would-be-actress Ulla, a very tall, very Swedish bombshell as their 'secretary-slash-receptionist' (who is also offered a role in the show). The only remaining task: to raise two million dollars. Much to the delight of Max and Leo, everything that can go wrong does go wrong. Except for one small thing: The show is a hit. Max is arrested when it's discovered the accounting ledgers were 'cooked', and Leo, who narrowly escapes police detection, 'betrays' Max and ends up on a beach in Rio with Ulla. Feeling remorse for abandoning

Max, Leo returns to NYC (with Ulla), and confesses his role in the scheme. He also reveals his gratitude for the belief Max expressed in him. Max and Leo both end up in jail. In true musical theatre fashion, they return to the Great White Way as producers of the new hit musical, *Prisoners of Love*.

It's not hard to see why David Geffen saw the musical comedy possibilities in the movie. The film is a love letter to the theatre and Brooks had already written two songs: the jailhouse number 'Prisoners of Love' and the over-the-top, Ziegfeld-follies inspired, showstopper, 'Springtime for Hitler'. Similarly, Leo and Max are not only a hilarious 'double-act' in the tradition of silver screen clowns, but also a figurative 'love story' – what we'd refer to today as a 'bromance'. Where no one else saw Max as being anything other than a shyster producer, Leo saw Max for his talent and offered the one thing Max never had – friendship. In turn, Max gave Leo a sense of purpose and helped him realise his theatrical dreams (albeit in a roundabout and illegal way).

The musical uses song and dance to flesh out the Max and Leo relationship. Its pastiche of musical styles and clever lyrics both honours and parodies musical theatre. The song styles adopted reference a range of genres: the Great American Songbook (Irving Berlin, Cole Porter); the musicals of the 1940s and 1950s; and Yiddish, German, and Russian folk music. Max's '11 o'clock number', 'Betrayed', is a direct descendent of 'Rose's Turn' in *Gypsy*. Yet none of Brooks' compositions feel derivative. It's an original musical comedy score that emerges organically and defines the world of *The Producers*. And it's also deeply funny. Brooks' lyric writing is endlessly clever, but it never needs to announce this fact.

What shouldn't be underestimated in Brooks' work is his politically and socially minded agenda. *The Producers* is a social farce with political undertones, wrapped up in a 'showbiz' musical. In a 2018 NPR article, Susan Stamberg states that

> Brooks has made a career of poking fun at horrible things: Hitler, racial prejudice, anti-Semitism. He says that's the job. 'The comedy writer is like the conscience of the king…He's got to tell him the truth. And that's my job: to make terrible things entertaining.'
>
> *(Stamberg 2018)*

## Farce and the Theatrical Adaptation

It is not uncommon for us to see contemporary reworkings of classical or 'canon plays.' The Greeks remain a constant source of inspiration for contemporary playwrights, adapting the stories of Oedipus or Medea and relocating them to contemporary locations. Playwrights continue to return time and again to Ibsen, Strindberg, Chekhov, and Shakespeare; not only translating but adapting these works for contemporary audiences. Historically speaking, playwrights have been drawn to either dramas or tragedies in order to comment on contemporary issues. Yet the 21st century has seen a number of successful farces, adapted from theatrical sources, including *other* farces. Some have adhered closely to the original material, hewing to plot and character. Others used the original as a jumping-off point to tell a new story. These farces transcended their original material through the distinct voice of their playwright or the circumstances/context in which the plays have been set.

### *Phil Porter:* Vice Versa *(2017)*

In 2017, the Royal Shakespeare Company programmed the majority of their season around 'Rome.' Alongside Shakespeare's 'Roman' tragedies, *Antony & Cleopatra, Coriolanus, Julius Caesar,* and *Titus Andronicus,* the RSC also produced *Salome, Dido of Carthage,* and also the world premiere of Mike Poulton's *Imperium: The Cicero Plays,* a six-play adaptation based on novelist Robert Harris's "The Cicero Trilogy." On paper, it was a season that tipped the scales towards more serious subject matter. To offset the political intrigue, assassinations, and high body count of the tragedies, the company offered British playwright Phil Porter's new play *Vice Versa (or The Rise and Fall of General Braggadocio at the Hands of his Canny Servant Dexter and Terence the Monkey)* as a farcical antidote. Porter was commissioned by the RSC to:

> …write something funny. They suggested I look at [Roman playwright] Plautus for inspiration and possible adaptation, which I was very happy to do as I'd enjoyed reading Plautus at university…With Pippa Hill, the RSC's Senior Dramaturg, I looked at a few plays, and *Miles Gloriosus* seemed the most exciting – the vain and boastful General at the centre of it seemed like a great character to be engaging with in the era of Trump, Putin and soon-to-be PM Boris [Johnson]. I guess the result is somewhere between adaptation and 'inspired by'. The first half of *Vice Versa* is quite true to *Miles Gloriosus* in its plotting. The second half is almost entirely my invention, based on the foundations created in the first. But most of all I was interested in capturing the anarchic, bawdy essence that leaps off the page from a good Plautus translation – something much sweatier, grubbier, rougher, more direct than the Feydeau plays that were my introduction to the genre.
> *(Porter 2022)*

Stories featuring a 'Miles Gloriosus-type' character (i.e. the not-too-bright, self-involved, 'braggart soldier') have appeared throughout theatre history in one form or another. This stock character can be found in various guises in Shakespeare, Moliere, *commedia dell'arte*, through contemporary works by Richard Bean, Martin McDonagh, and Ken Ludwig. Variations on the character even appear in sitcoms like *The Mary Tyler Moore Show, Community*, and *What We Do in the Shadows.* One of the most popular adaptations of Plautus's work, featuring the Gloriosus character, is the Stephen Sondheim, Larry Gelbart and Burt Shevelove musical *A Funny Thing Happened on the Way to the Forum*.

Porter's farce *Vice Versa* begins with Dexter, a wily servant, catching us up with an expositional prologue, presented in rhyming couplets no less. We find out her master, Valentin, was called away, and her mistress Voluptua has been kidnapped and held by General Miles Braggaddocio, as his concubine. Attempting to track down her master, Dexter's boat is captured by pirates (as is usually the case), coincidentally finds herself reunited with Voluptua, and is subsequently gifted as a slave to Braggadocio (whom the pirates apparently owed a favour). She is forced to work in Braggadocio's household with two other servants, Feclus (who is pretty feckless) and Omnivorous (who's usually hungry), and a mischievous monkey named Terrence. Dexter and Voluptua get word to Valentin, who promptly returns and moves in with Braggadocio's neighbour, Philoproximus, an elderly lawyer. To help reunite the young lovers, Dexter re-engineers the attic skylights of the two homes so Voluptua and Valentin can sneak across their respective roofs to be one with one another, hoping they can all be free from the bonds of Braggadocio.

Things grow dire after Voluptua is spotted in a state of undress by Feclus in Philoproximus' home, and proceeds to share the news with Braggadocio about his mistress's infidelity. Dexter and company scheme to protect the young lovers from the imbecilic, jealous General. The play's comic chicanery includes men pretending to be statues, and Voluptua pretending to be her own non-existent twin Greek sister (whose language is dominated by words such as hummus and souvlaki, and whose accent is over the top). Much fun is had at the expense of Feclus, double entendres are spewed, anachronisms are tossed, alcohol is imbibed, songs are sung, dances are danced, and pea soup is unceremoniously dumped on a certain General. In the end, lovers are reunited, servants are set free, and Braggadocio is left alone with the person he loves the most…himself.

Unlike the original source material or previous adaptations of Plautus, Porter's play empowers the female characters. They are not 'empty-headed', simple objects of desire, or shrewish. Instead, the female characters in the play are clever and driven; they take control of the situation, and 'own' the men.

One can see the echoes of Donald Trump and others in the characterization of Braggadocio. The General's narcissism exemplifies power-infatuated leaders who cannot see past their own nose. We delight in seeing them get their comeuppance. Although insults have flown, pain has been inflicted, and Romans have behaved badly, a farce like *Vice Versa* leaves us smiling. Porter offers this:

> I think a lot of the best farce productions engender a feeling of "why do I feel so warmly towards these various appalling characters?!" The answer, I suppose, is that we feel grateful to them for making us feel happy.
> 
> *(Porter 2022)*

### *Taylor Mac:* Gary – A Sequel to Titus Andronicus *(2019)*

Over the years well-known (or little-known) characters from classic plays, especially Shakespeare, have provided comedic inspiration to playwrights. The popularity of the 'Falstaff' character (a favourite of Queen Elizabeth's) in Shakespeare's *Henry IV Parts I & II*, led him to write *The Merry Wives of Windsor*, a 'stand-alone' farcical comedy around the 'Fat Knight.' In Canadian playwright Ann-Marie MacDonald's 1988 comedy *Goodnight Desdemona (Good Morning Juliet)*, university professor Constance Ledbelly uncovers a manuscript that might offer insight into the original sources for both *Othello* and *Romeo and Juliet*. Magically, she is transported back to the Elizabethan Age, where she finds herself caught up in the middle of both plays, taking on the archetypal character of the 'Fool', and, in the process, potentially altering the outcome of two of Shakespeare's great tragedies. Paula Vogel's *Desdemona: A Play About a Handkerchief* is a serio-comic retelling of *Othello* from the empowered perspectives of Desdemona, Emilia, and Bianca.

One of the most popular instances of reframing a Shakespeare tragedy for comic purposes is Tom Stoppard's 1966 play *Rosencrantz and Guildenstern are Dead*, a play that has been referred to as 'existential' or 'absurdist' through its invitation to audiences to see the story of *Hamlet* through the eyes of two of its minor characters, Hamlet's schoolfriends Rosencrantz and Guildenstern. With nods to both Samuel Beckett and Luigi Pirandello, Stoppard portrays these two comic characters as innocents, searching for meaning and understanding in a world where they seem to possess no discernible identity. Yet the two persist in their charge, even if

> Stoppard concedes that we are stuck in the middle of a world that is hard to understand. It might even be that we will never understand the really important things in life, but that does not mean the universe is meaningless…is our inability to uncover life's persistent questions really a bad thing?
>
> *(Demastes 50)*

Queer playwright, actor, performance artist, and drag performer Taylor Mac (who uses the pronouns 'he' and 'judy') has become one of the most provocative commentators of contemporary culture in the 21st century. Citing Charles Ludlam and the aesthetics of the Ridiculous Theatre as an influence (including a mutual affection for satire and pastiche), Mac's work draws on

> the Ridiculous genre by employing it as a tool for political satire and radical commentary…extend[ing] his approach to the Ridiculous sensibility into a broader context that attempts to address all Americans in the paradigmatic search for national identity in the post-9/11 era.
>
> *(Edgecomb 127)*

Although drag is Mac's predominant form of performance expression, he considers himself more in line with the archetypal character of the 'Fool.' In a 2008 *American Theatre* interview with Caridad Svich, Mac describes the Fool as:

> …a person who speaks truths that others, who do not have such a phantasmagorical aesthetic, are unable to get away with speaking. The Fool is dismissed as insane or is confused with the clown (an entertainer), and so the listener lets his or her guard down. It is when this happens that the Fool can present a truth not usually spoken – and the listener, endeared to the Fool, will actually listen. The Fool is a perpetual outsider. A shaman. A queer. And a queer is not exclusively or merely a homosexual but…a person who at an early age was ostracized by society to such a degree that [they] could never possibly ostracize another human being. The Fool brings an understanding of the social contract because [they were] born into it, but has the ability to release people from the social contract because [they were] rejected from it and can see what's on the outside.
>
> *(Svich 2008)*

The character of the Fool takes his rightful place in Mac's 2019 phantasmagoric comedy *Gary: A Sequel to Titus Andronicus* (2019), helping us make sense of a world that often feels like it has descended into nonsense. Mixing a variety of comic forms, including satire, farce, slapstick, vaudeville, and clowning, Mac has given contemporary audiences an allegory for our times. He has fashioned a world within which those with power have abused it, left chaos and destruction in their wake, and forced the powerless to pick up the pieces.

Set in the bloody aftermath of the events portrayed at the end of Shakespeare's tragedy, *Titus Andronicus*, *Gary* takes place in the 'opulent' banquet room of recently deceased Roman General Titus Andronicus. Following the recent coup, it is now filled from floor to ceiling with 1,000 corpses of soldiers, senators, and other civilians. Mac specifically states, though, that we should never see the bodies of any women or children.

Our protagonist, Gary, known only as 'Clown' in Shakespeare's play (and who only appears briefly in two scenes), was tasked to deliver a letter from Titus to Emperor Saturninus. Upon receiving the letter, Saturninus orders 'Clown' to be taken away and executed.

Taylor was interested in exploring what happened to this seemingly innocuous character after he was sentenced to hang. In this sequel, we find out Gary's life was spared, and he was promoted from clown to maid, in order to help clean up the mess. Working alongside Janice, the lone surviving maid from the coup (who apparently 'worked' the Ides of March), the two must clean and remove the bodies. An inauguration banquet for the new Emperor is scheduled for the morning; if they have not finished cleaning the hall by this time, they will be executed.

As the two maids work through the night, syphoning 'bodily fluids' and manipulating the corpses in order to help them expel excess gas, they carry on a scatological vaudeville act. In this they are joined by Carol, a midwife, who spends the evening staunching blood spurting from her slit throat, while bemoaning 'her inability to save the baby' (whom we take to be the bastard child of Shakespeare's Aaron and Tamora).

Gary, an aspiring court 'Fool', aka "a clown with ambition" (Mac 20), sees this job as a gateway to fulfil his comic destiny. Gary surmises

> now that I got a job in a fancy place, I could find me way to court, couldn't I? Become one of them blokes who changes the minds of Emp'rors. Someone who gets a promotion from clown, to maid, to Fool.
>
> *(Mac 23)*

As the evening wears on, the two maids remove entrails, mop the floors, and, in Gary's case, puppet the penises of the corpses. They regale each other with "…pseudo-philosophical speeches about societal power imbalances, how the little people are so often forced (literally in this case) to clean up after the bigwigs and the transformative power of art" (Scheck 2019). Halfway through the play, with the prospect of death looming, Gary proposes an 'Act of Fooling' (a Fooling being a new genre) that would leave an indelible mark on those who witness it, and in the process bring an end to tragedy. Gary pitches it as:

> …its own kind of coup…Not a violent coup. An artistic one. A sort of theatrical revenge on the Andronicus revenge. A comedy revenge to end all revenge. Well not just a comedy. A sorta folly. No a spectacle. Or a comedy folly that is a spectacle. Sorta a machination. That's full of laughter. But more than laughs. But with laughs. Well sorta a thinking man's laughter. But could be a knee-slapper.
>
> *(Mac 29)*

With Janice's help, they construct a Rube Goldberg-like contraption from the appendages, intestines, and genitalia of the dead. When it's 'released', it creates a ridiculous, show-stopping, chain reaction, domino impact. It is a bold 'artistic statement' that Gary hopes will touch those attending the inauguration. Optimistically, Gary believes:

> If two maids can turn the hopelessness of a massacre into a coup of beauty, they too can imagine a better world. New ways of government will spring forth, new mechanisms of distribution…laying themselves prostrate to servants, making love to enemies and outsiders, bleeding their hearts, flooding through the streets, until the entire world is saved by…WONDER!
>
> *(Mac 30)*

One could say *Gary* is Taylor Mac's 'Fooling.' Known as a 'downtown' theatre artist, the play was Mac's Broadway debut. Actor Nathan Lane, who originated the role of Gary, said "I love the fact that I don't know how people will respond…It's much quirkier and darker. We're doing a downtown show uptown…That's either going to be refreshing to people or bewildering" (Fierberg 2019). Contained within a structure featuring a host of comedic styles, Mac also writes in iambic pentameter, rhyme, and song.

In a subsequent interview, Lane goes on to say,

> It's about taking a risk…Taylor is a brilliant mind, but has a theatrical agenda. Part of the agenda is, I'm not here to make you comfortable, in fact, I might be here to make you uncomfortable and yet we're still going to have a lot of fun.
>
> *(Fierberg 2019)*

Speaking with the *New Yorker* in 2019, Mac said, "Right now, in our political system, we're living in a kind of revenge tragedy…We're trapped in a cycle where conflict is created and escalated and then created again; we're chasing sensation" (Pollack-Pelzner 2019).

Like Lucy Kirkwood's *Tinderbox*, although set in the distant past, Mac presents us with a shattered world that is the result of greed, corruption, and the abuse of political power. Who pays the price? The people. In his words,

> All of us have to clean up after our particular political system that's falling apart right now. Eventually, we are going to have to pick up the pieces rather than just continue to fight each other. 'What is that going to look like?' and 'Who is going to do it?' and 'How are we going to do it?' is the bigger question.
>
> *(Fierberg 2019)*

Mac has Janice echo this sentiment, when she points out to Gary who is blind to the reality facing him:

> JANICE: When ya refuse to pick up a mess so people see the error of their ways, they don't see the error, they get accustomed to it. They start thinking it's normal, and when something is normal it's your identity and when it's your identity, anybody who tries making something different out of normal things is trying to make you different and when someone is trying to make you different ya feel ya need to defend yourself, so what do you do? Ya make an even bigger massacre!
>
> *(Mac 43)*

*Gary* was Mac's response to the political turmoil shaped by the Trump presidency. Instead of focusing on those in charge,

Mac shifts the point of the play from exposing the excesses of power to the needs and dreams of the exploited general population. As a result, the human dimension endures through the gags: when Janice bemoans the plight of her mistress, Lavinia – she is raped and dismembered in the Shakespeare – it's genuinely poignant.

*(Karren 2022)*

Through the spectre of death and destruction, political upheaval, and debris, Mac offers hope through laughter. In Gary, we see a man who desperately wants to make the world laugh in the face of tragedy.

Clowns, fools, and jesters invite us to look at the world through their unique, innocent and uncensored perspectives. These characters appear throughout history, finding amusement in pain, using humour to point up humanity's flaws, and highlighting political and social tensions. We see it in the working-class comics of Trevor Griffiths' *Comedians* (1975) as they try to make a name for themselves as stand-up comedians; in the Elizabethan fool 'Lucius' who unwittingly gets caught up in political skullduggery against Elizabeth I in Stephen Jeffreys' satirical-farce *The Clink* (1991); or in 'Joss', an aspiring female comic, who must disguise herself as a man, in order to be taken seriously in the male-dominated, mediaeval world of 'Court Fools', in Theresa Rebeck's 2014 farce, *Fool*. Clowns, fools, and jesters teach us something about ourselves through their irreverence and comic bravery. They are stand-ins for the audience, saying and doing the things we wish we had the courage to. True, they sometimes cause more chaos in the process, but their commitment to enlightenment through laughter, and bringing light to a dark and disordered world, is rarely about them. It's about cleansing the muddy, and distilling the complicated to the simple.

Reimagining or 'resetting' a classic play requires consideration of at least three points of view: the play's original context, a contemporary point of view, and how the new setting is in dialogue with present-day audiences. We have seen playwrights take canon works and update them. By doing this, it can link past and present, with history helping us make sense of the world we live in. We can see how far we have (or haven't) evolved as a society. Over the years we have seen many successful adaptations of classic texts, including three Pulitzer Prize-winners: Jonathan Larson's *Rent* (based on Puccini's opera *La bohème*), Lynn Nottage's *Ruined* (based on Brecht's *Mother Courage and Her Children*), and, most recently, James Ijames' *Fat Ham* (based on *Hamlet*). Yet, we have seen far fewer classic comedies whose plots have been transposed or re-set in another time period, including the present day.

Tom Stoppard's farces *On the Razzle* and *Rough Crossing* are 'free' adaptations of Johann Nestroy's *Einen Jux will er sich machen* (which also inspired Wilder's *The Matchmaker* and the musical *Hello Dolly!*) and Ferenc Molnar's *Jatek a kastelyban*. These adaptations are characterised more so by Stoppard's characteristic brand of humorous dialogue, though the latter play was relocated to an ocean liner from its original 'palatial house' on the Italian Riviera. American playwright Aaron Posner has adapted two plays by Anton Chekhov, finding parallel resonances and absurdity within their contemporary settings. In both *Life Sucks* (based on *Uncle Vanya*), and *Stupid Fucking Bird* (based on *The Seagull*) Posner saturates his works with corrosive humour and emotional heft. He clearly has a strong affection for the source material, but is never beholden to it, often breaking the fourth wall with theatrical panache.

The reason that there might be a shortage for these types of farces is perhaps because of contemporary views on domestic, social or political issues, or advancements in technology which undermine the conceits that define the original writing, thereby lessening the stakes and the comedy. However, this did not stop British playwright Richard Bean from crafting one of the most popular and critically acclaimed farces of the 21st century.

### *Richard Bean:* One Man, Two Guvnors *(2011)*

In 2011, the National Theatre's Artistic Director, Nicholas Hytner, sought a play that would help balance a summer season that "looked particularly grim: Chekhov, Ibsen, Jacobean tragedy, the Ipswich serial killer" (Hytner 258). Hytner was looking to collaborate again with actor James Corden, and floated the idea to his season planning team. Sebastian Born, the National's literary manager, recommended Carlo Goldoni's 18th-century comedy *The Servant of Two Masters*. Hytner, who hadn't read the script since he had performed in it back in school, wasn't "interested in re-creating the world of commedia dell'arte…[or] dress James as a harlequin" (259) but began thinking of ways to capitalise on Corden's abilities. Asking himself what was "the English low-comedy equivalent of Italian low comedy? It could have a whiff of end-of-the pier farce, and the 'Carry On' films, and Ealing comedy" (259). Hytner saw the opportunity to combine the performer/audience by-play that characterised the source material with the variety acts that used to tour seaside towns during the 1960s.

Richard Bean, with whom Hytner had recently collaborated on a successful adaptation of the Dion Boucicault farce *London Assurance*, was enlisted to write the play. The two of them agreed that setting the play in 1960s Brighton offered "the energy, colour and music" (Hopkins 484) of the era.

In May 2011, the National Theatre premiered *One Man, Two Guvnors*. Transposed from 18th-century Venice, Italy, to Brighton, England circa 1963, Bean's robust farce hews close to Goldoni's original structure, while capturing the 'spirit' of *commedia dell'arte* in its characterisations and improvisational repartee between performer and audience. Lazzis (i.e. comic business or 'set pieces') abound, demanding expert timing, demonstrations of wild physical comedy, and the verbal dexterity of the Marx Brothers. This all had to be performed with not only clarity, but also effortlessness. Hytner brought physical comedy expert Cal McCrystal on board as his associate director (he was credited on Broadway as 'Physical Comedy Director') to help work out the intricacies of the comedy.

The 'servant' in question is Francis Henshall, who has been recently fired from the skiffle band he founded. Francis is hired as a 'minder' by Roscoe Crabbe ('Guvnor #1), a London hood who has unexpectedly come to Brighton to collect a £6000 debt from Charlie "The Duck" Clench, the father of Roscoe's fiancée Pauline. Roscoe's arrival is unexpected because everyone believed that Roscoe had been murdered. Pauline is now engaged to Alan, an aspiring actor, who does not take kindly to Roscoe's arrival.

We soon learn that 'Roscoe' is none other than his twin sister 'Rachel', pretending to be 'Roscoe' in order to collect the money. This throws a wrench into the engagement plans of Pauline and Alan. Complications mount when Stanley Stubbers, Rachel's boyfriend, and the man responsible for killing Roscoe, arrives in Brighton to hide from the police. He hopes to reunite with Rachel (even though he has killed her brother). Francis, who is in a perpetual state of hunger throughout Act I, has a chance meeting with Stanley, which results in Francis being hired on to serve a second 'Guvnor.' With the promise of more money and therefore more food, Francis must now juggle two Guvnors, ensuring that neither finds out about the other. As he digs a deeper hole for himself, mixing up letters and steamer trunks, while creating a fictional character named 'Paddy' upon whom to blame his actions, Francis finds himself embroiled in escalating dilemmas. Act I culminates in a madcap set piece with Francis and the waitstaff of two, attempting to serve dinner to both guvnors simultaneously. Striving to keep his two guvnors from discovering one another, amid swinging doors and constantly appearing food, he is further distracted by the presence of Alfie. Alfie is an 87-year-old, almost deaf, slow-moving waiter who endures countless mishaps. He is knocked over, whacked across the face, has his pacemaker abused, and falls down a flight of stairs multiple times. The good news is, by the end of Act I, Francis finally gets to eat.

With a satiated belly (at least for now), Francis must find a new objective for Act 2. With the reappearance of Dolly (an employee of Charlie's), whom Francis shamelessly flirted with upon their first meeting, his motivation stems from his loins. In a private, metatheatrical aside with the audience, Francis asks us if we "see how *commedia dell'arte* works? In the first half I'm driven by my animal urges, hunger, but in this second half, because I've eaten, I am humanised, civilised, and I can embrace the potentiality of love" (Bean 73). As Francis tries to win a date with Dolly, he continues to find himself entangled in everyone's romantic and financial knots.

All is reconciled by the end. Stanley has been given a legal 'out' for killing Roscoe, Rachel receives her money, three pairs of lovers are brought together, and the entire cast sums up the play's outcome with the song 'Tomorrow Looks Good From Here'.

Approaching this new adaptation of *The Servant of Two Masters*, Bean acknowledged that "the main problem was to find a new central framing. What needed to change in order for the play to have currency for a modern audience?" (Hopkins 484). The first decision was re-setting the play in 1960s Brighton, "a sort of weekend retreat for mods, where you would find gangsters, crooks, a seedy underworld, violence, death, and gangs" (485). The 'arranged marriage' plot device that drove Goldoni's play also needed to be re-thought for a 21$^{st}$-century audience (and 1960s setting). Bean latched onto the idea of a 'lavender marriage', "when a gay man marries a straight woman to mask his true identity" (485). Added into the mix is a bit of blackmail, raising the stakes for Charlie who has agreed to support the sham marriage in order to pay off a debt to Rachel and Roscoe's father.

Drawing on the improvisational nature of *commedia* throughout the performance Francis often breaks the fourth wall, directly addressing and/or interacting with the audience. At various moments we are his confidant, ally, and even assistants. These interactions become important because they set up 'theatrical magic tricks' later on. At one point volunteers are recruited from the audience to help Francis move a trunk. At another, in an attempt to feed his hunger, Francis asks if anyone in the audience has a sandwich. Finally, an audience member is asked to guard a tureen of leftover soup for Francis. This same audience member gets roped into the dinner scene as an extended prop. At the end of the act, a Crepe Suzette goes up in flames and our poor audience member is not only doused with water but also covered from head to toe with fire extinguisher foam. We are initially shocked, but soon realise all is not as it seems, as the line between what's real and what is 'performance' becomes blurred.

In addition to many of the classic farce tropes, *One Man, Two Guvnors* revels not only in the slapstick violence (including one comic lazzi that sees Francis literally engaging in fisticuffs with himself), but showcases a level of wit in the dialogue that runs the gamut from clever to absurd.

The text is propelled by wordplay, non-sequiturs, and running gags. Numerous scenes feel like comedy double-acts, hearkening back to the old school British comedians referenced in Terry Johnson's *Dead Funny*. The following exchange between Francis and Stanley epitomises this aspect of the play:

*Stanley:* What did he die of?
*Francis:* He was diagnosed with diarrhoea but died of diabetes.
*Stanley:* He died of diabetes did he?
*Francis:* He did, didn't he?
*Stanley:* Were you there?

> *Francis:* When?
> *Stanley:* When he was diagnosed with diarrhoea but died of diabetes.
> *Francis:* No, I was in Didcot, and he was diagnosed with diarrhoea but died of diabetes in Dagenham.
>
> *(Bean 75)*

Music was known to be incorporated into *commedia dell'arte* scenarios, whether it was incidental music or songs accompanied by dance. Additionally, characters might enter singing a song, playing a guitar, or serenading a lover under a balcony. Bean recommended to Hytner that they draw on the popularity of skiffle music from the 1960s, incorporating it into the event of the performance. Skiffle, a kind of folk music that originated in early 20th-century America, was adopted by British musicians in the 1950s, including John Lennon, Mick Jagger, and Van Morrison, finding favour among many who would go on to make names for themselves as pop-rock artists.

Grant Olding, the composer, lyricist, and original lead singer of the onstage band, 'The Craze', wrote fifteen original tunes for the play, capturing the 'upbeat' skiffle sound, which was driven by guitar, bass, percussion, washboard, and tight harmonies. The Craze both functioned as a pre-show, warm-up act for the audience, and also offered musical entertainment during the interval. The band also accompanied cast members who came out in character during transitions and performed songs or 'specialty acts' (like the ones seen during a summer seaside season in Brighton), that slyly commented on or anticipated events in the play.

Artist and teacher Didi Hopkins, who was Bean's *commedia* advisor, states that in the case of *One Man, Two Guvnors*, Bean "has transformed what was, for some, an arch, archaic and antique tradition into something that now has currency for a modern audience. He has resurrected Commedia and offers a new template for the twenty-first century" (Hopkins 489).

When asked to comment on the play's continued popularity, Bean says,

> There's no messaging in the play. There's no playwright behind it saying that you're bad, you're wrong, you're privileged, and the world needs to change in order to right these injustices. It is the human condition laid bare. The first thing we learn as human beings is that we're idiots - we can't walk, we can't talk, we can't drive a car, we poo our pants - we must be idiots, and that stays with us. Put a lovable idiot on stage and deep down we recognise ourselves.
>
> *(Bean 2020)*

(Interestingly, Bean returned to classic source material in late 2022, with the National Theatre's premiere of Bean's and Oliver Chris's new farce *Jack Absolute Flies Again*, based on Richard Brinsley Sheridan's 18th-century play *The Rivals*. Updated to July 1940, their adaptation focuses on a group of RAF pilots who must balance their romantic rivalries with their military responsibilities.)

## Farce and the Cultural Icon

Cultural icons throughout history have inspired numerous late 20th- and 21st-century farces, offering playwrights the chance to filter serious themes through significant characters, populating well-known or little-known historical or cultural events. In the process, issues related to the following are explored: art, science, religion, legacy, politics, and gender.

### *Terry Johnson:* Hysteria *(1993)*

What happens when the father of psychology encounters the (arguably) most famous painter of the surrealist movement? Terry Johnson's 1993 play *Hysteria (or Fragments of an Analysis of an Obsessional Neurosis)*, reimagines an actual meeting that took place between a cancer-stricken Dr. Sigmund Freud and the artist Salvador Dali, as a farce. Set in November of 1938 in London's Hampstead, on the eve of Kristallnacht, Freud (who had recently fled Vienna from the Nazis), is interrupted one rainy night by a drenched Jessica, a young woman from the local college, seeking answers regarding her mother, one of Freud's patients from thirty years ago.

Freud invites her in, and, as they converse, she (much to Freud's chagrin) gradually removes her soaked clothing. His physician, Abraham Yehuda, has been imploring Freud to retire for the sake of his health. Meanwhile, a scheduled appointment with Salvador Dali looms, and Freud spends the entire evening trying to hide the girl from both Yehuda and the libidinous surrealist.

Johnson's play "raises the question of the relationship between farce and tragedy, laughter and insight. Freud is dying from cancer of the jaw, and we are laughing at a dying man's visions, expressive of his disquiet and fear" (Gilleman 113). Towards the end of the play, as Freud's morphine-induced state sees the farce turn nightmarish, a series of escalating stage directions drawn from the dream-like surrealist works of Dali, describe how Freud

> goes for the door. He pulls the handle, but the door has become rubber-like. It bends without opening", "Freud picks up the phone. It turns into a lobster", and "The clock strikes. Freud, terrified, compares his watch. The clock melts."
> *(Johnson 71–72)*

A 2013 revival confirmed

there is far more to Johnson's confection than mere laughter and clever jokes involving underwear and Freudian slips. It shows us that farce is a very serious business, drawing on subconscious fears and long-buried repressions. This is, after all, a drama that takes us from dropped trousers to the gates of Auschwitz, and where the naked woman in the closet is asking hard questions about why, after developing a theory that the distress of many of his female patients arose from sexual abuse within the family, Freud subsequently recanted.

*(Gardner 2013)*

### *Itamar Moses:* **Bach at Leipzig *(2005)***

The year is 1722. Johann Kuhnau, the celebrated organist of the Thomaskirche in Leipzig, Germany, dies unexpectedly, and his position becomes one of the most coveted in Europe. With seven of the best organists in Germany vying for it, *Bach at Leipzig* (2005), by the American playwright Itamar Moses, is literally a fugue-like farce that structurally echoes the musical form practised by the musicians in the play. Two characters have a scene together. One propositions the other with a 'deal'. That person subsequently has a scene with a new character who enters the room, and propositions them with their own offer. Moses builds on a theme and adds the complications. Speaking about his inspiration for the play, Moses says,

> Bach was always my favourite composer. His music is so highly constructed, it's almost mathematically perfect. And a comedy of manners is also highly constructed, almost musical in its setups and payoffs, so I could use it as a kind of Baroque form.
>
> *(Berson 2005)*

More witty and bawdy than knockabout (save for the penultimate scene which is filled with chases and swordplay), Moses' elegant farce showcases men in strident times. Whether it's providing their families with economic stability, having the opportunity to be artistically and musically daring, or proving themselves a force to be reckoned with, obtaining this position means something different to each of them. The stakes could not be higher.

Based on real people and events, three different 'Johanns' and three different 'Georgs' compete for the open position, leading to both nomenclature confusion and high levels of scheming, including blackmail, bribery, betrayal… and attempted murder.

When dust and egos have settled, Johann Sebastian Bach has quietly swooped in and been hired as the new organist. The others move on, having learnt more about themselves and those they love.

*Bach at Leipzig* is a historical, cultural farce that uses rapier wit and physical humour to grapple with issues of religion and faith, artistic bravery, and ambition. What could have been a dry lesson in classical music history, instead becomes a means of underlining the lengths we go to in order to earn being seen as 'artists.' It is about jealousy and how we reconcile personal happiness with striving for excellence in our chosen art form.

It is also about validation. Each character sees this potential position as validation of the hard work they have invested in their chosen profession. Without it, they are simply 'second best', relegated to being one who 'never rose to the occasion' or met their true potential.

Moses crafted a farce that humanises differences and invites us to see the divides in our own country. Written during the Bush era, and in the wake of 9/11, the US was (and continues to be) a divided place. The play highlights various schisms and the extreme behaviours we exhibit when obsessed.

### Liz Duffy Adams: Or, (2009)

American playwright Liz Duffy Adams has three actors portray a handful of cultural icons, concocting the Restoration-era play *Or,*. Having recently been released from debtors' prison by a disguised King Charles II, the novelist, poet, spy, and would-be playwright Aphra Behn is on a deadline. Trying to complete her first play by morning, Behn must juggle her writing, with attending to the needs of her three lovers, including the actress Nell Gwynne, the aforementioned King Charles II, and William Scot, her ex-lover and another spy whom she thought was dead, but who is very much alive and intent on murdering the king.

Combining comedy of manners, bawdy anachronisms, and elements of the domestic 'sex farce', Adams has crafted a comedy that celebrates the

> …hope and change of the 1660s, 1960s and 2008 against the background of a long, unpopular [Civil] war and the fear of religious terrorists (Catholic, in this case) promised a special place in heaven. Hope prevails, in great waves of laughter…
>
> *(Hurwitt 2010)*

The title of the play comes from a dictum laid out by the 'impresario', Lady Davenant, who is keen on producing Behn's work but says she will not have "one of those 'or' titles, you know what I mean, one of those greedy get-it-all-in titles, 'the something something OR what you something,'…they take up half the poster and the typesetter charges by the word, make up your mind and pick one, thank you…" (Adams 31). For contemporary 'or' examples, please see *Hysteria* and *POTUS*.

The unintentional subtext in Lady Davenant's comment, beyond the superficial annoyance of a long title, is the notion that we have to choose to be 'one thing', to be with 'one type of person', to define ourselves in a narrow way. The 'Or,' reminds audiences that there is more to us than one label. That we can be 'this' *or* that. Adams allows Behn to enjoy multiple vocations, to write what inspires her, and to take lovers of any gender without feeling judgement.

Almost fifteen years on, the play remains "refreshing as a straight-out celebration of free love, as none of the main characters are the least bit monogamous and they make no bones about it.

But it's a celebration of so many things: of women, of sex, of writing, of the hope of a new era, and especially of theater" (Hurwitt 2010).

### *Steve Thompson:* **No Naughty Bits** *(2011)*

*No Naughty Bits* by Steve Thompson (*Whipping it Up*) fictionalises the real-life culture clash between one of the world's most popular sketch comedy ensembles, and corporate television.

In 1975, riding a crest of popularity in their native Britain, the six members of Monty Python were looking forward to the broadcast debut of their groundbreaking sketch comedy series *Monty Python's Flying Circus* on American television. Unfortunately, the show's premiere on ABC did not go as planned, as the network decided to cut out all of the 'naughty bits' from the show. Subsequently, the 'Pythons' sued ABC not

> for monetary damages; they were trying to prevent creative meddling, a non-economic and somewhat ethereal claim. To put it in a language a federal court would understand, [Terry] Gilliam and [Michael] Palin – the two Pythons who appeared in person – argued that the specials would essentially make their work unappealing, and adversely affect the sales of their albums and books.
>
> *(Rossen 2017)*

As the play interrogates issues of censorship, intellectual property, and artistic integrity, there is a scrutiny of the very nature of what constitutes 'funny' between two different cultures.

The play lands Palin and Gilliam stateside, as 'fishes-out-of-water', going toe to toe with network executives. Yet the true farce emerges in the courtroom, with the two Pythons forced to justify why their work is funny. The proceedings border on a sketch worthy of the Pythons, if it wasn't actively subverting the point of their comedy. Ironically, "what the play conveys superbly, and humorously, is the sense of how talking about comedy kills it stone dead" (Coveney 2011).

### A Few More Contemporary Cultural Farces

Based on the 1946 film by Ernst Lubitsch of the same name, British playwright Nick Whitby's 2008 adaptation of *To Be or Not to Be* feels as timely today as the original movie must have been when it premiered in cinemas just over 75 years ago. With a noticeable rise in antisemitic rhetoric, and white supremacist groups being enabled by far right leaders, we welcome stories about those using their art as a defiant form of resilience. Within this work comedy becomes an active weapon to disarm hate.

A character comedy with elements of farce, *To Be or Not to Be* takes place in the period 1939–1940, in Nazi-occupied Poland. A Warsaw theatre troupe, led by the husband and wife actors Joseph (a ham-fisted egotist) and Maria Tura (a diva), are trying to maintain their work in the wake of the Nazi invasion. Their most recent production, *A Gift from* Hitler, is shut down by censors, who fear the production will needlessly provoke the Nazis. When a plot is uncovered to quash the Polish resistance, the Turas and their eclectic ensemble of actors are enlisted by Polish Air Force Lieutenant Sobinsky to help prevent Silewsky, a double agent, from carrying out the Nazis' nefarious plan.

For us to invest in the plight of the characters, the stakes must again be high and we must believe they can do this – even if they're afraid. Speaking about his approach to the adaptation, Whitby writes that his

> real contribution as the play's adapter has been to realise that the Polish troupe at the heart of the story had to be credible as a genuine theatre company. On film this sense of reality could be created with mise-en-scène, in set-ups, details and background business etc, but on stage you can't do this. It must be in the script, embodied in the characters and the story.
>
> *(Whitby 2012)*

By the close of the play, utilising their costumes, sets, and necessary impersonations of Gestapo personnel, the troupe foils Silewsky's plan and finds their way out of Warsaw. *To Be or Not to Be* remains resonant today because it presents a group of people unifying, and using their artistry, to achieve a 'life or death' goal.

The German playwright David Gieselmann's black farce *Herr Kolpert* ("Mr. Kolpert") gleefully channels the work of Joe Orton, but is inspired by cinematic vocabulary. Bored twenty-somethings Ralf (a chaos researcher) and his girlfriend Sarah decide to enliven their evening by inviting Sarah's colleague Edith, and her husband Bastian, over for pizza, drinks, and Botticelli. The play takes a macabre turn when Ralf informs the couple that the trunk sitting in the middle of the room contains the corpse of Sarah and Edith's colleague, Mr. Kolpert. Is Ralf telling the truth? Or is a sick joke being played for personal entertainment? With pop cultural echoes of Alfred Hitchcock's *Rope*, Edward Albee's *Who's Afraid of Virginia Woolf?*, and an ending straight out of a Quentin Tarantino film, Gieselmann's play, written in 2000, invites audiences to consider the lengths they will go to in order to feel 'alive.' Reviewing the original production, Michael Billington wrote that Gieselmann seems to be "saying that in Germany, and elsewhere, there is an urban ennui and emotional deadness that drives people to ever greater extremes to discover lost feelings" (Billington 2001).

The 21st century has also seen a selection of adaptations that adhere closely to their source material, updating the setting or the language to reflect a contemporary voice. Sean Foley's *The Painkiller* (2011) is the first English-language adaptation of playwright Francis Veber's 1969 boulevard farce, *Le Contrat* ("The Contract"). Updated to contemporary England, suave hitman Ralph and meek photographer Brian have checked themselves into adjacent hotel rooms; each brought there because of the high-profile trial taking place across the street. Brian is there to photograph the proceedings. Ralph is there to assassinate an infamous gangster who has been summoned to testify. Brian is also suicidal, despondent about his wife leaving him for her psychiatrist. When Brian's first suicide attempt goes awry, Ralph is inadvertently pulled into Brian's situation by the hotel's porter. This does not bode well for Ralph, as a suicide would attract unwanted attention, and interrupt his task at hand. Soon Ralph finds himself playing rescuer instead of killer. As he works to keep Brian out of difficulty, and complete his 'job', Ralph and Brian's problems continue to mount with the arrival of a policeman, a psychiatrist, and Brian's wife, Michelle (who was called by the psychiatrist, and turns out to be the one for whom Michelle left Brian). Mistaken identities abound, confusion reigns, fights break out, clothes are exchanged, people are caught in various states of undress, and Ralph is injected with horse tranquiliser, causing him to lose all control of his body. At play's end, Brian has found new confidence and Ralph, unable to complete his contract, is reduced to tears.

Steve Martin's *The Underpants* (2002) is a faithful adaptation of German playwright Carl Sternheim's 1910 farce *Die Hose*. While she is watching a parade for the King, Louise's underpants accidentally fall down. Enraged and embarrassed, Louise's husband Theo is convinced that this public display will ruin them financially and make them social outcasts. Instead of being scandalised, multiple men soon appear at Louise and Theo's flat, vying to rent their open room (though really hoping to seduce Louise). Infused with Martin's trademark brand of absurd whimsy, ribaldry, and gentle insight, the play points up the negative aspects of celebrity and the perceived limits of gender roles.

At the beginning of this chapter, the question "Will they pull it off?" was offset by the question "How will they pull it off?" In many ways, this question is what makes cultural farce unique. With contemporary playwrights drawing on and reimagining cultural touchstones that include literature, film, theatre, and well-known figures from history, these works often carry much more expectation than the farces found behind our other four doors. Not only is cultural farce measured by the work onstage, but the play itself is under heightened scrutiny. In addition to whether the play works as a theatrical entity, the contemporary playwright must decide how to mine and transcend the source material, capturing the essence of (and at times baggage accompanying) the original work, while steering away from a plethora of in-jokes that may alienate audiences unfamiliar with the source.

The theatricalisation of a novel forces the writer to distil not only the story but also the language into an active and playable form. It is easier to find the farce in serious, epic novels rather than comedic ones. These pieces are ripe for parody and farce, oftentimes because of their length. Unlike with a novel, one cannot take their time watching a play. Speed and engagement become imperative.

Visuals are the earmarks of cinematic storytelling. As we've seen, this requires the contemporary playwright to rethink the detailed worlds conjured for cinema, in order to transpose the storytelling for the strictures of the stage. Within these limitations, playwrights can exploit the film medium for comedy, co-opting the audience as accomplices, and activating their imagination with transformative props and set-pieces. Like novels, films have beloved followings and, in many cases, are cherished for their artistry. Additionally, because they are so accessible, movies can reach a wider audience more quickly than either literature or theatre.

The contemporary playwright inspired by canon works must decide how to resituate the original play so that it speaks to today's audience. It need not be set in contemporary times, or be a direct adaptation, but there needs to be a strong point of view and an energy that resonates with and activates contemporary audiences.

Finally, as offered in farces such as *Hysteria* or *Bach at Leipzig* featuring cultural icons, these characters must be allowed to be silly, vulnerable, and questionably behaved. The comedy emerges from observing 'respected' or 'esteemed' characters thrust into recognisable situations which make them not only fallible, but humanised.

We readily see the allure of cultural farces. Their titles have name recognition, feature popular characters, and provide high-wire acts of artistry. When executed poorly, we question their purpose. No one wants to see a favourite work of art treated shabbily. However, when these 'remixed' farces 'find the funny and the heart', they leave audiences breathless.

## Works Cited

Adams, Liz Duffy. *Or,*. Dramatists Play Service, 2010.
Barlow, Patrick. *The 39 Steps*. Samuel French, 2009.
Barlow, Patrick. *Ben Hur*. Samuel French, 2012.
Basden, Tom (after Fyodor Dostoyevsky). *The Crocodile*. Nick Hern Books, 2015.
Bean, Richard. Email Interview. 13 Jul. 2020.
Bean, Richard. *One Man, Two Guvnors*. Oberon Books, 2011.
Bean, Richard, and Chris, Oliver. *Jack Absolute Flies Again*. Methuen Drama, 2022.
Bean, Richard, and Coleman, Clive. *Young Marx*. Oberon Books, 2017.
Berson, Misha. "What Would You Do to Beat out Bach?" *The Seattle Times*, 29 Apr. 2005, www.seattletimes.com/entertainment/what-would-you-do-to-beat-out-bach
Billington, Michael. "No Naughty Bits – Review." *The Guardian*, 26 Mar. 2020, www.theguardian.com/stage/2011/sep/14/no-naughty-bits-review

Billington, Michael. "Mr Kolpert." *The Guardian*, 20 Sept. 2017, www.theguardian.com/culture/2000/may/11/artsfeatures4

Coveney, Michael. WhatsOnStage. "No Naughty Bits." *WhatsOnStage.com* –, 22 June 2023, www.whatsonstage.com/west-end-theatre/reviews/no-naughty-bits_7024.html

Demastes, William. *The Cambridge Introduction to Tom Stoppard*. Cambridge University Press, 2012, p. 50.

Doyle, Sir Arthur Conan, Canny, Steve, and Nicholson, John (Adapters). *The Hound of the Baskervilles*. Nick Hern Books, 2015.

Edgecomb, Sean F. *Charles Ludlam Lives!*. University of Michigan Press, 2017, p. 127

Fierberg, Ruthie. "Taylor Mac Explains Broadway's Gary: A Sequel to Titus Andronicus." *Playbill*, 5 Jan. 2022, playbill.com/article/taylor-mac-explains-broadways-gary-a-sequel-to-titus-andronicus

Fierberg, Ruthie. "Why Nathan Lane Follows up Angels in America With Taylor Mac's Gary." *Playbill*, 16 Dec. 2021, playbill.com/article/why-nathan-lane-follows-up-angels-in-america-with-taylor-macs-gary

Fitzpatrick, Sean. "The Thirty-Nine Steps by John Buchan: The Importance of the Impossible." *Crisis Magazine*, 12 June 2014, crisismagazine.com/opinion/thirty-nine-steps-john-buchan-importance-impossible

Flaubert, Gustave, Nicholson, John, and Marzan, Javier. *The Massive Tragedy Madame Bovary!* Nick Hern Books, 2016.

Foley, Sean. *The Painkiller*. By Francis Veber. Nick Hern Books, 2011.

Fricker, Karen. "Variety." *Variety*, 16 Sept. 2011, variety.com/2011/legit/reviews/no-naughty-bits-1117946121

Gardner, Lyn. "Hysteria – Review." *The Guardian*, 26 Mar. 2020, www.theguardian.com/stage/2013/sep/13/hysteria-review

Gieselmann, David. *Mr. Kolpert*. Nick Hern Books, 2000.

Gilleman, Luc. "Terry Johnson's *Hysteria*: Laughter on the Abyss of Insight." *Theatre Symposium*, vol. 16, no. 1, Jan. 2008, pp. 110–120, https://doi.org/10.1353/tsy.2008.0011

Goodale, Robert, and David (under The Goodale Brothers). *Jeeves & Wooster in Perfect Nonsense*. Nick Hern Books, 2014.

Hemming, Sarah. "No Naughty Bits, Hampstead Theatre, London | Financial Times." *Financial Times*, www.ft.com/content/5b8f2e2a-debf-11e0-a228-00144feabdc0

Hopkins, Didi. "Roots and Routes." *The Routledge Companion to Commedia Dell'arte* (Edited by Judith Chaffee and Oliver Crick). Routledge, 2017.

Hurwitt, Robert and SFGATE. "'Or, Review: Liz Adams' Hilarious History Lesson." *SFGATE*, 12 Nov. 2010, www.sfgate.com/performance/article/Or-review-Liz-Adams-hilarious-history-lesson-3246275.php

Hurwitt, Sam. *A-Plus is for Aphra – The Idiolect*. theidiolect.com/theater/a-plus-is-for-aphra

Hytner, Nicholas. *Balancing Acts: Behind the Scenes at London's National Theatre*. Vintage Books, 2017.

Johnson, Terry. *Hysteria*. Methuen Drama, 1993.

Karren, Howard. "In Gary, a Shakespeare Sequel, WHAT Slays the Summertime Blues." *The Provincetown Independent*, Sept. 2022, provincetownindependent.org/arts-minds/2022/08/03/in-gary-a-shakespeare-sequel-what-slays-the-summertime-blues

Le Navet Bete. "Le Company." *lenavetbete.com*, 2016, lenavetbete.com

Locher, Whitney. Personal Interview. 28 Oct. 2020.

Ludwig, Ken. *Ken Ludwig's Baskerville: A Sherlock Holmes Mystery*. Samuel French, 2015.
Ludwig, Ken. *Ken Ludwig's The Game's Afoot or Holmes for the Holidays*. Samuel French, 2012.
Linehan, Graham. *The Ladykillers*. Samuel French Ltd., 2012.
Mac, Taylor. *Gary: A Sequel to Titus Andronicus*. Dramatists Play Service, 2019.
Martin, Steve (Adapter). *The Underpants*. By Carl Sternheim. Hyperion, 2002.
Moses, Itamar. *Back at Leipzig*. Faber and Faber, 2005.
Nicholson, John, and Le Navet Bete. *Dracula: The Bloody Truth*. Nick Hern Books, 2017.
Nicholson, John, and Le Navet Bete. *The Three Musketeers*. Nick Hern Books, 2019.
Nicholson, John, and Le Navet Bete. *Treasure Island*. Nick Hern Books, 2020.
Paice, Jill. Email Interview. 20 Aug. 2020.
Peepolykus. "What We Do." *peepolykus.com*, 2016, www.peepolykus.com
Pollack-Pelzner, Daniel. "In 'Gary: A Sequel to Titus Andronicus,' Taylor Mac Takes on Shakespeare—And Trump." *The New Yorker*, 20 Apr. 2019, www.newyorker.com/culture/culture-desk/in-gary-a-sequel-to-titus-andronicus-taylor-mac-takes-on-shakespeareand-trump
Porter, Phil. *Vice Versa*. Oberon Books, 2017.
Price, Mark. Personal Interview. 8 Aug. 2020.
Richardson, Jay. "It's Great – Now Make It Funnier: Interviews 2011: Chortle: The UK Comedy Guide." *Copyright Chortle 2023. All Rights Reserved.*, 20 May 2011, www.chortle.co.uk/interviews/2011/05/20/13328/its_great_%E2%80%93_now_make_it_funnier
Rossen, Jake. "When Monty Python Took American Television to Court | Mental Floss." *Mental Floss*, 6 June 2017, www.mentalfloss.com/article/501461/when-monty-python-took-american-television-court
Rustin, Sandy. *Clue*. Playscripts, 2020a.
Rustin, Sandy. Email Interview. 18 Jul. 2020b.
Scheck, Frank. "The Hollywood Reporter." *The Hollywood Reporter*, 22 Apr. 2019, www.hollywoodreporter.com/news/general-news/gary-a-sequel-titus4-andronicus-theater-review-1203525
Sheridan, Karen. Email Interview. 4 Sept. 2020.
Sierz, Aleks. *Good Nights Out: A History of Popular British Theatre Since the Second World War*. Methuen Drama, 2021. pp. 142–143.
Spencer, Charles. "Hysteria: Review." *Hampstead Theatre*, n.d., www.hampsteadtheatre.com/news/2013/09/hysteria-from-the-telegraph
Stamberg, Susan. "Mel Brooks Says It's His Job to 'Make Terrible Things Entertaining'." *NPR*, 26 Apr. 2018, www.npr.org/2018/04/26/605297774/mel-brooks-says-its-his-job-to-make-terrible-things-entertaining
Svich, Caridad. "Glamming It up with Taylor Mac." *AMERICAN THEATRE*, 19 Apr. 2019, www.americantheatre.org/2008/11/01/glamming-it-up-with-taylor-mac
Thompson, Steve. *No Naughty Bits*. Nick Hern Books, 2011.
Vogel, Paula. *Desdemona: A Play about a Handkerchief*. Dramatists Play Service, 1994.
Whitby, Nick. *To Be or Not to Be*. True West Ltd., 2012.

# 5
# BACKSTAGE FARCE

Theatre artists are a unique breed of people. The majority are paid little to do what they love, yet will go to extraordinary lengths to ensure the show will go on, even in the midst of catastrophe.

Audiences love watching shows about theatrical disasters. Even if they are not 'in-the-know' as theatre people, they recognize the blood, sweat, and make-up it takes to get ready for something, and the subsequent mishaps that take place when putting on a 'metaphorical show.' The 'show' could be preparing and serving a fancy dinner, creating and pitching a new product to potential investors, or conducting a research experiment. If we draw parallels with the theatre, rehearsals are the preparation and the presentation is the performance. At every step of the way, be it in the kitchen, the boardroom, or a laboratory, there is always the possibility that something will go wrong. The key is: how do we remain resilient when things go awry? Backstage farces help us understand a bit more about our humanity and relationship to survival in the face of disaster.

We look to the theatre as a beacon for overcoming. The plays and characters exemplifying this are found behind our final door, marked 'Backstage Farce'.

Backstage farces feature a collective of artists striving to put on a show, often in the face of pandemonium. The types of plays 'mounted' in these farces range from serious dramas to period pieces, mysteries to actual farces. For the characters in these pieces, putting on the show is a direct reflection of them as artists. Fragile egos, the fear of tarnished reputations, and potential fame and fortune motivate the characters in backstage farce. No one wants to fail, especially before an audience. Failure for such characters means admitting they are not good actors. It also causes them to face an existential crisis of professional identity. Who are they if they're not actors, writers, or directors? Being a part of the theatre consumes the characters in these plays. We are not interested in watching characters doing this for a hobby, or who have 'day jobs'. The theatre is their passion and their life. Without the theatre, these characters have no purpose. Without purpose, they have no place in the world. Those are the stakes.

Watching characters in a farce attempt to maintain decorum in public, when all is falling apart around them, is cause for much amusement. For this reason, dinner parties, government spaces, and workplace meetings, are ripe scenarios for farce. In backstage farces, there is considerable fun watching 'actors' attempt to maintain poise, even grace, while 'in character' as sets collapse, costumes malfunction, and offstage issues bleed onto the stage.

Playwrights delight in writing backstage farces as a delicious opportunity to skewer their profession and highlight how challenging, if not outright ridiculous, it can be to make theatre. These elements are what we come to love about such plays.

One of the most important aspects of this type of farce is, no matter how far proceedings spiral out of control, everyone is seeking a positive outcome. Even in Mel Brooks' *The Producers*, despite Max and Leo's efforts to mount a flop, everyone else involved with *Springtime for Hitler* truly believes they are making high art. And that is where the comedy flourishes.

The contemporary farces discussed in this chapter fall primarily into two major categories: Farce in Rehearsal and Farce in Performance. These are followed by a short selection of other backstage farces that spotlight understudies and critics, among others. To usher us in, we must consider the impact of Michael Frayn's play *Noises Off*, one of the finest farces ever written.

### Michael Frayn: Noises Off (1982)

> LLOYD: Think of the first night as a dress rehearsal. If we can just get through the play once tonight for doors and sardines. That's what it's all about. Doors and sardines. Getting on – getting off. Getting the sardines on – getting the sardines off. That's farce. That's the theatre. That's life.
>
> *(Frayn 20)*

One night, while watching his first play *The Two of Us* (1970) from the wings, British playwright Michael Frayn marvelled at the spectacle of his two actors running around backstage, having to make quicksilver costume changes, scurrying between multiple doors simply trying to make their entrance on time. In a profile for the *Washington Post* in 1983, Frayn discussed how fascinating it was to watch the backstage action of his play, and how, in its own way, it mirrored our own lives:

> We all do a certain amount of desperate fixing behind the scenes in order to keep a presentable social front going to the world. We all feel terrified when it's threatened. And I thought then that I'd like to do something about a farce seen from behind.
>
> *(Frayn 133–134)*

This would lead arguably to the most brilliant of farces, *Noises Off*. A farce about the staging of a farce that devolves into farce.

A three-act play, *Noises Off* is about a touring troupe of actors rehearsing and performing a cottage sex farce of the Whitehall variety, called "Nothing On". Although Frayn's play is regularly referred to as a 'farce', original director, Michael Blakemore, believes that "this is only half true. Up to the midpoint it is actually a comedy, involving real people in a real situation, namely a dress rehearsal" (Blakemore v). Act One introduces us to the company, each of whom have recognisable quirks: Lloyd, the philandering director; Dotty, the faded character actress; Gary, the inarticulate actor; Belinda, the busybody; Brooke, the inflexible blonde who keeps losing her contacts; Frederick, the fragile leading man whose nose bleeds whenever faced with confrontation; Poppy and Tim, the put-upon stage manager and assistant stage manager, respectively; and Selsdon, the 'seasoned' actor, an alcoholic who keeps disappearing. Losing their technical rehearsal due to a delay in the set's construction, the company finds itself on the play's unit living room set, the night before their official opening, simply trying to get through a dress rehearsal before facing a paying audience. Frayn uses this first act to plant the metaphorical bombs that we know will detonate later in the show, both on- and offstage. He sets up myriad relationships – professional and personal – that the audience may deduce will blow up and wreak havoc on the production.

Act Two takes place one month later, after the show has gone on tour. The living room set is spun 180 degrees and the audience now watches the show from a backstage vantage point, bearing witness to what becomes a literal 'backstage farce'. It is immediately apparent from the outset of Act Two that all is not right with the company. After Poppy gives the 'place's call' for "Act One beginners, please…", Tim offers up a hopeful "And maybe Act One beginners is what we'll get" (Frayn 71). Within a page and a half of Act Two, tension permeates the production, relationships have fractured, and backstage drama is taking a significant toll on the company. In an artful piece of writing, requiring a deft directorial hand and intricate choreography, Frayn gives the audience 20 minutes of expert theatre, with essentially two parallel plays being performed. Before us is a pantomimed section which sees actors and the stage management team attempting to keep the show from going completely off the rails. Actors are at each other's throats, they disappear, or come perilously close to missing their entrance cues.

Simultaneously, the actors still manage to perform "Nothing On" (ironically to an upstage wall). They pull the performance off without a hitch, committed to the play they have rehearsed. They make their entrances and exits, executing the onstage show without incident, with the audience unaware of the spiralling chaos backstage. It is a tour-de-force of writing, performance, direction and design. If any of those components were out of sync, the tower of farce would topple.

Almost two months have passed when the curtain rises on Act Three. The set has spun another 180 degrees, returning the audience to the living room of the Brent country home. By now, the bedraggled "Nothing On" company is barely making it through the performance. ASM Tim often steps in for Selsdon, actors improvise new lines and business, while bringing their offstage baggage onstage. We could be watching a nihilistic version of "Nothing On", a hilarious existential farce that builds on the disaster we watched backstage in Act Two, and now extends to absurd heights in Act Three, where the actors must finish the show. If not, they cease to be actors. They could give up. They could quit. But they do not. Instead, they must endure for the sake of the art. A failure to make an entrance is failure. The real audience is painfully aware of what is going on, but one has to wonder what the fictional paying audience thinks of the production. Would they detect something is 'off'? What is at stake for these actors? Their careers. Their livelihoods. Their sense of identity. They will do everything they can to finish the show. The show must go on.

Navigating seven different doors, a full-length window, newspapers, sardines, phones, bags, boxes, luggage, tea sets, costume pieces, and temperamental curtains, the company must never let on to their audience that things are going awry. These are not 'bad actors' either. We have to believe that these are actually decent performers who simply get in their own way. Act One needs to set this up, showing us that although the play-within-the-play might be a bit clunky, the actors are talented enough to handle it.

Since its premiere in 1982, *Noises Off* has received three West End revivals (2001, 2019, 2023), a major production at the Old Vic (2011), and two Broadway revivals (2001 and 2016) in the 21st century alone. Whenever a play or musical incorporates storylines about 'backstage mishaps' or theatrical processes falling apart, *Noises Off* is often referenced as a cultural touchstone – the backstage farce to end all backstage farces.

As an example of a farce which could go very wrong, making for an unbearable night at the theatre, *Noises Off* would be it. All it takes is for one actor to be out of step with the rest of the ensemble, or a poorly rendered scenic design hindering entrances, exits and the overall rhythm of the piece. Why does *Noises Off* continue to resonate with audiences and artists, and invite companies and commercial producers to keep producing it?

American stage director Meredith McDonough, who has directed *Noises Off* on two different occasions, refers to the play as Frayn's "…love letter to the theatre". She goes on to say that it appeals to audiences because

> …they know all of the inside jokes. And the brilliant thing is that *Noises Off* isn't a sex farce. "Nothing On" is a sex farce. It is the parts of the form that are, perhaps in the sexual politics of today, "troubling", the play acknowledges. A lot of the time, sex farces can be like you're laughing at the characters. And with this, you are actually inside of it.
>
> *(McDonough 2020)*

To combat the perceived sexism that may occur with the casting of an older actor playing Lloyd, McDonough took a different approach, removing an element that may no longer appeal to contemporary audiences:

> What helps the sexual politics inside of the group, is that I cast Lloyd as an early thirties dude in a hoodie and some Chuck Taylors…and it's not the vision of a director that is an older man who is preying on younger women. It is rather a younger man who's doing this thing between his two bigger gigs. And so therefore, he's badly behaved. Like don't sleep with two people in the same company(!)…but he's not a predator.
>
> *(McDonough 2020)*

Multiple practitioners consistently invoke the word 'mathematical' to describe not only *Noises Off*, but also how to approach it. McDonough says, referring to the script "…its math is perfect. It's just perfect" (McDonough 2020).

The intricacies or 'mathematics' of the play can come down to the single placement of a set piece or prop. British director Jeremy Herrin, whose revival of *Noises Off* opened on Broadway in 2016, and was remounted in London in 2019, discovered while rehearsing the show, that the positioning of the phone in Act One impacted on a sequence of comic business in Act Three. Herrin recalls:

> In the London production of *Noises Off*, I remember realising that the phone was on the wrong side of the sofa at the top of Act Three…[H]aving gone through about… five pages [of staging] with the phone on that side…I wasn't able to do the next sequence of jokes as effectively. So having to go back to Meera [Syal], who was playing Dotty, and say all of that opening stuff…I'm going to change it and I know that you['ll] hate me, and I know what I'm asking you to do…how serious it is, but we've just got to do it.
>
> *(Herrin 2020)*

*Noises Off* speaks to our contemporary need to rise up in the face of failure, even doom. It is a fine example of the fragility, but also the resilience, of human behaviour. Act Three could very quickly become a dead-end endeavour of comedy where the characters abuse one another. In fact, there have been productions that don't know what to do with Act Three, and have actually cut it. Both McDonough and Herrin state that the importance of the laughs continuing and growing into Act Three should lead to the funniest of the three acts. Herrin offers this observation:

> The big mistake is to try and make one [of the Acts] too funny…it's like a long-distance run. It's not a sprint…If you start making the audience laugh at the surface of things now, you're not going to get them to where you need to get them, which is the kind of giddy high. And I think that's the thing – is just to be truthful and then play a long game. Allow Act Two to be the peak of comedy. And then if you're any good and you can get the scene change between Act Two and Act Three quick enough, then you can maintain those laughs into Act Three…That's what I was aiming at. I was aiming at hitting a kind of summit plateau, probably like a couple of pages into [Act Two] when the show itself starts and they're backstage…and maintaining that to the end – which is really challenging. The original, from what I can remember, was pretty effective. But all the other subsequent productions that I've seen…faded away in Act Three. Act Three was never funny. Act Three never worked, and that was largely to do with design. With the two different designers that I worked with on the show, the first thing that I said to both of them was that the change between Act Two and Act Three needs to be 30 seconds. Otherwise we don't have a show…I know that to be true.
>
> I suppose it's like any show, it's about the clarity of your storytelling. You know what is happening and how do you realistically allow the audience to understand it in a way that doesn't sacrifice plausibility for a laugh? Because that would be a very short term strategy. You've got to believe when that stage manager comes out in the interval between 2 and 3, that he's just having a horrible, horrible day. You've got to be believing that he's never going to be stage managing again. He's had enough.
>
> *(Herrin 2020)*

Frayn wants us to see the actors in existential desperation, finding ways to survive. To go on. So that they can continue to be actors.

Actor Rob McClure, who played Tim, the Assistant Stage Manager, in the 2016 Broadway revival, calls the play:

> …a masterpiece. The reason that it lands so beautifully, time and time again, is because all of the comedy is born of desperate necessity. There is not a single "bit". The second act in particular is a monumental achievement in

writing. Michael Frayn actually wrote two Act Two's. One is happening backstage and one is happening onstage. But our audience gets to see both of them…After 4 pages of silent action, something will occur that requires perfect synchronicity between the two plays to meet in moments of brilliance. But can you imagine the logistical nightmare of having two hands land on opposing sides of a door knob at the exact same time after 7 minutes of silence? There's only one way. Rehearsal. Rehearsal. Rehearsal.

*(McClure 2020)*

Actor, Clown, and Physical Movement Director, Lorenzo Pisoni, was hired as the 'Comedy Stunt Coordinator' for the 2016 Broadway revival. Speaking to the power of farce and specifically *Noises Off*, he says,

> it can be so razor sharp. And speak truth. But also allow people to 'hear' truth. And when done well, even something as silly and effervescent as *Noises Off*, there's still the act of trying to stay calm and carry on. And community and sticking together and ultimately caring about one another.
>
> *(Pisoni 2020)*

Perhaps the greatest thing *Noises Off* teaches through farce is how to keep going in the face of disaster. How to adapt when things don't go right. How to be flexible. How to be a team player. And how to keep finding love in the work, no matter what happens. In Frayn's introduction to his 'Plays 1', he writes,

> The actors in *Noises Off* have fixed the world by learning roles and rehearsing their responses. The fear that haunts them is that the unlearned and unrehearsed – the great dark chaos behind the set, inside the heart and brain – will seep back on to the stage. The prepared words will vanish. The planned responses will be inappropriate. Their performance will break down, and they will be left in front of us naked and ashamed.
>
> *(Frayn xiv)*

### Farce in Rehearsal

The rehearsal room is a magical place where discoveries are made, moments crystallise, and performers find the essence propelling them to opening night. However, the course of true theatre never runs smoothly. And the rehearsal process is fodder for great farce because, inevitably, things go wrong. Here we have an opportunity for audiences to peek behind the velvet curtain and glimpse the controlled (or not-so-controlled) chaos that goes into rehearsing a show. The three farces in this section take place at different points in the rehearsal process, showcasing characters valiantly struggling to get to opening night.

*Sarah Ruhl:* **Stage Kiss *(2011)***

The plays of Sarah Ruhl, a Pulitzer Prize finalist and Tony-nominated playwright, "are often about love and intimacy…but love-as-subject-matter is less the point than dramatizing the problem of getting close to another" (Muse 63–64). Her plays, including *The Clean House*, *In the Next Room (or the Vibrator Play)*, *Dead Man's Cell Phone*, feature characters who, in their own ways, long for and struggle with issues of intimacy and connection. In their efforts to find meaning in their relationships, Ruhl's characters, especially her female characters, often get 'lost' along a journey of self-discovery and 'rediscovery.' In matters of the heart, she allows them to be messy, confused, and flawed. In particular, Ruhl "is a playwright who knows how to explore the contours of *adult* love and marriage" (Muse 65).

The characters in her plays are often in static marriages or relationships at a crossroads. A 'stranger' or 'person from the past' or an 'outsider' comes into their life at this specific moment and makes them question aspects of themselves, including their happiness and sense of self, that have long been buried, repressed, or repurposed.

In her 2011 play *Stage Kiss*, Ruhl continues to interrogate these themes through the lens of a backstage, domestic farce. Propelled by her own curiosity, she decided to examine the idea of the 'kiss' in the theatre and how this staged act of intimacy and affection can impact the lives of actors both on- and offstage, with comical consequences. For Ruhl, the play was an "experiment to explore 'the phenomenon of actors kissing on stage. I think it's so wonderful and so weird, to kiss in front of people for a job'" (Muse 89). Ruhl probes the grey area between reality and fantasy, and the power a kiss can hold within and outside the theatre.

With echoes of Coward's *Private Lives*, *Stage Kiss* finds actors 'She' and 'He', two former lovers who had an affair many years ago, unknowingly cast as romantic leads in *The Last Kiss*, a long-forgotten (and not very good) melodramatic musical comedy from the 1930s, about two former lovers who had an affair many years ago. As they begin to rehearse the play, at first attempting to maintain professionalism, reality and fantasy blur as their onstage affair follows them offstage. She is forced to re-evaluate her marriage, as she wrestles with the legitimacy of the manufactured sparks between herself and He. Ruhl seems to be asking: at what point does the repeated act of kissing, this required action that is part of one's job, eventually transcend the work and reveal itself as authentic beyond the rehearsal room and performance space? Can those feelings be trusted?

Both She and He are in committed relationships. She is married with a sixteen-year-old child. He is with a schoolteacher. Neither are unhappy per se. But once they start rehearsing the play, a play filled with a multitude of kisses, the mutual attraction and passion they once shared years ago is reignited. It brings them back to their youthful days twenty years before, reminding She of what life was like before marriage and family. It is a passion that invites She to question her happiness, eventually leading He and She to announce they are 'in love' and leaving their significant others. Things become more complicated when She's husband, Harrison, takes in and takes up with Laurie, He's (now) former girlfriend.

What soon becomes obvious is that the heightened intensity which has been kindled throughout the production process is unable to be sustained. Once the curtain falls and the house lights come up, the imperfections of life hidden by the stage world re-emerge.

She finds herself faced with the stark reminder of who 'He' really is, calling him 'scary' and a "seventeen year old in man pants. Peter Pan is great in the book – but in real life, people who don't grow up, they're a fucking nightmare" (Ruhl 109). She misses her daughter and sees herself losing the family that means so much to her, sacrificing a home she has built for something that may not be real. The grass is always greener on the other side of the footlights.

One could say that it is the power of the 'stage kiss' that sets off the farce. When faced with the first moment in rehearsal where they are supposed to kiss, they are tentative, uncertain, awkward, even scared. When they kiss, which leads to more kissing, it gives way to something absurdly flammable. The stage kiss results in comedic concealment, revelation, and eventual reconciliation.

> The indefinable slipping point between the actuality of the kiss and the illusion of the kiss reminds me of the actuality of love and the stories we tell ourselves about love. The ordinariness of a long and stable relationship is non-narrative by nature, whereas the combustible romance (and I think the word "romance" almost implies an ending) has extraordinary narrative power over us. Our imaginations want a romance, our practical natures want a marriage.
>
> *(Ruhl 2015)*

### *Peter Houghton:* A Commercial Farce *(2009)*

Australian actor-playwright Peter Houghton's *A Commercial Farce* manages to pull off a high wire act featuring only two actors – the smallest cast of a 21st-century farce discussed in this book. Houghton's play finds a director and actor rehearsing a farce within a farce.

The play takes place the night before the opening of fictional playwright Dylan Crackbourn's Whitehall-inspired farce, "Living Today". Hoping for a professional and financial success that will save his career and marriage, Bill, the play's director, calls in his lead, Jules, to rehearse 'bits' of farcical business that the actor simply does not seem to grasp. As the offstage farce of Bill's life becomes entangled with the onstage farce he is rehearsing, things go horribly wrong with Houghton's play ending in brutal violence.

Set in a rehearsal room, the two characters rehearse the end of Act I of Crackbourn's play. Houghton pits two generations of artists against each other: Bill, the middle-aged, veteran theatre director who is having a midlife crisis and on the verge of a mental breakdown, versus Jules, the young, handsome, and famous television actor who has been cast to draw audiences, even though he's ignorant of theatre convention, let alone farce. Bill is a 'man of the theatre', steeped in its history. Jules, by contrast, is a product of the celebrity machine, who ably executes what is asked of him on the small screen. Bill wants to remain relevant, yet has cleaned out his savings to produce a thirty-five-year-old farce, a play that Bill freely admits is "not trying to be original, [it's] trying to be effective…to 'effect' the audience…It's old. It works" (Houghton 21). Bill has chosen what he believes is a tried-and-true 'commercial farce'. When Jules asks what that means, Bill replies "It means that the audience is paying by the laugh. We're in the laugh delivery business" (Houghton 31). Bill has chosen a play hoping it will appeal to all audiences and make back his investment – throw in a famous actor and it ought to be a surefire hit.

Bill doesn't expect to be challenged by Jules, who dismisses dusty physical comedy bits like slipping on a banana peel, stepping on a rake and having it hit one in the testicles, or recurring gags like the 'Moo' sound cue that plays every time the set's front door opens. As Bill attempts to teach Jules the 'rules' of farce, the audience gets its own crash course in the genre as well. Jules is completely in the dark when it comes to comedy, unable to understand why these classic gags are funny. Yet, when Bill demonstrates pieces of staging and accidentally slips on the peel, or gets whacked by the rake, Jules laughs uproariously at Bill's pain, proving Bill's point that the old gags still work.

> Farce, as Bill says in the play, is a "race against time", a form which viscerally invokes our own race against the ticking clock of life. The play winds the clock tight, so its hands fly maniacally around the dial causing panic and confusion. It is life sped up. In middle age, we enter the last half of existence and our identities, our caution, our fears and dreams crumble in the face of the inevitable end.
>
> *(Houghton 3)*

As the two men attempt to rehearse the last five minutes of Act I, tensions escalate as time ticks away and the need to get it right becomes crucial. Unfortunately, they are constantly derailed as Bill's offstage life (it is his anniversary and his wife has announced that she wants a divorce) sends him spiralling. Bill

> guzzles more and more of the sponsor's wine and Jules takes a greater interest in Bill's "real" life, the staple diet of panic, fluster and outrage intensifies

and becomes even more hilarious. The cliché jokes that are being directed and performed in the original farce cleverly begin to play out in Bill's "real" life. We become the audience he is wishing to impress, he becomes the fool he is seeking to direct.

*(Thomas 2009)*

Ironically, it is only when true feelings and personal secrets are revealed, that Jules becomes the expert 'non-thinking' farceur Bill has been seeking all night, executing expert pratfalls and delivering the work with ease. In Houghton's words, "*A Commercial Farce* uses the confused identities and situations standard to the [farce] form to unravel the central identities of its (hopefully) three-dimensional dual protagonists" (Houghton 3).

Houghton's 'farce-within-a-farce' acknowledges the rickety nature of past farces, but uses those tropes to explore and explode his own farce with contemporary verve. As Bill's life implodes, so does the rehearsal set with Bill taking his pain and frustration out on it. The themes that have been running through Crackbourn's play have bubbled to the surface in Bill's life.

In the foreword to the digital edition of the play, Tom Healey, Australian Script Centre Literary Manager, observes that:

> Traditional farce is not a form that one readily associates with early millennial Australian theatre and Houghton tackles this expectation directly, just by making it his form of choice. The deep water under this argument has to do with our cultural values. Theatre is, of course, a fashion-driven art, this goes without saying because it can't retain its currency if it ignores popular culture. Having said that, our youth-oriented culture of disposability, with its lack of historical regard, sometimes leaves us in very shallow water. How do we make a contemporary theatre culture that both embraces the present and contains the wisdom of the past?
>
> *(Healey 1)*

### Anne Washburn: 10 out of 12 *(2015)*

After spending weeks in the rehearsal room, the company moves into the performance space. By this point, sets have been built and loaded in, costumes sewn and altered, lights hung and focused, sound cues created, and props acquired. These design elements must now be integrated with the performers' work. As onstage and offstage worlds meld, with upwards of thirty people or more sharing the space, the goal becomes tying all the theatrical elements together to form a cohesive production.

There are several examples of backstage farces taking audiences into the rehearsal room. What is rare is a farce that puts an emphasis on the technical rehearsal or 'tech'. Those who have experienced a 'tech', know that it is both an artistically revelatory time, and one defined by 'the clock'. 'Tech' can be a long and tedious ordeal. As each department does their best to execute painstaking work, driven by the need to 'get it right', to ensure everyone's safety, and to tell the most effective story, things inevitably go awry. Be it unpredictable technical glitches, actors missing entrances, or simple miscommunication, having to 'reset' and 'run it again' leads to impatience and frayed tempers, especially when time is short. Tech involves considerable waiting around; for those who do not understand the process, it can be hard to see why things aren't moving faster. So how does one milk this part of the production process for an evening of amusement.

Anne Washburn's play *10 out of 12* places the audience at the proverbial tech table observing a technical rehearsal for an unnamed play traversing multiple time periods. Upon entering the theatre, audience members are handed a pair of headsets. Encouraged to listen with at least one headphone on throughout the performance, patrons literally have the production team in their ear, immersed in technical jargon, mundane conversations, and moments of chaos as they play out in the theatre.

The title *10 out of 12* refers to the ten hours of onstage time equity actors are allowed to work over the course of a 12-hour tech day. Presiding are the director, the stage management team, designers, the assistant director, backstage crew, and the actors. Conspicuously absent is the playwright. This is not surprising since Washburn has been quoted as saying that,

> she first began taking notes at rehearsals, because "a playwright is useless at tech, and it's too dark to read". She wanted to capture how a technical rehearsal is "immensely boring, but then immensely sort of interesting and weird". She started thinking about braiding all of these notes, these "little odd moments of behavior", into a script.
>
> *(Soloski 2015)*

By mixing disembodied voices with live actors who appear both in the audience (or 'house') and on the set for the play-within-the-play, Washburn makes the audience privy to private and public conversations between actors and various members of the production team. As they watch egos derail the process, they hear crew members mock the actors over the headset. Opinions are offered about everything from the director's abilities to salami and cheese sandwiches.

The play employs insider humour, peppered with theatrical jargon that will sound like a foreign language to the uninitiated. However, anyone who has collaborated on a team project will find parallels to their own experience. The play pulls back the curtain on a magic trick and reveals the machinery creating the illusion. Tech rehearsals lay bare character. The farce may be subtler, but the passion and obsession to pull everything off well is no less engaging. Watching and listening to these characters strive to complete their tasks before the clock runs down, we feel the pressure in the room intensify, leading to characters' behaviour that is downright awkward and uncomfortable.

Although Washburn is having satirical fun within the container of the technical rehearsal, for those 'in-the-know', her attention to detail is staggering. At times bordering on naturalism, one might refer to the play as a 'slice-of-life' farce. "Partly a documentary piece, '10 out of 12' is…also a backstage farce, a workplace drama and a melancholy meditation on why anyone would want to make live theater in the first place" (Soloski 2015). Tech rehearsals can leave a production team exasperated, panicked because of constricted schedules, but fully aware they cannot give up. They must persevere, because an audience is expecting a great show. In his review for Theatre Wit's 2017 production of the play, Chris Jones observes that tech rehearsals "…can be occasions for a beautiful coming together. Or occasions for panic, as all of the fundamental fissures in the enterprise start to widen before everyone's terrified eyes" (Jones 2017).

At the end of the play, Paul, one of the seasoned actors in the cast, shares an inner monologue capturing the joy and mess of what it used to mean to put on a show. For all the ups and downs experienced while producing a new play

> …we knew that this was a splendid, a glorious way to live. We knew that this was the best way to live. Because we believed in what we were doing. Utterly. We believed in ourselves. Utterly. We were heroes of art. We were heroes.
>
> *(Washburn 104)*

While he speaks, the action surrounding the audience takes on a moment of fantasy. A cacophony of voices begins to drift in; technical chatter mixes with snippets of songs heard throughout the show. Casual gestures from the characters onstage and in the 'house' morph into the entire company singing and dancing in an act of momentary harmony. This dream sequence is snapped back to reality, when the stage manager announces that the rehearsal is over and they can all go home.

What emerges at the end of the play is surprisingly moving; a paean to the theatre that is "…an engaging and unexpectedly poignant tribute to all the mess and waste and hurt and boredom and bother and idiocy and passion and brilliance and devotion and love that goes into the premiere of any new play" (Soloski 2015).

And they will come back and do it all again tomorrow.

### Farce in Performance

This next section focuses on a selection of farces that take place 'in performance'. Rehearsals have occurred, tech has been completed, and now the play is set to be shared with an audience. Exposed to varying degrees with nowhere to hide onstage, eager actors or comedians perform before us, bound to carry on no matter what goes wrong. We are simultaneously the paying audience for a carefully prepared production shaped by talented artists, *and* the audience for a performance-within-a-performance that doesn't quite go according to plans.

*Farce Goes Wrong: 'Mischief Theatre'*

When it comes to making theatrical mishaps an art form, not since the Rude Mechanicals held court with their performance of "Pyramus and Thisbe" in Shakespeare's *A Midsummer Night's Dream*, has a company mastered this sub-genre of farce better than Britain's Mischief Theatre.

The Olivier and Tony-Award winning Mischief Theatre, led by Artistic Director Henry Lewis and co-writers Jonathan Sayer and Henry Shields, along with their stalwart repertory of actors Charlie Russell, Dave Hearn, Nancy Zamit, Greg Tannahill, Rob Falconer, and Bryony Corrigan, have seen their work explode in popularity, crafting a series of plays that comprise their 'Goes Wrong' canon.

Talented improvisers with a penchant for genre material, Mischief Theatre is a new generation of performers, injecting comedy with a youthful approach that delights in its theatrical roots while pushing the physical and technical boundaries of farce to new and exciting places. Although the plays are predominantly co-authored by Lewis, Sayer, and Shields, the entire company is involved with the development of the plays, bringing expert timing, fertile imagination, and love of 'play' to the rehearsal room. Carefully scripted and meticulously staged, there is an element of 'farce through devising' that emerges in their process, lending a true sense of collective creation.

Michael Green's book *The Art of Coarse Acting* and his subsequent series of plays influenced Mischief's work. In 1964, reporter Green published his satirical take on the profession, an amateur performer's manifesto taking on everything from how an actor prepares to how to work with a directorial czar. The success of the book led Green to adapt it into play form, called *The Coarse Acting Show*. Multiple volumes have been produced, parodying everything from Shakespeare to musicals. What ties them all together is that we are watching a group of amateurs attempt to produce a play. Mischief Theatre is a direct descendant.

Mischief's 'Goes Wrong' series of plays are brought to life with pluck and optimism by a repertory of talented actors and writers who excel in improvisation. These plays feature members of the fictional drama club known as the Cornley Polytechnic Drama Society. This group of 'dedicated' theatre makers are living out their dreams, 'putting on a play'. Watching Cornley's ragtag ensemble of artists valiantly try to execute their productions is to be reminded of those who aspire to the stage. Perhaps they aren't as well trained or don't have as much experience under their belts, but they are a company of performers delighting in being in front of an audience. We have the actor who becomes enthralled whenever someone applauds, the writer/director/actor who will do everything in his power to protect the integrity in his work, the ingénue who keeps going no matter what is thrown at her, the character actor who can never remember his lines, and the stage management team who are constantly putting fires out backstage, or stepping in when an actor goes down.

The 'Goes Wrong' plays in performance are defined by the improv artist's credo: 'Yes, and…' With failure not an option, there is a certain glee in witnessing the company say 'yes, and' to every mishap and situation. And there is nowhere to hide from the audience when calamity strikes. If props break, set pieces collapse, costumes tear, or sound cues are late, the company must carry on. It's what endears them to us. If someone was to say 'no' to what was in front of them, or ignore the 'problem', the innocence of the experience would fall apart and we would stop cheering for them. As audience members, the fun is watching these characters problem-solve in the moment. We know things will go wrong (it's right in the title of the plays), yet we do want them to succeed. It's also important to note that, unlike the company of professional actors and stage managers in Frayn's *Noises Off*, the Cornley Society is composed of young people working (usually) on limited budgets, bringing blissful naivety to the work. It's why it's also poignant to see these characters stuck in a world that is literally falling apart.

The canon includes *The Nativity Goes Wrong* (produced by the Christian Humanitarian Reading Initiative for Spiritual Theatre, or C.H.R.I.S.T.), and the 'Cornley Presentations' of *Peter Pan Goes Wrong*, *The Play That Goes Wrong*, and, most recently, *Magic Goes Wrong* (in collaboration with magicians Penn and Teller). The company has recently branched out and produced a series for the BBC, taking the 'Goes Wrong' brand and adapting it for television.

Numerous aspects of Mischief's work demand recognition. First, there is deeply embedded trust within the ensemble. A repertory of actors appear regularly in Mischief's work, and the 'give-and-take' between them is filled with ease. The actors know when to punch a moment, but also when to give up that moment to another player in order to garner an even bigger laugh. Their inventiveness is laudable. Technical expertise allows the scenic design to become its own character.

Originally a one-act play entitled *The Murder Before Christmas*, *The Play That Goes Wrong* (2013) began life at London's Old Red Lion Theatre Pub, before transferring to Trafalgar Studios as a two-act version. After touring the UK, the 'little farce that could' found its way to the West End where it played the Duchess Theatre, eventually winning Best New Comedy at the 2015 Olivier Awards. The play moved across the pond and opened on Broadway in 2017 with the original cast, where it won the Tony Award for Best Scenic Design.

To illustrate:

Cornley Polytechnic Drama Society is set to open their production of Susie H.K. Brideswell's *Murder at Haversham Manor*, a 1920s Agatha Christie-esque murder mystery. The play-within-the-play is not a parody. The company has decided to present a serious 'whodunnit'. The melodramatic premise of the story allows the comedy to flourish. If the play they were performing was a parody, the audience wouldn't be able to tell what was intentional and what were 'accidents'.

Admittedly, trying to keep track of the *Haversham* plot becomes a challenge with so much going wrong onstage. From the outset, as the audience is finding their seats, touch-ups are still being made to the set, and crew members are searching for Winston, a missing dog who is supposed to appear later in the play. When Chris, the play's director and also the portrayer of 'Inspector Carter', comes out to give the curtain speech, the spotlight cuts his head off, forcing him to have to step into it. The audience is already getting a taste of the theatrical car wreck they are about to witness.

The convoluted plot of *The Murder at Haversham* revolves around the murder of Charles Haversham, on the night of his engagement party to Florence Colleymoore. Inspector Carter is called in to unmask the culprit. Adultery, fraud, betrayal, and even more murder are all on the menu as the suspects are held at Haversham Manor for interrogation.

From a writing perspective, Mischief has done their homework, crafting an intricately plotted mystery that, if played straight, would offer audiences a classic, 'well-made' play. Discussing the multifaceted rehearsal process, Associate Director (USA) Matt DiCarlo shares that he'll "…always start by talking about the play and then having the cast read *The Murder at Haversham Manor*…Then, we work through the play in a linear way, making sure that everyone understands what would be happening if it was going RIGHT before we explore how it goes WRONG" (DiCarlo 2020).

Of course, as the opening moments make apparent, things only get progressively worse: props go missing, actors jump lines causing actions to happen before they've been prompted, corpses have trouble remaining dead, and the leading lady is accidentally rendered unconscious. Yet the 'professional' actors must have a firm handle on *The Murder at Haversham Manor*, even if their character counterparts lose the thread. We have to see them constantly playing the objective of the story and not the circumstantial obstacles. Watching the characters do everything in their power to push the story forward, even as the world around them is crumbling, showcases marked perseverance. There is something gratifying (and laugh-inducing) when we see a character freeze in place, unsure of how to deal with a moment gone wrong, and then choose at that moment how to keep going.

Actor Alex Mandell, who played the character of 'Max' on Broadway, notes that,

> …these characters are genuinely trying to…perform the play as best as they can…[the Broadway replacement company] made our own [backstory] that we had a number of positive rehearsals. We had a really great dress rehearsal…perhaps missing some elements that we'll throw in on opening night, and now opening night is here. And when there's the pressure of an audience, there's no stopping [the performance].
>
> *(Mandell 2020)*

One of the keys in all of the 'Goes Wrong' plays is to have the audience invest in the characters' plight to pull off the show. We want to see them succeed. Otherwise, the performance becomes a sadomasochistic exercise in laughing at fools we don't care about. DiCarlo echoes that when he says: "No matter what happens onstage, the resilient Cornley cast and crew are so determined to make it to the last line of their murder mystery – and they do! I think audiences really root for them" (DiCarlo 2020).

There are traps, though, that surface in plays like this, where actors can become indulgent and 'comment' on their characters and the action, showing us that the characters are bad actors. This becomes problematic because the proceedings take on a mean-spiritedness where we laugh at the characters for the wrong reasons. In addition, if the farce is not played for truth, with high stakes and passion, the audience will get ahead of the action and anticipate the jokes or gags.

Mischief company member and actor, Dave Hearn, in discussing the science of farce, says:

> …farce really leans into that idea of speed and precision…To always control the rhythm of the audience. To always be one step ahead or allow them to be one step ahead so that we can undercut them. So, in fact, we're two steps ahead…We found there is a science behind how you can manipulate certain jokes and certain rhythms to get certain laughs. And how one look, purely based on where it comes in the joke, can bring the house down. But then actually, do you want that moment? Do you want to sacrifice a joke five seconds later or two seconds before for this laugh…?.
>
> *(Hearn 2020)*

In the introduction of the acting edition of *The Play Goes Wrong*, the playwrights present a very important dictum for all of the 'Goes Wrong' plays:

> The actors of Cornley Drama Society are not bad actors but the victims of unfortunate circumstance. The comedy comes from their unwavering endeavour to continue, their bad choices in trying to get out of the situations they find themselves in and their optimistic belief that their luck will

change…it is vital everyone works to present "the play that goes wrong" not "the play that's being done badly.

*(Lewis, Sayers and Shields 8)*

As of this writing, *The Play That Goes Wrong* has been "performed in over 35 countries across 6 continents…" (Mischief 2023). This speaks to the ability of both the show and, more broadly, the genre of farce to connect across cultures. Whether the play is set in a theatre, a kitchen, or in an office, the inherent struggle to carry on in the face of disaster, inevitably unleashes laughter.

Actress Bryony Corrigan, who has performed in a number of 'Goes Wrong' plays, including *The Play That Goes Wrong*, surmises:

…the reason that '…Goes Wrong' has been so successful across the world is because I feel like farce is a language that everybody understands. It's physical. You don't necessarily need to be talking to understand what is going on in a farce. You can watch and laugh at people just falling over things, dropping things, tripping up, laughing at each other. And I love that it's a universal thing. It's not about intellect, it's not about politics, you can be anybody and watch it and go, yeah, that is just fundamentally silly and funny and has made me laugh. So I think that's why I enjoy it. Just like laughing at myself and at my friends.

*(Corrigan 2020)*

Mischief Theatre has gone on to produce a series for the BBC entitled *The Goes Wrong Show*. Drawing on elements of their stage shows, the Cornley company has been given a budget and studio space to put on a weekly 'live' television show. This allows them to play with everything from sets being built in the wrong scale or incorrect position, to cameras not following the action. All of this combines with moments of slapstick, missed lines, and the need to improvise around mistakes and mishaps.

The company continues to practise their art, touring a live show called *Mischief Movie Night*, in which they improvise a new 'movie' each night based on audience suggestions.

It should be noted, too, that Mischief's work offers inclusive casting, where actors bring their unique selves to the table. Their characters are identifiable because they all struggle against a familiar world that is eroding around them. Farce is a form transcending culture, race, gender, and sexual orientation. It has a power that actor Mandell calls,

…a unifier. There's a reason shows like *The Play That Goes Wrong*, and *One Man, Two Guvnors* are so broadly successful; at their purest core they are about people trying to do their best, and failing. This is such a universal truth of the human condition, it transcends politics and other dividing forces. I think farce, when done well, can remind us of all the things we have in common with one another, and hopefully inspire some deep-level empathy and understanding of others. There's so much to despair about these days, laughter might be the singular universal antidote.

*(Mandell 2020)*

### Ben Ashenden and Alex Owen: The Comeback *(2020)*

In 2018, Ben Ashenden and Alex Owen, the comedy duo known as The Pin, appeared at the Edinburgh Fringe Festival with a one-act play entitled *Backstage*. Playing versions of themselves, Ben and Alex are the openers for the headlining act of 'old school' comedy duo, Phillip and Robin (also played by Owen and Ashenden). Following their fifteen-minute set, the two work their material backstage, lament their careers, and brainstorm how they can ascend to the top rung.

What Owen and Ashenden crafted was

> a giddy slice of *Noises Off*-style knockabout, overlaid with the Pin's signature meta-comedy, as Owen, Ashenden, Philip and Robin chase one another on stage and off, identities get scrambled and a chair on the stage miraculously reappears – and vanishes from – behind the scenes.
>
> *(Logan 2018)*

Amidst their own unique brand of sketch comedy, whilst portraying two generations of comedians, the work flourished because at the "…heart of this piece…is the friendship (or otherwise) between two halves of a double act…a brilliant send-up of the perils of working in a double act, only to reconfirm the true friendship behind this hilarious show" (Dessau 2018).

Following its success at the Fringe, the play moved to London, where it was seen by British producer Sonia Friedman, who invited the duo to expand the play into a longer piece, resulting in *The Comeback*.

The essence of the original remained. In *The Comeback*, Ben and Alex still portray a young up-and-coming comedy duo named Ben and Alex who are opening for Sid and Jimmy, an older comedy act in the vein of Morecambe and Wise. The first part of Act I finds the pair honing and presenting their two-man sketches, struggling to get laughs. We witness the pair onstage and in the Green Room. When the duo get wind that a famous 'Hollywood Director' is coming to see the show that night, they plot to sabotage the older duo with the hope of impressing the Director. Alas for the young comics, the older duo overhear the news about the director's visit and likewise plot to torpedo the younger act.

On the surface, this would be a fun concept to play with – watching two thirty-somethings going head to head with two octogenarian comics. Maintaining their Fringe conceit, Ashenden and Owens continue to portray the older comedians. As the play accelerates, both actors must not only make lightning-fast quick changes but also age up and down before our eyes. Showcasing dynamic farce skills, Ben and Alex are still playing stage versions of themselves – Alex the optimist, and Ben the cynic – while playing their opposite traits when they portray the elder comic statesmen, Jimmy and Sid. With mere physical changes and the addition of a costume piece, we watch the two actors transform before our eyes.

The play finds comic lineage in Shakespeare's *The Comedy of Errors*, Charles Ludlam's *The Mystery of Irma Vep*, the Two Ronnies, Monty Python, and Sean Foley and Hamish McColl's play, *The Play What I Wrote*.

The latter play and *The Comeback* both feature a 'guest performance' from the audience who is asked to be part of some of the 'bits'. There is also an element of Christopher Guest's mockumentary *Waiting for Guffman* with the unseen Hollywood director never quite making an appearance. The play also has a sweetness to it that should not be underestimated. Without becoming sentimental, the younger duo find that despite their struggles and lack of success, it is their friendship that must be treasured. In their own way, they make each other better – professionally and personally.

The term 'comeback' has multiple meanings in the play. There is the 'comeback' insult, which puts someone down or in their place. For the older duo, the 'comeback' may mean an opportunity for rediscovery. And, finally, we have the sense of 'coming back' to the stage, returning to something lost or given up. Surrounding the farcical shenanigans of the four characters, and their attempts to one-up each other in order to prove their mettle, we also see the four characters grapple with mortality and comic identity. Comedians need a laughing audience. Who are they if audiences don't want to see them? If they are no longer funny, or have nothing to offer, where does this leave them? What is at stake is the life and death of not only their act, but their careers.

The meta farce of *The Comeback* is more than a play within a play. It is an 'act' within a farce. The Pin have created a contemporary farce that pays homage to those British duos of yesteryear, and to *Noises Off*. It builds on the current trend of a small ensemble playing multiple characters to glistening comedic effect.

Interviewed for *Broadway World* prior to the show's November 2020 reopening, Alex Owen said:

> It's a very silly play, and hopefully, people will be in the mood to come and see something like this. It's going to be a bit of an escapist moment of nonsense and fun. The play also has themes appropriate for the current situation such as companionship, community, and not giving up on the relationships that are important, no matter how difficult they get. I say that, but 95% of the show is people falling over and throwing things at each other!

*(Drugeot 2020)*

The Pin found themselves in an unfortunate position with *The Comeback*. It opened in February 2020 and was promptly shut down at the start of the COVID-19 pandemic. As venues opened up again, the play was scheduled for a July 2021 presentation and subsequently was pushed to a December opening. It appeared the play was going to have its own artistic 'comeback'. Alas, the West End debut of the show was felled again within days of its reopening by the COVID virus, forcing its closure.

Prior to its shuttering, the play was heralded as "an energetic old-school farce…the pair bring verve and invention to the genre, and to the double act tradition, both of which they clearly respect" (Chortle 2020). Using actor doubles and some tried-and-true stagecraft magic,

> the moment all four [comedians] discover the famous director sitting out front, everything, most especially everyone's rampant ambition, instantly ratchets up several gears. And when Ben 'accidentally' knocks out Sid, it's not so much a case of rivalry as total back-stabbing, and suddenly, in rising director Emily Burns' expert hands, we have two actors playing four characters in a furiously funny, wonderfully escalating, high-stakes, 'Noises Off-style farce'.
>
> *(Benedict 2020)*

Committing their new work to audiences while paying tribute to those same comedic acts revered in Terry Johnson's *Dead Funny* and echoed in Bean's *One Man, Two Guvnors*, *The Comeback* is an 85-minute farce complete with

> [s]light gags, impersonations, door-slamming, comedy chases: all the ingredients are in play with increasingly crazy situations growing satisfyingly out of the initial material. It's all an inch away from chaos and, since it's perfectly timed and ruthlessly controlled, uproariously funny…
>
> *(Benedict 2020)*

### Farce and the Understudy

Once a play has been rehearsed and opened, a small group of unsung heroes wait in the wings should trouble befall an actor. We've learned that it doesn't take much for a COVID-like intruder to take down multiple cast members. Understudies, standbys, covers, and swings, ensure the show can still go on. Never before in the modern era of theatre have we relied so heavily on those actors whose job is to be ready to go on at a moment's notice. If they're fortunate, they have a few hours' warning and are given a 'put-in' rehearsal. Occasionally, an actor goes down mid-show and the understudy must complete the performance.

Theresa Rebeck's *The Understudy* (2008) and Dave Hansen's *Waiting for Waiting for Godot* (2013) offer farcical but affectionate looks at the life of understudies and what it means to be 'just out of the limelight'.

Theresa Rebeck's *The Understudy* is a three-character, backstage satire/farce that focuses its comedic attention on an understudy 'put-in' rehearsal for a lost Franz Kafka play that recently opened on Broadway. Harry, a journeyman actor with a chip on his shoulder, is the understudy for Jake. Jake is a rising movie star, keen to be seen as a 'legitimate' actor. He is also starring opposite a famous (unseen) action star named 'Bruce'. Jake also happens to be Bruce's understudy. Running the rehearsal is Roxanne, the production's exasperated stage manager and Harry's ex-fiancée, whom he unceremoniously ghosted, six years earlier. This put-in rehearsal has been deemed necessary not only per union rules, but also because Bruce is on the verge of securing a multi-million dollar movie deal, and may have to leave the production.

Taking place in 'real time', over the course of 90 minutes, tensions run high as the three characters are continually sidetracked by professional and personal issues, while attempting to rehearse the three-hour(!) Kafka play. Not helping matters is a live intercom system transmitting onstage conversations to backstage. Additionally, Laura, an unseen ASM and sound and lighting board operator, is also stoned, resulting in wrong cues being called and incorrect scenery flying in and out of the space.

Rebeck is clearly drawing on her own experiences in the theatre. Skewering everything from Broadway's penchant for casting 'celebrities' over trained theatre creatures trying to make their mark, to money-oriented producers putting dollar signs before art. Rebeck manages to find connective moments where we see the genuine impact the theatre has on the three characters. In a 2014 interview with *The Atlantic*, author Ben Marcus describes the key elements that define Kafka's literary work as an "affecting use of language, a setting that straddles fantasy and reality, and a sense of striving even in the face of bleakness – hopelessly and full of hope" (Fassler 2014). This not only describes the plight of the characters in *The Understudy*, as they navigate the personal and professional roller coaster of show business, but also encapsulates the tension inherent in farce as well: how to move forward optimistically when all is darkening.

Part parody, part farce, *Waiting for Waiting for Godot* (2013) finds its inspiration from Samuel Beckett's existential, absurdist classic. Dave Hanson's play focuses on Val and Ester, the two understudies covering the characters of Vladmir and Estragon in a production of *Waiting for Godot*. As the two men wait for the Director (i.e their 'Godot') to let them know when they'll go on, their act of waiting and the various ways they pass time, paint a picture of "…the trivial purgatory Ester and Val share. Most likely the understudies will never tread the boards in the theater – their performance is limited to the ways they can waste time in their closeted paralysis" (Greenham 2017).

The two men engage in malapropistic discussions about various acting techniques, and the particular play they're understudying:

*Ester:* We are a part of a very important production. I mean Beckett…you know…Beckett.
*Val:* Who?
*Ester:* Sam Beckett.

Blank stare from VAL

*Ester:* Samuel Beckett…? The author? He's very well respected
*Val:* Is he? Do you think he'll come?
*Ester:* He's dead.
*Val:* Don't say that!
*Ester:* My friend, he's been dead for years. They all have.

*(Hanson 16)*

Hanson pays homage to Beckett's writing style, interpolating lines of text from the original play at specific moments for effect. Like the characters they are understudying, Ester and Val find themselves caught in circular conversations evoking hoary vaudeville routines.

For Ester and Val, performing gives their life meaning. For Ester, being seen is a gift to audiences, and a validation of his inflated sense of self (even if he can't remember the roles he has played). When they believe their Director has arrived – which can only mean that something has gone wrong onstage – Ester's confidence melts and he becomes a puddle of insecurity. Meanwhile, Val wants to go on so he can make his Aunt Mary proud. Mary has been coming to the play every night hoping her nephew will finally get his chance to shine. Unfortunately, Aunt Mary proves to be the undoing of the show.

It would be easy to dismiss the play as a simple parody of *Waiting for Godot*, an extended 'theatre insider''s sketch. Recasting Beckett's classic hobos as understudies, Hanson offers an apt metaphor for the industry. Beyond the 'waiting to go on', Hanson's play highlights one of the harsh existential truths about the business: if no one sees us perform, are we actors? The perpetual act of 'waiting' is something to which all theatre artists can relate. When is our next job? When will we finally be noticed? Who or what does our existence depend on, in order to find professional success? Beyond the walls of the theatre, the play can be viewed as an allegory for everyone who doesn't feel seen. It is easy to see Val and Ester's plight and feel themselves in those characters: the person who is continually passed over for promotion, the minor league baseball player never called to the major leagues, or the child always in the shadow of a favoured sibling.

Hanson, who was cast as an understudy in a Los Angeles production of *Waiting for Godot*, talks about how his experience as an understudy inspired the work, saying:

> There's a strange effect when you ingest Beckett's work over and over again. The world around you starts to transform into the absurdist reality you're reading. Things get a little darker, pursuits seem a little more useless and every action carries its own sardonic irony. And then you stop reading it, the world snaps back to how it was…almost. This happened to me when I was cast as an understudy for a terrible production of *Waiting For Godot* in Los Angeles, many years ago. I sat backstage, for no pay, almost no rehearsal time and no guaranteed performances, and came to the panicked realization that I was living Beckett's play. I was my own parody and reference joke. But since my first love is parody and reference jokes, this tragic realization seemed pretty funny to me.
>
> *(Hanson 2016)*

Many look at theatre artists and see the farce embedded in our industry. Consider what we do on a regular basis: playing pretend and dress-up, building structures and clothes, singing, dancing, and making fools of ourselves for other people's enjoyment, and little money. The vocation may appear frivolous to outsiders, but for those in the theatre, nothing could be more important. Hanson and Rebeck's plays, seen through the eyes of understudies, underscore the fragility of the business. Simultaneously, we are reminded that what we offer is unique, that one day our time to shine will come, and we need to be ready. For those in the wings, and their audiences, Hanson hopes the play "offers an inspiring, comedic look into the existence of artists. Especially those you never hear of, the ones who are waiting" (Hanson 2016).

### Farce and the Critics

Where would the theatre be without critics? To this point, we have examined backstage farces presenting the follies of actors and other creative types in rehearsal and performance. Loved or loathed by theatre artists, critics, however, are rarely featured in plays. The musical *Curtains* (2006) by John Kander, Fred Ebb, Peter Stone and Rupert Holmes, has fun with this contradiction, satirising critics and their reviews in the song "What Kind of Man". Disheartened by a series of scathing reviews of their new musical *Robbin' Hood*, the producer and creatives question why anyone would want to become a critic. That is, until they receive one glowing review, and suddenly the critic who wrote it becomes a genius.

Playwrights must be strategic if they are going to present the figure of the critic in their work, especially in a satiric or parodic capacity. Cheap characterisations of the critic make the playwright appear bitter or petty, potentially teeing them up for even more criticism. Critics may try to be objective, but they are human, and tasked to share insights and opinions for their readers (and publishers). Some offer thoughtful perspectives of the work they've observed; others may seem simply cruel. In the end, like it or not, they have become an integral part of the production process.

One early appearance of the critic as a featured character occurs in Richard Brinsley Sheridan's rarely performed *The Critic, or a Tragedy Rehearsed* (1779). This play satirises the theatre conventions of the day and parodies the types of plays that were written during the mid to late 18th century. Sheridan sends up the self-important artist, the misplaced power bestowed on critics, and the universal need for validation from those in positions of influence.

Tom Stoppard's one-act, metatheatrical whodunnit *The Real Inspector Hound* (1968) mixes genres including mystery, farce, parody and melodrama, eventually blurring the line between 'theatre' and reality. At the top of the play, the audience observes two critics watching an Agatha Christie parody. Birdboot and the second string critic, Moon, each from rival newspapers, are seated in theatre stalls meant to replicate the ones the audience sits in, as if we are looking at a mirrored version of ourselves. Birdboot and Moon (who is there in place of his colleague, and first-string critic, Higgs) speak in hushed tones throughout the performance, commenting on the action with an air of critical superiority. At the play's interval, the onstage phone rings. When nobody picks it up, Moon irritatedly enters the stage area and answers. It turns out to be Birdboot's wife, 'calling him at work'. Taking the phone from Moon, Birdboot is subsequently 'caught' onstage by a character in the play and is unwittingly integrated into the action.

The play takes a turn, the familiar structural mechanics of the murder-mystery parody shatter, and the critics are drawn deeper into the proceedings. While 'performing', Birdboot discovers that the corpse lying onstage is that of Higgs. A shocked Birdboot believes he knows what has happened and attempts to reveal the truth. Before he can do so, he is shot and killed. Moon leaves his seat, realises that Birdboot is dead, and proceeds to take on the role of the play's detective, Inspector Hound, in order to solve his fellow critic's murder. In the end, Moon is the one implicated in the two murders, and is shot trying to escape from the 'real' Inspector Hound, who is revealed to be Puckeridge, the 'third-string' critic for Moon's newspaper. Puckeridge is the mastermind behind the entire affair, a vile scheme that would see him promoted to first-string critic.

When it first premiered,

> critics loved the new play, finding themselves both the subject of, and commentators on, the satire.... Exploring the fantasy of critics wanting to cross the footlights and showing what might happen if, in fact, they did so, Stoppard confronted their dreams with theatrical reality.
>
> *(Nadel 203)*

The genre of the murder-mystery intrigues audiences because it keeps them guessing,

> asking what is true and false…[whereas here] we are called on to ask what is reality and what is illusion…Stoppard not only playfully critiques our faith in reason and logic; he also challenges the idea that art holds a mirror up to life, suggesting instead that art influences, interacts, and intertwines with life in ways the mirror metaphor fails to include.
>
> *(Demastes 61)*

The farce in watching real life meld with theatrical life provides for laughs, as it puts the focus on critics who compete for status and power. Once they are dropped into the theatrical proceedings, the playing field is evened. Ironically (even though it turns out to be a fellow critic), we first believe that an actor has *literally* killed a critic, in the same way critics have been known for killing a show (or careers).

In 2016, the Shakespeare Theatre Company in Washington D.C. paired *The Real Inspector Hound* with a shortened, one-act adaptation of Sheridan's *The Critic*, by Jeffrey Hatcher. Complementing one another, and set almost 190 years apart, both plays have fun at the expense both of the mechanisms of theatre and of those that write about it. Hatcher observed that

> both plays have critics watching a play…They're both the only plays I can think of where you're watching an audience watching a play and those members of that audience are becoming involved in the play that they're watching. There's a meta theater going on.
>
> *(Loutchko 2016)*

For many in our field, reviews are the most anticipated and dreaded part of the theatrical process. A show can rise and fall based on the swift strike of the keyboard. Reviews have been known to make or break a show.

Terrence McNally's 'opening night' comedy *It's Only a Play* (1985; revised in 2014) is infused with a healthy dose of anticipation and dread. Unlike the previous plays discussed, McNally's satirical farce of the showbiz industry takes place *after* the curtain has come down.

Playwright Peter Austin has made his Broadway debut with the new play, *The Golden Egg*. Following the performance, a motley crew of narcissists gather at the townhouse of novice producer Julia Budder, to celebrate Peter's achievement. These include James Wicker, Peter's best friend, who declined the lead role because of his television series; Frank Finger, 'boy-wonder' British director and kleptomaniac; Virginia Noyes, the substance-abusing lead actress; Ira Drew, the vitriolic theatre critic (and would-be-playwright); and Gus, a coat check boy dreaming of being a serious theatre artist. As everyone awaits the post-show verdict from the critics – in particular, the

*New York Times* – petty insecurities and jealousies mount, friendships are tested, egos are brandished, and secret artistic desires are revealed.

In his Introduction to the 1990 collection, *Three Plays by Terrence McNally*, the playwright wrote *It's Only a Play*

> is a comedy, but it's one of the most serious plays I have ever written. It's my attempt to describe exactly what it was like to work in the Broadway theater in the 1980s. It is probably the closest thing I will ever write to a documentary.
>
> *( McNally X )*

The play offered McNally an opportunity to poke fun at the current state of theatre, and indulge in 'bitchy' showbiz gossip (all in good fun for the most part), dropping names of actors, directors, media pundits, and other playwrights. When the play was revived on Broadway in 2014, McNally updated it to the present day, adding the presence of cell phones (allowing reviews to be texted), and replacing referenced celebrities like Rita Moreno, Candice Bergen, David Mamet, and *La Cage aux Folles* with contemporary pop culture figures Kelly Ripa, Harvey Fierstein, Alec Baldwin, and Lady Gaga. McNally playfully skewers performers he regularly collaborates with, including theatre icons Liza Minelli and Audra MacDonald. Ben Brantley is substituted for Frank Rich as the 'feared' and 'lacerated' chief theatre critic of the *New York Times*. And Gus finally gets his moment to shine, singing a clarion "Defying Gravity" from the musical *Wicked* to make everyone feel better.

In the end, as the company nurses their artistic wounds, and bemoans what is sure to be both their opening and closing night, Julia challenges Peter to write what he knows. Peter flippantly offers a suggestion for a new play, a play that sounds suspiciously like the play we've been watching, featuring an eclectic group of people sounding very much like the ones currently gathered in Julia's townhouse bedroom.

For all of the backbiting, inflated egos, insecurities, and bad reviews, *It's Only a Play* reminds us that putting on a piece of theatre is an accomplishment unto itself. Peter does not set out to write a bad play. Julia has no interest in producing a flop. The actors recognise that they are the ones in front of the audience bound to give it their all. The director is determined to lift the story off the page in the most exciting way possible. No one wants the production to fail. With money, reputations, and future opportunities on the line, what everyone strives for is success. What may get lost at times, in an effort to please audiences, and placate reviewers, is the living essence of theatre. Locating the beating heart beneath the satiric barbs and farcical stakes, becomes imperative. In McNally's own words:

> *It's Only a Play* is a much more complicated play about theatre, the mystery of it, the agony of it, and also the big joy it can be when it all works. It's

much more than some funny lines about theatre people. I think it's a much more serious play than people notice when they just hear some of the name-dropping and some of the bitchy lines; there's a lot of heart in the play too.

*(Frontain 150)*

**One Modern and a Few More Contemporary Backstage Farces**

Ken Ludwig has a fondness for theatre people, often setting his work in and/or around the performing arts. Although we have previously labelled *Lend Me a Tenor* and *A Comedy of Tenors* as domestic farces, there is also a backstage element to those two plays. Both take place mere hours before the opening of an operatic performance with the farcical action of the two plays casting doubt as to whether the performances in question will even happen. With allusions to 'opera buffa', domestic farce intersects with backstage farce.

Ludwig's 1995 modern farce *Moon Over Buffalo* paints a fading picture of longtime married couple, George and Charlotte Hay, modelled on famous theatre icons like the Barrymores, the Lunts, and the Oliviers. The Hays have not had a hit in years, and are touring *Cyrano de Bergerac* and *Private Lives* in repertory (currently in Buffalo). They hope to rekindle some of their old glory in the eyes of fans, as well as Hollywood. With the film director Frank Capra expected to attend the matinee, their newly engaged daughter, Rosalind, arrives unexpectedly with fiancé, Howard, in tow, while two of the younger members of their rep company throw romantic wrenches into the gears. The play, in Ludwig's words, "is about second chances and about the courage that is needed to take a second chance" (Ludwig xvii). *Moon Over Buffalo* is equal parts backstage and domestic farce. There are not only professional second chances at stake, but also romantic ones.

In 2003, Ludwig adapted Ben Hecht and Charles MacArthur's 1931 *Twentieth Century*. Although it doesn't take place in a theatre, Ludwig's backstage and cultural farce features an array of 'showbiz' folk travelling on the famous express train from Chicago to New York. Chief among these is theatre director and impresario Oscar Jaffee, seeking to sign Academy Award-winning actress, Lily Garland, who is expected to be on the train as well. Oscar 'discovered' Garland when she was a chorus girl and her name was still Mildred Plotka. They became involved professionally and personally, with neither relationship working out. Jaffe, now bankrupt and trying to save his theatre, hopes to entice movie star Garland to take the lead role of 'Mary Magdalene' in his new Broadway mounting of the *Passion Play*, and perhaps win back the 'one who got away'. Providing unnecessary obstacles are Garland's agent and current lover, George Smith, rival director Max Jacobs, looking to sign Lily to a new movie, and Matthew (or Myrtle) Clark, a middle-aged, Bible thumper who papers the train with stickers extolling the word of God, and who is mistaken for a big-time producer. With the entire play taking place in three railway berths, comic hijinks mix farce and romance.

With a nod to the cross-dressing and 'pants roles' convention found in the plays of Shakespeare, Farquhar and the operas of Mozart, Ludwig's 2006 play *Leading Ladies* also tips its hat to Brandon Thomas' classic 19th-century farce, *Charley's Aunt*.

Both out of work and out of money, British thespians Leo and Jack are touring their two-man *Scenes from Shakespeare* around the Amish counties of Pennsylvania. The two men hear that Florence Snider, a wealthy old woman in the York, PA, area is on the verge of death, and wants to leave her fortune to her two long-lost English nephews. Leo and Jack scheme to impersonate the two nephews and 'inherit' her money. All does not go according to plan as Leo and Jack discover that the heirs aren't two nephews, but two nieces. This leads them to 'assume' the roles of 'Maxine' and 'Stephanie.' As the two men struggle to maintain their female roles, Leo falls in love with Florence's other niece, Meg. Disguises abound and a romantic entanglement forces the men to make decisions about what is actually in their best interest – money, art, or love.

Shakespeare's *A Midsummer Night's Dream* has provided the inspiration for a couple of Ludwig comedies containing farcical elements. *Midsummer/Jersey* (2011) is a contemporary retelling of Shakespeare's play, set on the boardwalk of a seaside town in New Jersey. More prominently, Ludwig's *Shakespeare in Hollywood* (2004) is based on the true events surrounding the trials and tribulations of famed European stage director, Max Reinhardt, and the filming of what would be his only movie, based on *A Midsummer Night's Dream*. Combining screwball comedy, satire, and farce, Ludwig's play takes us inside Warner Brothers Studio, where Reinhardt is trying to make his movie. Less a backstage farce than a 'backlot' farce, the play follows Reinhardt as he contends with egos, the Hays Production Code, and Jack Warner's mistress (who insists he produce a 'prestige pic' for her to star in). The play features a who's who of Hollywood icons: from gossip columnist Louella Parsons and Groucho Marx, to James Cagney and Dick Powell.

In a bit of fairyland magic, Shakespeare's characters Oberon and Puck accidentally end up in Hollywood (and Ludwig's play) when Puck mistakes a prop sign that says 'A Wood Near Athens'. Soon they find themselves taken by the celebrity lifestyle Hollywood has to offer, while becoming embroiled in the lives of those involved in the movie. It is no surprise that magic flowers and love potions find their way into the action of the play. The process of making a celluloid version of *A Midsummer Night's Dream* starts to resemble the source material.

Ludwig's 'backstage' comedy addresses contemporary topics of censorship, artistic politics, commercial art versus high art, all the while celebrating the idiosyncratic process of moviemaking.

Although this book has not focused on farces written and produced for film and television, it is the backstage farce that has found a home on both the silver and small screens. Movies like *Tootsie*, *Waiting for Guffman*, *Soapdish*, and

*Birdman* have elements of backstage farce woven into their storytelling. If anything, backstage farce has found great success in television, where the act of producing a television show or a talk show has become weekly fodder for farce. *The Dick Van Dyke Show*, *The Larry Sanders Show*, *30 Rock*, *Curb Your Enthusiasm*, *Extras*, and *Episodes* are just a few examples of the genre. The Canadian series *Slings & Arrows* takes us behind the scenes of the fictional New Burbage Festival in Ontario, Canada (modelled after the Stratford and Shaw Festivals). Over the course of three seasons, we watch the artists and administrators of the fictional Festival struggle hilariously to keep it afloat amid mounting artistic and financial concerns.

Most theatre artists know that putting on a show is no easy task. With so many elements and egos to juggle, one marvels how we ever get a play up in front of an audience. In seeing a project to its fruition, we admire the resilience and commitment in those that sew the seams, light the lights, paint the flats, and tread the boards. Of course, if all went according to plan, we wouldn't have any material to draw on. It is for this reason that backstage farces epitomise the four 'P's we articulated in "Entrances": the characters share a *passion*, even an obsession for putting on a show. They *persist* despite myriad obstacles that threaten to derail the show…because the show must go on. Inevitably, the process takes a dire turn and *panic* ensues, begging the question 'Will the show go on?' By the end, the ensemble of merry misfits populating these plays have found a way to survive, to *preserve* their reputations, their dignities, and their lives as theatre artists in order to perform another day.

We opened the chapter by looking at Michael Frayn's *Noises Off*, a play often quoted or referenced whenever quirky actors and backstage goings-on are the focus of the story. Yet the backstage farces discussed use the genre to dissect not only the act of performing in front of an audience, but also to take us inside the production process: from the beginning of rehearsals, through technical rehearsals, to opening night and beyond, while offering a glimpse into the lives of the understudy, and the inevitable role of the critic.

Theatre people love to 'poke fun' at the theatre; a place where characters crave acceptance, seek adulation, and dream of bigger and better things in the entertainment industry. It is also a place where the onstage and offstage lives of characters become blurred, resulting in wounded prides, broken 'showmances', and the threat of not finishing the show.

What is so fascinating about watching people put on a play? For those who have never spent time in an actual rehearsal room or on stage, it offers a peek behind the curtain, a certain glimpse, perhaps gleeful, perhaps morbid, into the 'secret' magic of theatre.

No one *wants* to put on a bad play. The characters in a backstage farce want to do a good job and please their audiences (and be loved, too?). We don't want to watch 'bad actors' trying to put on a show. We want to see the artists in a backstage farce persevere and triumph. For this reason, backstage farces are an apt metaphor for life. How can we remain steadfast, and carry on, when everything is going wrong?

This brings us to the end of our 'hallway of farce'. Having surveyed a wide selection of modern and contemporary farces featured behind our five doors, where does farce go from here? What lies ahead for this oft-misunderstood and maligned genre?

Let us exit.

## Works Cited

Ashenden, Ben, and Owen, Alex. *The Comeback*. Nick Hern Books, 2021.

Benedict, David. "Variety." *Variety*, 14 Dec. 2020, variety.com/2020/legit/reviews/the-comeback-review-ben-ashenden-alex-owen-1234853421

Bennett, Steve. "The Comeback with Ben Ashenden and Alexander Owen: Reviews 2020: Chortle: The UK Comedy Guide." *Copyright Chortle 2023. All Rights Reserved.*, 14 Dec. 2020, www.chortle.co.uk/review/2020/12/14/47489/the_comeback_with_ben%C2%A0ashenden_and%C2%A0alexander%C2%A0owen

Corrigan, Bryony. Personal Interview. 16 Sept. 2020.

Demastes, William. *The Cambridge Introduction to Tom Stoppard*. Cambridge University Press, 2013, p. 61.

Dessau, Lily. "Edinburgh Fringe Review: The Pin, Pleasance Courtyard." *Beyond the Joke*, 21 Aug. 2018, www.beyondthejoke.co.uk/content/6118/review-pin

DiCarlo, Matt. Email Interview. 13 Sept. 2020.

Fassler, Joe. "What It Really Means to Be 'Kafkaesque'." *The Atlantic*, 17 Jan. 2014, www.theatlantic.com/entertainment/archive/2014/01/what-it-really-means-to-be-kafkaesque/283096

Drugeot, Constance. "SOLT and UK Theatre Launch Theatre for Every Child Campaign." *BroadwayWorld.com*, 16 Oct. 2023, www.broadwayworld.com/westend/article/BWW-Interview-Ben-Ashenden-and-Alex-Owen-Chat-THE-COMEBACK-at-Nol-Coward-Theatre-20201126

Frayn, Michael, and Blakemore, Michael (Introduction). *Noises Off*. Methuen Drama, 2021.

Frayn, Michael. *Plays 1*. Methuen Drama, 1985, p. xiv.

Frayn, Michael. *Understanding Michael Frayn*. University of South Carolina Press, 2006, pp. 133–134.

Frontain, Raymond-Jean. *Conversations with Terrence McNally*. University Press of Mississippi, 2023, p. 150.

Hanson, Dave. *Waiting for Waiting for Godot*. Oberon Books, 2017.

Guest Blogger: Dave Hanson. "NYLON Will Be Performed as Part of Southbank Centre'S London Literature Festival." *BroadwayWorld.com*, 10 Oct. 2023, www.broadwayworld.com/westend/article/Guest-Blog-Playwright-Dave-Hanson-On-WAITING-FOR-WAITING-FOR-GODOT-20160822

Greenham, David. "Theater Review: 'Waiting for Waiting for Godot' -- No Exit from the Green Room - The Arts Fuse." *The Arts Fuse*, 10 Oct. 2023, artsfuse.org/161677/theater-review-waiting-for-waiting-for-godot-no-exit-from-the-green-room

Hearn, Dave. Personal Interview. 10 July 2020.

Herrin, Jeremy. Personal Interview. 30 June 2020.

Houghton, Peter, and Healy, Tom (Foreword). *A Commercial Farce*. Red Door, 2015.
Jones, Chris. "Review: Just Like a Real Tech Rehearsal, '10 Out of 12' Can Get Tedious." *Chicago Tribune*, 21 Mar. 2017, www.chicagotribune.com/entertainment/theater/ct-10-of-12-review-ent-0322-20170321-column.html
Logan, Brian. "The Comeback: The Farce with James Corden, Catherine Tate and Stephen Fry Onboard." *The Guardian*, 24 Nov. 2020, www.theguardian.com/stage/2020/nov/24/pin-comeback-stephen-fry-catherine-tate-james-corden-farce-french-saunders
Loutchko, Danylo. "Two Critical." *The Minnesota Daily*, mndaily.com/219672/arts-entertainment/theater/two-critical
Ludwig, Ken. *Lend Me a Tenor and Other Plays*. Smith and Krauss, 2010.
Mandell, Alex. Personal Interview. 15 Jul. 2020.
McClure, Rob. Email Interview. 10 Jul. 2020.
McDonough, Meredith. Personal Interview. 16 Jul. 2020.
McNally, Terrence. *Three Plays*. Penguin Publishing, 1990.
Mischief. "MISCHIEF." *The Play that Goes Wrong | Our Work | MISCHIEF*, www.mischiefcomedy.com/our-work/the-play-that-goes-wrong/about
Muse, Amy. *The Drama and Theatre of Sarah Ruhl*. Methuen Drama, 2020, pp. 63–89.
Nadel, Ira. *Tom Stoppard: A Life*. Palgrave Macmillian, 2002, p. 203.
Pisoni, Lorenzo. Personal Interview. 22 Jul. 2020.
Ruhl, Sarah. *Stage Kiss*. Samuel French, 2015.
Ruhl, Sarah. "Sarah Ruhl on Stage Kiss: The Metaphysics of Backsides - Trailers + More: Playwrights Horizons." *Playwrights Horizons*, www.playwrightshorizons.org/shows/trailers/sarah-ruhl-stage-kiss
Soloski, Alexis. "10 Out of 12 Review – More than Just an Avant Garde Noises Off." *The Guardian*, 26 Mar. 2020, www.theguardian.com/stage/2015/jun/22/10-out-of-12-review-anne-washburn
Stone, Peter, et al. *Curtains*. Theatrical Rights Worldwide, 2011.
Thomas, Nikki. *A Commercial Farce | Malthouse Theatre*. 17 Jun. 2009, www.australianstage.com.au/200906172638/reviews/melbourne/a-commercial-farce-%7C-malthouse-theatre.html
Washburn, Anne. *10 out of 12*. Samuel French, 2016.
Wiki, Contributors to Goes Wrong Extended Universe. "The Murder at Haversham Manor." *Goes Wrong Extended Universe Wiki*, theplaythatgoeswrong.fandom.com/wiki/The_Murder_At_Haversham_Manor

# EXITS

## Farce and the Future

In the Spring of 2020, stages all over the world went dark. COVID didn't just shutter theatres; it shuttered the globe. Unable to gather in communal settings to share stories, and with artists suddenly finding themselves out of work, the theatre community sought ways to reach audiences.

Apps and platforms like FaceTime, Skype, Google Meet/Hangouts, and especially Zoom, became integral avenues for us to connect online. The ability to appear in a digital box and connect with friends, colleagues, and loved ones became a lifeline for communication during some very dark times. Ironically, they also became a tool for inadvertent comedy.

To this day, how many of us find ourselves in a meeting, beginning to speak, only to have a colleague say "You're muted!"? Or similarly, an awkward personal chat is overheard because someone has forgotten to mute their button. Bad Wi-fi causing faces to freeze, conversations buffered, pets jumping on a keyboard, children crying, half-clothed family members nonchalantly strolling by, and people caught attending trouserless, have all made for moments of 'Zoom Farce'.

It's not surprising that after spending so much time trapped in our little boxes (never mind our own homes), artists began exploring the parameters of online platforms like Zoom, to create works of theatre. Theatre companies and universities began to stream readings – live or pre-taped for their audiences. Audiences could watch their favourite actors perform virtual monologues, musical numbers, or conduct their talk shows from kitchens, living rooms, basements, or backyards. Although we were no longer able to share 'breath' in a theatrical space, the pandemic connected us in more intimate ways. Without the veneer of performance, artists could be seen as vulnerable, afraid, flawed, and, especially, relatable. We were all in this together.

DOI: 10.4324/9780429268809-8

For all the tragedy that the pandemic wrought, one could imagine Beckett or Ionesco seeing absurdist potential in the existential dread many of us have felt. The need to make sense of our situation while grieving unimaginable loss, manifested itself in digital presentations, using Zoom as a 'creative partner'. Dramatic works brought about quarantine catharsis. And as governments tried to contain the outbreak of COVID, with varying degrees of success, we saw examples of artists grasping the opportunity to laugh in the face of the tragic farce we were all living through.

Less than a month after universities and colleges went online, Saint Louis University Program Director of Theatre, Nancy Bell, created *MUTE: A Play for Zoom* (2020) Speaking about the project, and the decision to present the piece as a 'Zoom farce', she wrote at the time,

> I have been doing research on farce, and messing around with writing farces for a while...When COVID-19 struck, and everyone was piling on Zoom, the idea for "MUTE" came to me whole cloth – an apocalyptic farce on Zoom – and I wrote the first draft in about a week.
>
> *(Rotermund 2020)*

With productions being cancelled, accompanied by heartbreak and hard work never to be seen, Bell summed up a feeling many of us had, when she said, "We were doing theatre during a time when theatre was impossible and it felt amazing. We theatre folk love our work fiercely, and we miss it so much. It felt defiant to perform live, like an act of resistance" (Rotermund 2020).

The Old Globe in San Diego presented *In-Zoom* (2020), a 10-minute play featuring expert stage clowns Bill Irwin and Christopher Fitzgerald. Written by Irwin, the short play finds the two friends ruminating on this particular moment early on in the pandemic while navigating the ins and outs of 'Zoom'. Commenting on everything from 'where to look in the camera' to replicating a 'frozen screen' (which sees the two actors holding their faces in place for an extended period of time), and 'speaking in delays' (as if the Wi-fi connection keeps cutting out), the two men even play with their Zoom frames, having an arm starting in one screen and 'pushing through' into the other. At one point Fitzgerald says, "We're heads now...We talk in windows" (The Old Globe 2020).

They find unique ways to play with many of the recurring farce elements we have explored in this book, especially the notion of needing to persevere in the face of tragedy, and find resilience in uncertainty. They offer a funny and heartbreaking look at the impact of being trapped in isolation.

Towards the end, Irwin asks Fitzgerald to share an inspirational quote, and they each stare into the camera and offer words of wisdom encompassing the idea that despite forced separation, with love and faith, we will endure beyond death. It is a sobering and touching moment that emerges from the comedy. 'Leave Meeting', completes a decidedly Beckett-like experience.

There's some old school farce to be had with Zoom, and some Godot-esque moments as well. It is as if the gags of *Commedia Dell'arte* and French Farce have been adapted for this moment, and for this new technology (which is exactly what Irwin is attempting).

*(Teicholz 2020)*

One-third 'showbiz' satire, one-third cultural/backstage farce, and one-third metatheatrical experiment, *Staged* (2020–2022) presents close friends and stars of stage and screen, David Tennant and Michael Sheen, playing fictionalised versions of themselves, trying to stay sane during lockdown. When the pandemic cancels their West End production of Pirandello's *Six Characters in Search of an Author*, Sheen and Tennant find themselves trapped in their respective homes in Wales and London, driving their families crazy. The two friends pass time over Zoom chatting about the mundanity of life, while bickering with one another. Worried that his big break is going to pass him by, their *Six Characters* director, Simon Evans, suggests they continue rehearsing online. Unfortunately, the proceedings of Season One are derailed by egos, lies, and the restrictions of Zoom.

As the series returns, apropos of the multi-realities of Pirandello's *Six Characters*, Season Two delivers a metatheatrical 'show-within-a-show.' Because of the popularity of the 'actual' Zoom series *Staged*, Simon (who is the creator of *Staged*) has now achieved the big break he always sought. Hollywood wants to capitalise on the success of *Staged* and produce an American version of the Zoom Series, *without* Tennant and Sheen. Season Three finds the world emerging from the pandemic, with Sheen and Tennant keen to move on with their lives and determined to have nothing further to do with Simon. Predictably and riotously, Simon manipulates them into recording a Christmas radio play. The pleasure in the series is watching the 'bromance' between the two actors and their undeniable chemistry.

In May 2020, award-winning playwright Jordan E. Cooper wrote and directed *Mama Got a Cough*, a domestic/social farce using the Zoom platform to highlight how COVID heightened racial and class disparity, and its impact on the African American community. Worrying about their mother's ongoing cough and the possibility she may have contracted COVID-19, five siblings gather over Zoom to formulate a strategy on how they might convince her to go to the hospital. Unfortunately, the conversation is sidetracked whenever a new sibling enters the Zoom room. Familial mocking makes for a hilarious Zoom call, pointing up the love these characters have for one another, while demonstrating the helpless feeling we all experienced, of not being able to look after our loved ones while in quarantine. All six characters are coping in their own way with the pandemic. Casey seems to be imbibing her fair share of wine. Ashley is not at home, cohabitating with a 'white conservative' man. Yolanda is struggling to help her disinterested son with math homework that is completely foreign to her. Jamel appears online with a new girlfriend, prompting his sisters to call him out on his three-month turnaround with women. Their youngest sibling, Malik, brazenly calls in from a house party or a 'quaranturna'. When Mama finally arrives on the call, we are presented with an irascible, tart-tongued, intelligent woman who fears dying alone. When Mama cites a recent neighbour who passed away in hospital from COVID with only tubes surrounding her, she

> proclaims that going to the hospital is useless because no one will care about her there – a recognition of the racial disparities in health care that make COVID-19 even deadlier for the black people who contract it – Ashley suggests Mama take her elderly white neighbour with her…'Look, good things happen when you hustle white people,' Ashley said.
>
> *(McDonald 2020)*

Underneath the sibling jabs and joshing, you can feel the impact the virus is having on all of these characters. Cooper is unafraid of letting the characters 'have at' one another with gleeful abandon in one moment, and pivot to the reality of their circumstances in the next. In a mere 14 minutes, Cooper and Company capture the earthy love within this family and the poignancy of loss and loneliness. With characters entering and exiting Zoom rooms and overcoming internet glitches, *Mama Got A Cough*

> is a testament to what's possible with a keyboard, an internet connection and a few friends. And it provides heaps of what remains an essential, priceless elixir: laughs.
>
> *(McDonald, 2020)*

Actor Rob McClure created 'ConductorCam', a 15-episode web series in lockdown. Shot from the perspective of a 'conductor's camera', and showcasing McClure's gift for physical comedy, these short pieces, many lasting no more than two minutes, drop the viewer inside a Broadway orchestra pit. We watch our resilient maestro (played by McClure), navigate everything from performers not paying attention to cutoffs, showboating for 'friends in the audience', to disappearing amidst an abundance of *Phantom of the Opera* 'fog' as it spills into the pit. In one particular episode, we see our conductor having to keep his orchestra and actors 'in-time' as he battles an audience's poor sense of rhythmic clapping during a performance of *Jersey Boys*.

In addition to the 'farcical' pieces, three of the episodes offer an urgent and poignant tone. Premiering in the wake of the George Floyd murder and Black Lives Matter protests, Episode 13 ("Poco a poco accelerando") finds McClure exuberantly conducting the opening number of *Ragtime* until everything comes to a sudden halt. Recognising the need to 'pass the baton', McClure hands over his conductor's wand to Kalena Bovell, African American poet, author, and conductor, who proceeds to speak words of power about what it means to be Black in America. The episode concludes with her finishing the number and offering the baton to the camera. Episode 14 finds McClure in the pit listening to a recorded speech of Donald Trump dismissing COVID and disrespecting the city of Philadelphia. Leaving the pit, McClure defiantly walks the streets of his hometown of Philadelphia, conducting an orchestral version of John Lennon's *Imagine*, in the process imploring everyone to exercise their right to vote.

There was only one episode crafted for 'Season Two', and for good reason. It had been recently announced that Broadway was re-opening. In this moving episode, while McClure goes through his preparation for the 'first show back', we hear the voice of a Production Stage Manager calling everyone to 'places'. A chorus of voices from productions all over Broadway, specifically those of unsung backstage crew members, respond with their own unique version of 'standing by'. These three episodes are not farcical, but their emotional weight lands because of the comedy that has preceded it. In fifteen short episodes, we have become invested in McClure's Maestro, as he tries to get through his performances without incident. In this final episode, his anticipation of the return of live theatre powerfully mirrors that of his colleagues and underlines our own devout wish and need. Reflecting on ConductorCam and its impact, McClure writes:

> Legendary director Jerry Zaks, has said to me repeatedly "Laughter is the sound of an audience falling in love with you…so therefore…when something befalls you…they care."
>
> ConductorCam was born out of a fascination with conducting. I've always considered it magical, like those fireworks of music shooting out of Mickey Mouse's fingertips in *Fantasia*. In the world of musical theatre, conductors, and conductor monitors in particular, can be the source of hysterical specificity and eccentricity for the actors who stare at them for instruction. I made the first episode during the pandemic, with no intention of making more than one, for the sole purpose of making a handful of friends chuckle. I quickly realized that this Conductor character was striking a nerve. I think people needed to laugh, and musical theatre people needed a reminder of home.
>
> Influenced greatly by Charlie Chaplin, Jim Carrey, Bill Irwin, Michael Jeter and Victor Borge, I know they were subconsciously pulling the strings inside me as I was creating the minute long episodes from Covid Quarantine in our home in Philadelphia. I didn't realize I was clowning at the time. The sketches were so specific in their humor, and yet their appeal seemed to be universal…a sure fire sign that the clown inside me must have been driving the whole time.
>
> When George Floyd was murdered, the cry for social Justice was rightly dominating the media, and I stopped making episodes to use my social media for the amplification of more imminent need.
>
> I began to wonder if there was a way to do a bait and switch.

Could I give people a new episode, where they would click to laugh, but then subversively deliver a poignant message. Charlie Chaplin's Tramp character did this in perhaps the most powerful example in "The Great Dictator."

I reached out to a Black Conductor that I was inspired by online named Kalena Bovell, who conducts the Memphis Youth Symphony. I asked if she'd be willing to partner with me on a Black Lives Matter episode of ConductorCam. We created something really powerful that we're both really proud of.

Cut to the 2020 presidential election. I again saw an opportunity for the Conductor character to have something more pressing to say.

And finally, as Broadway was reeling, closed for more than a year, I saw an opportunity to unite the community in a celebratory episode that I still get tearful thank you messages for almost daily.

Jerry Zaks was right. If you can make them laugh, you can make them care.

*(McClure 2023)*

Throughout this book, although focused primarily on the 21st century, we have referenced the origins, evolution, and impact of farce going back to the Greeks, through to the 20th century. We have encountered plays from all over the globe, entering worlds dominated by laughter, but also pain and sadness. Playwrights are exploding the boundaries of farce, no longer confined to the strictures that have come to define the form. Surveying work world-wide reminds us that human nature is a funny business. We respond universally to characters behaving irrationally, yet humorously. Farce speaks a global language.

The plays discussed herein, primarily from Europe, Australia, or the Americas, provide unique perspectives, styles, and use of language speaking to the playwright's moment. The hope remains that further study of farce will invite exploration of new works emerging from many countries in Asia and Africa.

Contemporary farce is daring and unpredictable, and it no longer relies on the classic tropes of the genre. It allows us to interrogate a world that can take itself too seriously, and through humour we are able to pay clearer attention. A good farce doesn't preach. Instead, it lures us in, makes us laugh and leaves us recognising part of ourselves in the characters onstage. As we have seen, contemporary farce, in its continued evolution, understands that its audience is broader and no longer confined to the exploits of the middle or upper classes. Contemporary playwrights are finding storytelling opportunities that mirror a greater diversity in its audience. The farces produced today have the potential to resonate with a wider audience because they are unafraid to plumb difficult topics featuring a more inclusive cast of characters. The stories feature lower-status, working-class characters, are racially, sexually, and gender inclusive, and have the courage to let us sit in the dark with comical discomfort.

As a contemporary society, we need farce more than ever, especially in our post-pandemic world. Its value is paramount when we recognise the omnipresence of 'real-world' issues demanding fine farcical commentary. Whether blessed with a generous budget, or working on a shoestring, farce can be fashioned effectively, entertainingly, and successfully. Twenty-first-century farces may function equally well with box sets, sturdy doors, and lavish costumes, or with two chairs, a bare stage, and actors portraying several roles. In either case, the audience's imagination and laughter complete the storytelling.

Our five doors were designed to help us see the world of farce beyond the frivolous, beyond simply light entertainment. They are meant to aid practitioners in not only recognising types of farce, but also identifying the elements that will help both 'pitch' and focus a production.

Clearly, most farces don't fall neatly into one category. They may have structural similarities. Cultural farces can have political leanings. Political farces can include domestic subplots. Domestic farces can have social overtones. In general, however, playwrights construct specific worlds that allow them to explore personal agendas. By situating farces into specific categories, practitioners can best target their work, and invite audiences to engage in meaningful dialogue with the plays.

As stages all over the world have reopened, the future of farce appears filled with possibilities and hope. Contemporary artists are seeing the genre as a viable and exciting means to reflect, comment on, and highlight our chaotic existence.

Appearing on Amber Ambam's podcast, "More to Talk About", to discuss her play *POTUS*, playwright Selina Fillinger was interviewed alongside the writer, commentator and feminist activist Jamia Wilson, and the renowned journalist and socio-political activist, Gloria Steinem. At one point, Steinem says:

> I would like to thank Selina for taking laughter seriously, because it turns out that laughter is actually the only emotion that can't be compelled. You can obviously make someone feel afraid. You can even make someone feel they are in love if they are dependent for long enough, because you enmesh in order to survive. But laughter is a free emotion. It is the proof of freedom. And in Native American cultures, they recognize that, because there was a Spirit of Laughter who was neither male nor female, and the spirit of laughter was important to everything else, because if you couldn't laugh and break into the unknown, you couldn't pray. So you might say that Selina taking laughter seriously here, is part of a great, grand tradition.
>
> *(Ambam 2022)*

Farce recognises, accepts, and addresses the absurdities of the world. The characters in these plays endure their hardships, manage their trials, and (hopefully) survive to behave 'farcically' again. Through laughter, contemporary audiences can cope with their own real-life absurdities for another day.

And thus, we have offered and honoured 'serious laughter' as a transformative power for catharsis.

**Works Cited**

Ambam, Amber. "Feminism & the White House Ft. Gloria Steinem, Jamia Wilson, & Selina Fillinger." *Apple Podcasts*, 10 Jun. 2022, podcasts.apple.com/us/podcast/feminism-the-white-house-ft-gloria-steinem-jamia/id1609713679?i=1000566013121

The Old Globe. "In-Zoom: A World Premiere Play." *YouTube*, 8 Jun. 2020, www.youtube.com/watch?v=Do8tXJLQgK0

"Mama Got a Cough." YouTube, uploaded by Cookout Entertainment, 18 May 2020, https://www.youtube.com/watch?v=YeOqzQedwHE

McDonald, Soraya Nadia. "'Mama Got a Cough' Is a Zoom Comedy for the COVID-19 Era." *Andscape*, 28 May 2020, andscape.com/features/mama-got-a-cough-a-zoom-comedy-for-the-covid-19-coronavirus-era

McClure, Rob. "CONDUCTOR CAM Episode 1-15." *YouTube*, 18 Sept. 2020, www.youtube.com/watch?v=Mm8Qtzs1UYk

McClure, Rob. Email Interview. 16 Oct. 2023.

Rotermund, Maggie. *SLU Playwright Pens, Produces "MUTE: A Play for Zoom"*. Saint Louis University, May 2020, www.slu.edu/news/2020/may/mute-zoom-play.php

Teicholz, Tom. "Zooming in on Bill Irwin's in Zoom Performance." *Forbes*, 14 May 2020, www.forbes.com/sites/tomteicholz/2020/05/14/zooming-in-on-bill-irwins-in-zoom-performance/?sh=4f348ec1a1fe

# APPENDIX

## List of Modern and Contemporary Farces from Around the World

**Modern & Contemporary Farces**

The following is a list of modern and contemporary farces from around the world. Modern farces encompass those written in the 20th century. Contemporary farces are those that premiered in the 21st century. In addition to those specifically mentioned throughout the book, I have included additional titles that came to my attention throughout my research. The following are broken down geographically, including their year of premiere and their predominant 'door.' If there is a clear crossover, I have listed multiple 'doors.'

| Geographical Location | Year of Premiere | Farce Door |
|---|---|---|
| **AFRICA** | | |
| South Africa | | |
| Uys, Pieter-Dirk | | |
| *Macbeki* | 2009 | Political |
| *The Merry Wives of Zuma* | 2012 | Political |
| **ASIA** | | |
| Japan | | |
| Motoya, Yukiko | | |
| *Vengeance Can Wait* | 2008 | Domestic |
| **AUSTRALIA** | | |
| Green, Declan | | |
| *The Homosexuals, or Faggots* | 2017 | Social/Domestic |
| Houghton, Peter | | |

*(Continued)*

| Geographical Location | Year of Premiere | Farce Door |
|---|---|---|
| *A Commercial Farce* | 2009 | Backstage |
| Lui, Nakkiah | | |
| *Black is the New White* | 2018 | Social/Domestic |
| Williamson, David | | |
| *The Department* | 1974 | Political |
| **EUROPE** | | |
| Denmark | | |
| Knutzon, Line | | |
| *The Builder* | 2008 | Domestic |
| France: | | |
| Camoletti, Marc | | |
| *Boeing-Boeing* | 1960 | Domestic |
| *Don't Dress for Dinner* | 1987 | Domestic |
| Poiret, Jean | | |
| *La Cage aux Folles* | 1973 | Social/Domestic |
| Reza, Yasmina | | |
| *Art* | 1998 | Social/Cultural |
| *Life x 3* | 2000 | Social/Domestic |
| *God of Carnage* | 2008 | Domestic/Social |
| Veber, Francis | | |
| *The Painkiller* (adaptation by Sean Foley) | 2011 | Cultural |
| Vos, Rémi de | | |
| *Till Death* | 2006 | Domestic |
| Germany | | |
| Geiselmann, David | | |
| *Mr. Kolpert* | 2000 | Cultural |
| *The Pigeons* | 2009 | Domestic/Social |
| Schimmelpfennig, Roland | | |
| *The Woman Before* | 2005 | Domestic |
| Von Mayenburg, Marius | | |
| *Perplex* | 2010 | Domestic |
| *The Ugly One* | 2007 | Social |
| Ireland | | |
| Cantan, Mark | | |
| *Jezebel* | 2012 | Domestic |
| Friel, Brian | | |
| *The Communication Cord* | 1982 | Domestic |
| Leonard, Hugh | | |
| *The Patrick Pearse Hotel* | 1971 | Domestic |
| McDonagh, Martin | | |
| *The Lieutenant of Inishmore* | 2001 | Political |

(*Continued*)

| Geographical Location | Year of Premiere | Farce Door |
|---|---|---|
| *A Behanding in Spokane* | 2010 | Social/Cultural |
| Walsh, Enda | | |
| *The Walworth Farce* | 2006 | Domestic |
| West, Michael | | |
| *Dublin By Lamplight* | 2005 | Cultural |
| Italy | | |
| Fo, Dario | | |
| *The Virtuous Burglar* | 1958 | Domestic |
| *Accidental Death of an Anarchist* | 1970 | Political |
| *Can't Pay? Won't Pay!* | 1974 | Political/Social |
| *Trumpets and Raspberries* | 1981 | Political |
| *Abducting Francesca* | 1986 | Political |
| Switzerland | | |
| Durrenmatt, Friedrich | | |
| *The Physicists* | 1962 | Social/Political |
| **UNITED KINGDOM** | | |
| Great Britain | | |
| Ashenden, Ben & Owen, Alex | | |
| *The Comeback* | 2020 | Backstage |
| Ayckbourn, Alan | | |
| *How the Other Half Loves* | 1970 | Domestic |
| *The Norman Conquests* | 1973 | Domestic |
| *Bedroom Farce* | 1975 | Domestic |
| *Ten Times Table* | 1977 | Political/Domestic |
| *Taking Steps* | 1979 | Domestic |
| *House & Garden* | 2000 | Domestic |
| Barlow, Patrick | | |
| *The 39 Steps* | 2008 | Cultural |
| *Ben-Hur* | 2020 | Cultural |
| Barnes, Peter | | |
| *Leonardo's Last Supper* | 1969 | Domestic/Cultural |
| *Laughter!* | 1978 | Political |
| *Not as Bad as They Seem* | 1989 | Domestic |
| Bean, Richard | | |
| *In the Club* | 2007 | Political/Domestic |
| *One Man, Two Guvnors* | 2013 | Cultural |
| *The Hypocrite* | 2019 | Political/Domestic |
| *Jack Absolute Rides Again* (with Oliver Chris) | 2022 | Cultural |
| Bennett, Alan | | |
| *Habeas Corpus* | 1973 | Domestic |

(*Continued*)

| Geographical Location | Year of Premiere | Farce Door |
|---|---|---|
| Buffini, Moira | | |
| *Dinner* | 2002 | Domestic |
| Churchill, Caryl | | |
| *Cloud Nine* | 1979 | Social/Political |
| *Serious Money* | 1987 | Political |
| Cooney, Ray | | |
| *Run for Your Wife* | 1983 | Domestic |
| *It Runs in the Family* | 1987 | Domestic |
| *Out of Order* | 1990 | Political |
| Elton, Ben | | |
| *Gasping* | 1990 | Political |
| *Silly Cow* | 1991 | Social |
| *Popcorn* | 1996 | Cultural |
| Frayn, Michael | | |
| *The Two of Us* | 1970 | Domestic |
| *Donkey's Years* | 1977 | Social |
| *Noises Off* | 1982 | Backstage |
| *The Sneeze* | 1988 | Cultural |
| *Alarms and Excursions* | 1998 | Domestic |
| Graham, James | | |
| *The Culture* | 2017 | Political |
| Hampton, Christopher | | |
| *The Philanthropist* | 1970 | Domestic/Social |
| Jeffreys, Stephen | | |
| *The Clink* | 1990 | Cultural/Political |
| Johnson, Terry | | |
| *Hysteria* | 1993 | Cultural |
| *Dead Funny* | 1994 | Domestic |
| Kirkwood, Lucy | | |
| *Tinderbox* | 2008 | Political/Domestic |
| Linehan, Graham | | |
| *The Ladykillers* | 2011 | Cultural |
| Mischief Theatre | | |
| *The Play That Goes Wrong* | 2012 | Backstage/Cultural |
| *Peter Pan Goes Wrong* | 2013 | Backstage/Cultural |
| *The Nativity Goes Wrong* | 2013 | Backstage/Cultural |
| *The Comedy About the Bank Robbery* | 2016 | Cultural |
| *Groan Ups* | 2019 | Domestic/Social |
| *Magic Goes Wrong* | 2019 | Backstage |
| Le Navet Bete & John Nicholson | | |
| *Dracula: The Bloody Truth* | 2017 | Cultural |
| *The Three Musketeers* | 2019 | Cultural |
| *Treasure Island* | 2019 | Cultural |
| Orton, Joe | | |

(*Continued*)

| Geographical Location | Year of Premiere | Farce Door |
|---|---|---|
| *Loot* | 1965 | Social/Domestic |
| *What the Butler Saw* | 1969 | Social |
| Peepolykus & John Nicholson | | |
| *The Hound of the Baskervilles* | 2007 | Cultural |
| *The Massive Tragedy of Madame Bovary* | 2016 | Cultural |
| Penhall, Joe | | |
| *Birthday* | 2012 | Domestic/Social |
| Porter, Phil | | |
| *Vice Versa* | 2017 | Cultural |
| Shaffer, Peter | | |
| *Black Comedy* | 1965 | Domestic |
| Stoppard, Tom | | |
| *Rosencrantz and Guildenstern are Dead* | 1966 | Cultural |
| *The Real Inspector Hound* | 1968 | Backstage |
| *After Magritte* | 1970 | Domestic/Cultural |
| *Dirty Linen* | 1976 | Political |
| Thompson, Steve | | |
| *Whipping it Up* | 2006 | Political |
| *No Naughty Bits* | 2011 | Cultural |
| Scotland | | |
| Beaton, Alistair | | |
| *Feelgood* | 2001 | Political |
| *The Arsonists* (after Max Frisch) | 2007 | Cultural/Social |
| Burke, Gregory | | |
| *Gagarin's Way* | 2001 | Social |
| Neilson, Anthony | | |
| *The Lying Kind* | 2002 | Social |
| **NORTH AMERICA** | | |
| Canada | | |
| Codrington, Lisa | | |
| *The Adventures of the Black Girl in Her Search for God* | 2016 | Cultural/Social |
| Sandler, Kat | | |
| *The Party/The Candidate* | 2019 | Political |
| Walker, George F. | | |
| *Escape From Happiness* | 1991 | Domestic |
| Wood, Tom | | |
| *Claptrap* | 1998 | Backstage |
| Mexico | | |
| Berman, Sabina | | |
| *The Agony of Ecstasy* | 1977 | Social |

(*Continued*)

| Geographical Location | Year of Premiere | Farce Door |
|---|---|---|
| United States | | |
| Benjamin, Nell | | |
| *The Explorer's Club* | 2014 | Social |
| Bradshaw, Thomas | | |
| *Intimacy* | 2014 | Social |
| Brooks, Mel and Meehan, Thomas | | |
| *The Producers: A New Musical* | 2001 | Cultural/Backstage |
| Busch, Charles | | |
| *The Tribute Artist* | 2014 | Social |
| Durang, Christopher | | |
| *Why Torture is Wrong and the People Who Love Them* | 2009 | Political/Domestic |
| *Vanya and Sonia and Masha and Spike* | 2012 | Cultural/Domestic |
| Erlbach, Matthew-Lee | | |
| *The Doppelganger* | 2018 | Political |
| FastHorse, Larissa | | |
| *The Thanksgiving Play* | 2015 | Social |
| Greenberg, Richard | | |
| *Hurrah, At Last!* | 1998 | Domestic |
| Guare, John | | |
| *The House of Blue Leaves* | 1971 | Domestic |
| *Six Degrees of Separation* | 1990 | Social/Domestic |
| *A Free Man of Color* | 2010 | Social |
| Hwang, David Henry | | |
| *Yellow Face* | 2007 | Social/Backstage |
| Guindi, Yuseff El | | |
| *Threesome* | 2016 | Social |
| Ives, David | | |
| *Is He Dead?* (after Mark Twain) | 2007 | Cultural |
| Jacobs-Jenkins, Branden | | |
| *Neighbors* | 2010 | Cultural/Social |
| *Appropriate* | 2014 | Social/Domestic |
| Lee, Young-Jean | | |
| *The Shipment* | 2009 | Social |
| Letts, Tracy | | |
| *The Minutes* | 2018 | Political |
| Ludlam, Charles | | |
| *The Mystery of Irma Vep* | 1984 | Cultural |
| Ludwig, Ken | | |
| *Lend Me a Tenor* | 1986 | Domestic/Backstage |
| *Crazy for You* | 1991 | Cultural/Backstage |
| *Moon Over Buffalo* | 1995 | Domestic/Backstage |

(*Continued*)

| Geographical Location | Year of Premiere | Farce Door |
| --- | --- | --- |
| *Shakespeare in Hollywood* | 2003 | Backstage/Cultural |
| *Leading Ladies* | 2004 | Backstage/Cultural |
| *Twentieth Century* | 2004 | Backstage/Cultural |
| *The Fox in the Fairway* | 2010 | Domestic |
| *The Game's Afoot* | 2012 | Cultural |
| *Baskerville* | 2015 | Cultural |
| *A Comedy of Tenors* | 2015 | Domestic/Backstage |
| *The Gods of Comedy* | 2019 | Cultural |
| Mac, Taylor | | |
| *Gary: A Sequel to Titus Andronicus* | 2019 | Cultural |
| Mamet, David | | |
| *Romance* | 2005 | Political |
| *November* | 2007 | Political |
| Martin, Steve | | |
| *The Underpants* (after Carl Weber) | 2002 | Cultural/Domestic |
| McNally, Terrence | | |
| *The Ritz* | 1975 | Social |
| *It's Only a Play* | 1982 | Backstage |
| Rebeck, Theresa | | |
| *The Understudy* | 2008 | Backstage |
| *Poor Behavior* | 2011 | Domestic |
| *Fools* | 2014 | Cultural |
| Rustin, Sandy | | |
| *The Cottage* | 2014 | Domestic |
| *Clue* | 2020 | Cultural |
| Simon, Neil | | |
| *Rumors* | 1988 | Social/Domestic |
| *The Dinner Party* | 2000 | Social/Domestic |
| Smith, Deborah Salem | | |
| *Faithful Cheaters* | 2017 | Domestic |
| Paul Slade Unnecessary Farce | 2006 | Social/Political |
| The Outsider | 2015 | Political |

# INDEX

*Accidental Death of an Anarchist* (Fo) 13, 103–110, 125
Ada, Kawa 107
Adams, Liz Duffy: *Or* 175–176
Adams, Tim 118
adaptation 145–146; cinematic 155–161; literary 146–155; theatrical 161–173; *see also* cultural farce(s)
*The Agony of Ecstasy* (Berman) 69; *El bigote* ("The Mustache") 69; *La casa chica* ("The Love Nest") 69; *La pistola* ("The Pistol") 69
Aitken, Maria 152
Albee, Edward: *Who's Afraid of Virginia Woolf?* 177
Ambam, Amber 220
American domestic farce(s) 44–50; *A Comedy of Tenors* (Ludwig) 45–48; *Faithful Cheaters* (Smith) 48–50; *Lend Me a Tenor* (Ludwig) 45–47
American political farce(s) 120–125; *The Minutes* (Letts) 120–123; *POTUS* (Fillinger) 120, 123–125
Aristophanes 101
*The Art of Coarse Acting* (Green) 195
Ashenden, Ben: *The Comeback* (Ashenden and Owen) 17, 200–202
*The Atlantic* 203
Ayckbourn, Alan 38–40, 135, 138; *Bedroom Farce* 39–40; *House & Garden* 40, 138; *How the Other Half Loves* 39; *The Norman Conquests* 40; *Taking Steps* 39; *Ten Times Table* 135

*Bach at Leipzig* (Moses) 174–175
backstage farce(s) 182–212; critics and 205–209; *Noises Off* (Frayn) 183–188, 196, 200, 201, 211; performance 194–202; rehearsal process 188–194; understudies and 202–205; *see also* Ludwig, Ken
Barlow, Patrick: *The 39 Steps* 6, 17, 152–155
Barnes, Peter 38; *Not As Bad as They Seem* 40–41
Barnett, Jeremy 65
Bartlett, Mike: *Cock* 80; *The 47th* 80; *Scandaltown* 80–81
Basden, Tom 109
*Baskerville* (Ludwig) 150–151
Bean, Richard 13, 162; *In the Club* 136; *The Hypocrite* 6, 116, 136; *Jack Absolute Flies Again* 172–173; *One Man, Two Guvnors* 13, 17, 18, 169–173, 202
Beaton, Alistair: *Feelgood* 111, 114–115, 135
Beckett, Samuel 23, 164; *Waiting for Godot* 203, 204, 205
*The Bedford Introduction to Drama* (Jacobus) 10
*Bedroom Farce* (Ayckbourn) 39–40

Bell, Nancy: *MUTE: A Play for Zoom* 215
Benjamin, Nell: *The Explorer's Club* 73–75
Bennett, Alan: *Habeas Corpus* 40
Bentley, Eric 22–23
Bergson, Henri 18, 21, 27
Berman, Sabina: *The Agony of Ecstasy* 69
Billington, Michael 33, 177
*Birdman* 210–211
*Birthday* (Penhall) 18, 41, 42–44
Bissett, Cora 82–83
*Black Comedy* (Shaffer) 25, 38, 41
*Black Is the New White* (Lui) 92–94
*Black Watch* 81
Blakemore, Michael 184
*Blue/Orange* (Penhall) 43
Boal, Augusto 107
*Boeing-Boeing* (Camoletti) 13, 18, 26, 30–33
Boenisch, Peter M. 72–73
Bogart, Anne 13
Borge, Victor 218
Born, Sebastian 169
*Boston Globe* 86
bourgeois farce 75–81; *The Dinner Party* (Simon) 76; *A Free Man of Color* (Guare) 6, 17, 76, 79–80; *Rumors* (Simon) 9, 75–76; *Six Degrees of Separation* (Guare) 76–79; *see also* Irish domestic farce
Bovell, Kalena 218, 219
Bradshaw, Thomas: *Intimacy* 16, 89–92; Jefferson on 89
Brantley, Ben 70, 90, 133
Brecht, Bertolt 102, 106; *Mother Courage and Her Children* 168; *The Resistible Rise of Arturo Ui* 128
British domestic farce(s) 37–44; *Bedroom Farce* (Ayckbourn) 39–40; *Birthday* (Penhall) 18, 41, 42–44; *Black Comedy* (Shaffer) 25, 38, 41; *Dinner* (Buffini) 13, 41–42; *Habeas Corpus* (Bennett) 40; *House & Garden* (Ayckbourn) 40; *How the Other Half Loves* (Ayckbourn) 39; *The Norman Conquests* (Ayckbourn) 40; *Not As Bad as They Seem* (Barnes) 40–41
British political farce(s) 111–120; *The Culture* (Graham) 17, 114, 115–117, 136; *Dirty Linen* (Stoppard) 112–114, 121; *Feelgood* (Beaton) 114–115, 135;

*Tinderbox* (Kirkwood) 111, 114, 117–120, 167
*Broadway World* 201
Brooks, Mel 1–2, 13; *All-American* 159; Broadway credits 159; lyric writing 161; *New Faces of 1952* 159; *The Producers* 13, 159–161, 183; *Shinbone Alley* (with Darion) 159
Brown, Blair 121
Brown, James: "I Got You (I Feel Good)" 115
Buchan, John 152, 154
Buffini, Moira 13; *Dinner* 13, 41–42; Sierz on 42
*The Builders* (Knutzon) 55–56
Bunt, Nick 147–148
Burke, Gregory: *Black Watch* 81; *Gagarin Way* 81, 82–83
Busch, Charles: *The Tribute Artist* 96

*The Cage of Madwomen* (Poiret) *see La Cage aux Folles* (Poiret)
Cagney, James 210
Callow, Simon 69
*The Candidate* (Sandler) 138, 139–140
Canny, Steve 147
Cantan, Mark: *Jezebel* 56–57
*Can't Pay? Won't Pay!* (Fo) 103
Capra, Frank 209
Carrey, Jim 218
Chaplin, Charlie 128, 218, 219
Chapman, John 38
character 19–20; *see also* specific farceurs
Chekhov, Anton 169
Chris, Oliver: *Jack Absolute Flies Again* 172–173
cinematic adaptation 155–161; *Clue* (Rustin) 157–158; *The Ladykillers* (Linehan) 155–157; *The Producers* (Brooks) 159–161
*The Civilized Reader* 154
*The Clean House* (Ruhl) 189
Cleese, John 30
*The Clink* (Jeffreys) 168
Clinton, Hillary 120
clowns, fools, and jesters 168
*Clue* (board game) 157
*Clue* (Rustin) 157–158
*The Coarse Acting Show* (Green) 195
*Cock* (Bartlett) 80
*The Code of the Woosters* (Wodehouse) 149

Index  **231**

*The Comeback* (Ashenden and Owen) 17, 200–202
*Comedians* (Griffiths) 168
comedy: as drama's broad form 12; physical 20–21; silence in 5; styles of 12
*The Comedy of Errors* (Shakespeare) 201
*A Comedy of Tenors* (Ludwig) 18–19, 45, 46, 47–48, 209
*A Commercial Farce* (Houghton) 190–192
*The Communication Cord* (Friel) 50–51
*Community* 162
ConductorCam (McClure's web series) 217–219
*Contemporary European Playwrights* 72
Cooper, Jordan E. 216–217; *Mama Got a Cough* 216–217
Corble, Simon 152
Corden, James 169
Corrigan, Bryony 195, 199
*The Cottage* (Rustin) 55
*The Coup* (Matura) 126, 128–129
COVID-19 pandemic 140, 202, 214–218
Coward, Noël 55, 63, 189
The Craze (band) 172
*The Cripple of Inishmaan* (McDonagh) 134
*The Critic, or a Tragedy Rehearsed* (Sheridan) 206, 207
critics, backstage farces and 205–209; *It's Only a Play* (McNally) 207–209; *The Real Inspector Hound* (Stoppard) 206–207
*The Crocodile* (Basden) 149–150
cultural farce(s) 144–179; icons *see* cultural icons; as models of adaptation 145–146; novel and *see* novels/literary adaptation; political leanings 220; as popular form 144; silver screen and *see* cinematic adaptation
cultural icons 173–176; *Bach at Leipzig* (Moses) 174–175; *Hysteria* (Johnson) 173–174; *No Naughty Bits* (Thompson) 176; *Or* (Adams) 175–176
*The Culture* (Graham) 17, 114, 115–117, 136
*Curb Your Enthusiasm* 17, 211
*Curtains* 205

Dali, Salvador 173
David, Larry 17

Davis, Jessica Milner 2–3, 5
*Dead Funny* (Johnson) 54–55, 171, 202
*Dead Man's Cell Phone* (Ruhl) 189
*Desdemona: A Play About a Handkerchief* (Vogel) 164
desperation *see* panic (hysteria and desperation)
De Vos, Remi 54
DiCarlo, Matt 197, 198
*The Dick Van Dyke Show* 211
*Die Hose* (Sternheim) 178
Dimon, Nobby 152
*Dinner* (Buffini) 13, 41–42
*The Dinner Party* (Simon) 76
*Dirty Linen* (Stoppard) 112–114, 121
domestic farce 25–57, 220; American 44–50; British 37–44; French 28–37; Irish 50–54
*The Doppelganger* (Erlbach) 137–138
Dostoevsky, Fydor 149
Doyle, Conan 150, 151; *The Hound of the Baskervilles* 147, 150; "A Scandal in Bohemia" 151
*Dracula: The Bloody Truth* (Le Navet Bete) 148
Dunn, Al 147–148
Durang, Christopher 44; *Why Torture is Wrong, and the People Who Love Them* 136–137

Ebb, Fred 205
*Einen Jux will er sich machen* (Nestroy) 168
El-Guindi, Yussef: *Threesome* 96
*Entertainment Weekly* 55
*Episodes* 211
Erdman, Nikolai 101
Erlbach, Matthew-Lee: *The Doppelganger* 137–138
*The Explorer's Club* (Benjamin) 73–75
*Extras* 211

*Faithful Cheaters* (Smith) 48–50, 64
farce(s): character 19–20; Davis on 2–3, 5; defining 10–13; as a divertissement 10; earliest roots 12; failures 9, 10, 14, 185; five doors 23–24; Foley on 3; Four P Story Arc 13–16; Frayn on 10, 15, 25; key ingredients 18; Kierkegaard on 3; language 21–22; machine-like quality of 5; mechanics 16–17; physical nature of 11; reductive language describing 10; Rourke on 4;

structure 17–19; themes 22–23; violence in 20–21; as white male-dominated genre 7; *see also specific farceurs*
*Farce: A History from Aristophanes to Woody Allen* (Bermel) 25
*Farce* (Davis) 2–3
"Farce is Far More Serious" (Kierkegaard) 3
farce remixed *see* cultural farce(s)
Farrell, Joseph 102
FastHorse, Larissa: *The Thanksgiving Play* 6, 94–95
*Fat Ham* (Ijames) 168
*Feelgood* (Beaton) 111, 114–115, 135
*Female Parts* (Fo and Rame) 103
Ferber, Edna 44
Feydeau, Georges 12–13, 28–30, 32, 33, 37, 41, 46, 47, 50, 51, 54, 58, 62, 63, 79, 102, 103, 130, 137
Fillinger, Selina: on Ambam's podcast 220; *POTUS* 120, 123–125, 175, 220
Fitzgerald, Christopher 215
Fitzpatrick, Sean 154
Floyd, George 108, 217, 218
Fo, Dario 29; *Accidental Death of an Anarchist* 13, 103–110, 125; bourgeois period 102; *Can't Pay? Won't Pay!* 103; *Female Parts* (with Rame) 103; *Kidnapping Francesca* 103; as people's playwright 103; *Trumpets and Raspberries* 103; *The Virtuous Burglar* 18, 103
Foley, Sean 3, 66; *The Painkiller* 178; *The Play What I Wrote* 201
*Fool* (Rebeck) 168
*The 47th* (Bartlett) 80
Foster, Hunter 157
Four P Story Arc 13–16; panic (hysteria and desperation) 15–16; passion (obsession) 13–14; persistence (perseverance) 14; preservation (survival) 16
Frayn, Michael 10, 25, 37, 38; *Noises Off* 19, 41, 46, 183–188, 196, 200, 201, 211; on panic 15; *Stage Directions* 15; *The Two of Us* 183
Freeman, Matt 147–148
*A Free Man of Color* (Guare) 6, 17, 76, 79–80
French domestic farce(s) 28–37; *Boeing-Boeing* (Camoletti) 13, 18, 26, 30–33; *God of Carnage* (Reza) 16, 33–37, 42
Freud, Sigmund 173

Friel, Brian: *The Communication Cord* 50–51
*Friends* 20
*A Funny Thing Happened on the Way to the Forum* 159, 163

*Gagarin Way* (Burke) 81, 82–83
*The Game's Afoot* (Ludwig) 150
*Gary: A Sequel to Titus Andronicus* (Mac) 165–169
Geffen, David 159
Gelbart, Larry 163
gender *see* identity, gender, and sexuality
*A Gentleman's Guide to Love and Murder* 159
Gieselmann, David: *Herr Kolpert* 177
Giguere, Amanda 34; *The Plays of Yasmina Reza on the English and American Stage* 35
Giles, Sarah 108–109
Gillette, William 150
*God of Carnage* (Reza) 16, 33–37, 42
'Goes Wrong' plays (Mischief Theatre) 11, 195–200
*The Goes Wrong Show* 199
Gogol, Nikolai 101
Goldoni, Carlo 102; *The Servant of Two Masters* 169, 171
*Goodnight Desdemona, Good Morning Juliet* (MacDonald) 164
*Good Nights Out* (Sierz) 153
government 110–111; American 120–125; British 111–120; *see also* political farce(s)
Gozzi, Carlo 102
Graham, James 17; *The Culture* 17, 114, 115–117, 136
Grandage, Michael 133, 134
Greek New Comedy 12
Green, Jesse 95
Green, Michael: *The Art of Coarse Acting* 195; *The Coarse Acting Show* (play) 195
Griffiths, Trevor: *Comedians* 168
*The Guardian* 36–37
Guare, John 44; *A Free Man of Color* 79–80; *Six Degrees of Separation* 76–79
Guenoun, Denis 34
Guest, Christopher: *Waiting for Guffman* 201

*Habeas Corpus* (Bennett) 40
Halevy, Louis 28

Halliwell, Kenneth 68
Hanson, Dave: *Waiting for Waiting for Godot* 203–205
Harris, Kamala 80
Hart, Moss 44
Hatcher, Jeffrey 207
Healey, Tom 192
Hearn, Dave 195, 198
Hecht, Ben 209
Hennequin, Maurice 28
Herrin, Jeremy 186, 187
*Herr Kolpert* (Gieselmann) 177
Hitchcock, Alfred 152, 177
Holmes, Rupert 205
homosexuality 64–65
Hopkins, Didi 172
Horace 102
Horvath, Odon Von 101
Houghton, Peter: *A Commercial Farce* 190–192
*The Hound of the Baskervilles* (Doyle) 147, 150
*House & Garden* (Ayckbourn) 40, 138
*How the Other Half Loves* (Ayckbourn) 39
Hull Truck Theatre 136
Hwang, David Henry: *Yellow Face* 85–89
*The Hypocrite* (Bean) 6, 116, 136
hysteria *see* panic (hysteria and desperation)
*Hysteria* (Johnson) 173–174
Hytner, Nicholas 169, 172

identity, gender, and sexuality 68–75; *The Agony of Ecstasy* (Berman) 69; *The Explorer's Club* (Benjamin) 73–75; *La Cage aux Folles* (Poiret) 68–69; *The Ritz* (McNally) 70–71; *The Ugly One* (Mayenburg) 6, 17, 71–73, 78
"I Got You (I Feel Good)" (Brown) 115
Ijames, James: *Fat Ham* 168
*Imagine* (Lennon) 218
*The Importance of Being Earnest* (Wilde) 66
*Independent* 31
interference 18–19
*In the Next Room* (Ruhl) 189
*Intimacy* (Bradshaw) 16, 89–92
inversion 18
'In-Yer-Face' Theatre movement 130
*In-Zoom* 215
Ionesco, Eugene 23, 72, 95, 101, 150, 215
Irish domestic farce 50–54; *The Communication Cord* (Friel) 50–51; *The Patrick Pearse Motel* (Leonard) 50; *The Walworth Farce* (Walsh) 51–54
Irwin, Bill 215, 218
*It's Only a Play* (McNally) 207–209

*Jack Absolute Flies Again* (Bean and Chris) 172–173
Jagger, Mick 172
Jain, Ravi 107
Jarry, Alfred 23, 101
*Jatek a kastelyban* (Molnar) 168
*Jeeves and Wooster in Perfect Nonsense* (Goodale Brothers) 149
Jefferson, Margo 89
Jeffreys, Stephen: *The Clink* 168
Jeter, Michael 218
Johnson, Terry: *Dead Funny* 54–55, 171, 202; *Hysteria* 173–174
Jones, Chris 194
Jordan, Eamonn 132
Juvenal 102–103

Kander, John 205
Kane, Sarah 130
Kaufman, George 44
*Kidnapping Francesca* (Fo) 103
Kierkegaard, Soren 3
Kirkwood, Lucy: *Tinderbox* 111, 114, 117–120, 167
Knutzon, Line: *The Builders* 55–56
Koenig, Rhoda 31
Korchinski-Paquet, Regis 108
Kuhnau, Johann 174

Labiche, Eugene 12–13, 28–29, 32, 37, 51, 62
*La Cage aux Folles* (Poiret) 68–69
*The Ladykillers* (Linehan) 155–157
Lane, Nathan 167
language 21–22
*The Laramie Project* 89
*The Larry Sanders Show* 211
Larson, Jonathan: *Rent* 168
*Leading Ladies* (Ludwig) 210
LeBlanc, Matt 20
Le Navet Bete 11, 147–148
*Lend Me a Tenor* (Ludwig) 45, 46–47, 209
Lennon, John 172
Leonard, Hugh 50
Letts, Tracy: *The Minutes* 120–123
Lewis, Henry 195
LGBTQ+ 49; rights 69, 78, 96
*The Lieutenant of Inishmore* (McDonagh) 13, 126, 129, 130–135

*Life Sucks* (Posner) 169
Linehan, Graham: *The Ladykillers* 155–157
Locher, Whitney 151
*Loot* (Orton) 63, 64–65
Louis-Dreyfus, Julia 20
Loveridge, Charlotte 119
*Lucky Stiff* 159
Ludlam, Charles 164; *The Mystery of Irma Vep* 201
Ludwig, Ken 44–48, 162; *Baskerville* 150–151; *A Comedy of Tenors* 18–19, 45, 46, 47–48, 209; *The Game's Afoot* 150; *Leading Ladies* 210; *Lend Me a Tenor* 45, 46–47, 209; *Midsummer/Jersey* 210; *Moon Over Buffalo* 209; *Moriarty* 151; *Postmortem* 150; *Shakespeare in Hollywood* 210
Lui, Nakkiah: *Black Is the New White* 92–94
Lukowski, Andrzej 133
*The Lying Kind* (Neilson) 16, 82, 83–85
Lynn, Jonathan 157

Maas, Danielle 67–68
Mac, Taylor 164–165; *Gary: A Sequel to Titus Andronicus* 165–169
MacArthur, Charles 209
MacDonald, Ann-Marie: *Goodnight Desdemona, Good Morning Juliet* 164
*Magic Goes Wrong* (Mischief Theatre) 196
*Mama Got a Cough* (Cooper) 216–217
Mamet, David: *November* 124
Mandell, Alex 197–198, 199–200
Marcus, Ben 203
Martin, Steve: *The Underpants* 178
Marx, Groucho 210
*The Mary Tyler Moore Show* 162
Marzan, Javier 147
*The Massive Tragedy of Madame Bovary* (Peepolykus) 147
Matura, Mustapha: *The Coup* 126, 128–129
Mayenburg, Marius Von: *Perplex* 95–96; *The Ugly One* 6, 17, 71–73, 78
Mayne, Andrew 64
McClure, Rob 45, 187–188; ConductorCam 217–219
McColl, Hamish: *The Play What I Wrote* 201
McCrystal, Cal 170

McDonagh, Martin 29, 38, 51, 138, 162; *The Cripple of Inishmaan* 134; *The Lieutenant of Inishmore* 13, 126, 129, 130–135
McDonough, Meredith 186, 187
McNally, Terrence: *It's Only a Play* 207–209; *The Ritz* 70–71
mechanics of farce 16–17
Meehan, Thomas 159
Meilhac, Henri 28
*Mein Kampf: Farce* (Tabori) 126–128, 132
Melendez, Priscilla 69
*Memoirs* (Simon) 76
Menander 12
#MeToo movement 28, 67, 74
Meyerhold, Vsevolod 4
*Midsummer/Jersey* (Ludwig) 210
*A Midsummer Night's Dream* (Shakespeare) 195, 210
*The Minutes* (Letts) 120–123
*Mischief Movie Night* (Mischief Theatre) 199
Mischief Theatre 11, 195–200; 'Goes Wrong' plays 11, 195–200; *Magic Goes Wrong* 196; *Mischief Movie Night* 199; *The Nativity Goes Wrong* 196; *Peter Pan Goes Wrong* 196; *The Play That Goes Wrong* 196–200
Molnar, Ferenc: *Jatek a kastelyban* 168
*Monty Python* 201
*Moon Over Buffalo* (Ludwig) 209
"More to Talk About" (podcast) 220
*Moriarty* (Ludwig) 151
Morrison, Van 172
Mortimer, John 14, 21
Moses, Itamar: *Bach at Leipzig* 174–175
*Mother Courage and Her Children* (Brecht) 168
Murphy, Tim 91–92
musical comedy 159
*MUTE: A Play for Zoom* (Bell) 215
*The Mystery of Irma Vep* (Ludlam) 201

National Health Service (NHS) 42, 43
*The Nativity Goes Wrong* (Mischief Theatre) 196
Neilson, Anthony 81–82, 130; *The Lying Kind* 16, 82, 83–85
Nestroy, Johann: *Einen Jux will er sich machen* 168
*Newsweek* 120
*New Yorker* 167

Nicholson, John 11, 147, 148
*Nobody Here But Us Chickens* 41
*Noises Off* (Frayn) 19, 41, 46, 183–188, 196, 200, 201, 211
*No Naughty Bits* (Thompson) 176
*The Norman Conquests* (Ayckbourn) 40
*Not As Bad as They Seem* (Barnes) 40–41
Nottage, Lynn: *Poof!* 96; *Ruined* 168
novels/literary adaptation 146–155; *Baskerville* (Ludwig) 150–151; *The Crocodile* (Basden) 149–150; *Dracula: The Bloody Truth* (Le Navet Bete) 148; *The Game's Afoot* (Ludwig) 150; *The Hound of the Baskervilles* (Doyle) 147; *Jeeves and Wooster in Perfect Nonsense* (Goodale Brothers) 149; *The Massive Tragedy of Madame Bovary* (Peepolykus) 147; *The 39 Steps* (Barlow) 152–155; *Treasure Island* (Le Navet Bete) 148
*November* (Mamet) 124

obsession *see* passion (obsession)
O'Hagan, Sean 131, 132
Olding, Grant 172
*One Man, Two Guvnors* (Bean) 13, 17, 18, 169–173, 202
*On the Twentieth Century* 159
*Or* (Adams) 175–176
Orton, Joe 38, 62–63, 86, 102, 118, 130, 132–133, 139, 177; *Loot* 63, 64–65; *What the Butler Saw* 63, 65–68, 132
'Ortonesque' fray 63
Owen, Alex: *The Comeback* (Ashenden and Owen) 17, 200–202

Paice, Jill 14, 154
*The Painkiller* (Foley) 178
panic (hysteria and desperation) 15–16; *see also* Four P Story Arc
Parker, Emma 67
Parsons, Louella 210
*The Party* (Sandler) 138–140
passion (obsession) 13–14; *see also* Four P Story Arc
*The Patrick Pearse Motel* (Leonard) 50
Peepolykus 11, 147, 148; *The Hound of the Baskervilles* 147; *The Massive Tragedy of Madame Bovary* 147
Penhall, Joe 130; *Birthday* 18, 41, 42–44; *Blue/Orange* 43; *Some Voices* 43
performance in backstage farces 194–202; *The Comeback* (Ashenden and Owen) 200–202; 'Goes Wrong' plays *see* Mischief Theatre
*Perplex* (Mayenburg) 95–96
perseverance *see* persistence (perseverance)
persistence (perseverance) 14; *see also* Four P Story Arc
*Peter Pan Goes Wrong* (Mischief Theatre) 196
Petosa, Jim 14
physical comedy 20–21
Pinero, Arthur Wing 37, 101
Pirandello, Luigi 86, 95, 164; *Six Characters in Search of an Author* (Pirandello) 216
Pisoni, Lorenzo 188
Plautus 12, 137, 162, 163
*The Plays of Yasmina Reza on the English and American Stage* (Giguere) 35
*The Play That Goes Wrong* 13, 196, 199
*The Play That Goes Wrong* (Mischief Theatre) 196–200
*The Play What I Wrote* (Foley and McColl) 201
playwrights 6–7
political farce(s) 101–140, 220; American 120–125; *see also* American political farce(s); British 111–120; *see also* British political farce(s); of Fo *see* Fo, Dario; government 110–111; radical 125–135; *see also* radical farce(s)
*The Politics of Farce in Contemporary Spanish American Theatre* (Melendez) 69
*Poof!* (Nottage) 96
Porter, Phil 13; *Vice Versa* 162–163
Posner, Aaron 169; *Life Sucks* 169; *Stupid Fucking Bird* 169
*Postmortem* (Ludwig) 150
*POTUS* (Fillinger) 120, 123–125, 175, 220
Powell, Dick 210
preservation (survival) 16
Price, Eric 157
Price, Mark 152–153, 154
Priestley, J.B. 151
*The Producers* (Brooks) 13, 159–161, 183
*Promises, Promises* 159
Pryce, Jonathan 86

race and racism 85–95; *Black Is the New White* (Lui) 92–94; *Intimacy* (Bradshaw) 16, 89–92; *The*

*Thanksgiving Play* (FastHorse) 6, 94–95; *Yellow Face* (Hwang) 85–89
radical farce(s) 125–135; *The Coup* (Matura) 126, 128–129; *The Lieutenant of Inishmore* (McDonagh) 126, 129, 130–135; *Mein Kampf: Farce* (Tabori) 126–128, 132
Rame, Franca 103; *see also* Fo, Dario
rape 67
Rattigan, Terence 63
Ravenhill, Mark 130
*The Real Inspector Hound* (Stoppard) 112, 206–207
Rebeck, Theresa: *Fool* 168; *The Understudy* 203
rehearsal process 188–194; *A Commercial Farce* (Houghton) 190–192; *Stage Kiss* (Ruhl) 189–190; *10 out of 12* (Washburn) 192–194
Reinhardt, Max 210
*Rent* (Larson) 168
repetition 18
reputation 9, 10
*Reservoir Dogs* (Tarantino) 82
*The Resistible Rise of Arturo Ui* (Brecht) 128
*Rewriting the Nation* (Sierz) 42
*The Ritz* (McNally) 70–71
*The Rivals* (Sheridan) 172
Rix, Brian 9, 38, 63
*Robbin' Hood* 205
*30 Rock* 211
*Roe vs. Wade* 124
Roman Comedy 12
*Rope* 177
Rose, William 155
Rourke, Josie 4
Royal Shakespeare Company (RSC) 162
Ruhl, Sarah: *The Clean House* 189; *Dead Man's Cell Phone* 189; *In the Next Room* 189; *Stage Kiss* 189–190
*Ruined* (Nottage) 168
*Rumors* (Simon) 9, 75–76
Russell, Charlie 195
Rustin, Sandy 55; *Clue* 157–158
Ryskind, Morrie 44

Sandler, Kat 138–140; *The Candidate* 138, 139–140; *The Party* 138–140
Sant, David 147
Sayer, Jonathan 195
"A Scandal in Bohemia" (Doyle) 151

*Scandaltown* (Bartlett) 80–81
*The Servant of Two Masters* (Goldoni) 169, 171
sexuality *see* identity, gender, and sexuality
Sexual Offences Act of 1967 64–65
sexual taboos 67
Shaffer, Peter: *Black Comedy* 25, 38, 41
Shakespeare, William: *The Comedy of Errors* 201; *Henry IV Parts I & II* 164; *The Merry Wives of Windsor* 164; *A Midsummer Night's Dream* 195, 210; *Othello* 164; *Romeo and Juliet* 164; *Titus Andronicus* 165
*Shakespeare in Hollywood* (Ludwig) 210
Sheen, Michael 216
Sheridan, Karen 153–154
Sheridan, Richard Brinsley 206; *The Critic, or a Tragedy Rehearsed* 206, 207; *The Rivals* 172
Shevelove, Burt 163
Shields, Henry 195
Sierz, Aleks 42; *Good Nights Out* 153
silence: in comedy 5
silver screen *see* cinematic adaptation
Simon, Neil 9, 44; *The Dinner Party* 76; *Memoirs* 76; *Rumors* 9, 75–76
*Six Characters in Search of an Author* (Pirandello) 216
*Six Degrees of Separation* (Guare) 76–79
Skiffle (folk music) 172
Smith, Deborah Salem: *Faithful Cheaters* 48–50, 64
*Soapdish* 210–211
social farce(s) 61–97; bourgeois 75–81; identity, gender, and sexuality 68–75; Orton and *see* Orton, Joe; race and racism 85–95; working class 81–85
*Some Voices* (Penhall) 43
Sondheim, Stephen 163
Soulpepper Theatre Company 107
*Spamalot* 159
*specific farceurs* 6
*Staged* 216
*Stage Kiss* (Ruhl) 189–190
Stamberg, Susan 161
status 9, 10
Steinem, Gloria 220
Stephen Joseph Theatre 39
Sternheim, Carl: *Die Hose* 178
Stirling, Rachael 81
Stone, Peter 205

Stoppard, Tom: *Dirty Linen* 112–114, 121; humorous dialogue 169; *On the Razzle* 168; *The Real Inspector Hound* 112, 206–207; *Rosencrantz and Guildenstern are Dead* 112, 164; *Rough Crossing* 168; *Travesties* 112
Stroman, Susan 159
structure 17–19; interference 18–19; inversion 18; repetition 18
*Stupid Fucking Bird* (Posner) 169
Sugarman, Bernie 86
survival *see* preservation (survival)
Svich, Caridad 165

Tabori, George: *Mein Kampf: Farce* 126–128, 132
*Taking Steps* (Ayckbourn) 39
Tannahill, Greg 195
Tarantino, Quentin: *Reservoir Dogs* 82
Tectonic Theatre 89
Tennant, David 216
*10 out of 12* (Washburn) 192–194
*Ten Times Table* (Ayckbourn) 135
Terence 12
*The Thanksgiving Play* (FastHorse) 6, 94–95
Theatre of the Oppressed 107
theatrical adaptation 161–173; *Gary: A Sequel to Titus Andronicus* (Mac) 165–169; *One Man, Two Guvnors* (Bean) 169–173; *Vice Versa* (Porter) 162–163
themes 22–23
*The 39 Steps* (Barlow) 6, 17, 152–155
Thomas, Brandon 37; *Charley's Aunt* 210
Thompson, Steve: *No Naughty Bits* 176; *Whipping It Up* 135–136
*The Three Musketeers* (Le Navet Bete) 148
*Threesome* (El-Guindi) 96
*Till Death* (De Vos) 54
Tillinger, John 67
#TimesUP movement 74
*Tinderbox* (Kirkwood) 111, 114, 117–120, 167
*To Be or Not to Be* (Whitby) 176–177
Tongue, Cassie 93
*Tootsie* 210–211
Torres, Gina 86
tragedies 12
Travers, Ben 37–38
Travis, Emlyn 55

*Treasure Island* (Le Navet Bete) 148
*The Tribute Artist* (Busch) 96
Trump, Donald 80, 120, 163, 218
*Trumpets and Raspberries* (Fo) 103
*Twentieth Century* (Hecht and MacArthur) 209
*The Two of Us* (Frayn) 183
*Two Ronnies* 201

*The Ugly One* (Mayenburg) 6, 17, 71–73, 78
*The Underpants* (Martin) 178
understudies, backstage farces and 202–205
*The Understudy* (Rebeck) 203
United States: domestic farce in *see* American domestic farce(s), American political farce(s), government, political farces

Veber, Francis: *Le Contrat (The Contract)* 178
*Veep* 20
*Vice Versa* (Porter) 13, 162–163
violence 20–21
*The Virtuous Burglar* (Fo) 18, 103
Vogel, Paula: *Desdemona: A Play About a Handkerchief* 164

*Waiting for Godot* (Beckett) 203, 204, 205
*Waiting for Guffman* 210–211
*Waiting for Guffman* (Guest) 201
*Waiting for Waiting for Godot* (Hanson) 203–205
Waititi, Taika 128
Walsh, Enda 38, 83, 133; *The Walworth Farce* 51–54
Walton, Tony 77
*The Walworth Farce* (Walsh) 51–54
Warchus, Matthew 31, 33, 36
Warner Brothers Studio 210
Washburn, Anne: *10 out of 12* 192–194
Weitz, Eric 11
well-made farce/play 29
*What's the Story* (Bogart) 13
*What the Butler Saw* (Orton) 63, 65–68, 132
*What We Do in the Shadows* 162
*Where Three Roads Meet* 38
*Whipping It Up* (Thompson) 135–136

Whitby, Nick: *To Be or Not to Be* 176–177
Whitehall Theatre 9, 38, 160, 184
*Who's Afraid of Virginia Woolf?* (Albee) 177
Wilde, Oscar: *The Importance of Being Earnest* 66
Wilder, Thornton 23, 44, 46, 168
Willstrop, James 117
Wilson, Jamia 220
Wing, Paula 107–108, 146, 159–160

Wodehouse, P.G. 149
working-class farce 81–85; *Gagarin Way* (Burke) 81, 82–83; *The Lying Kind* 16, 82, 83–85

*Yellow Face* (Hwang) 85–89
Young, Harvey 91

Zaks, Jerry 77, 218, 219
Zamit, Nancy 195
Zoom 214, 215–217

For Product Safety Concerns and Information please contact our EU
representative  GPSR@taylorandfrancis.com
Taylor & Francis Verlag GmbH, Kaufingerstraße 24, 80331 München, Germany

www.ingramcontent.com/pod-product-compliance
Ingram Content Group UK Ltd.
Pitfield, Milton Keynes, MK11 3LW, UK
UKHW022109180226
468177UK00020B/727